CHINESE:
AN ESSENTIAL GRAMMAR

Chinese: An Essential Grammar is a clear and concise reference guide to the grammar of modern Chinese (Mandarin). It presents a fresh and accessible description of the language, focusing on the real patterns of use in today's Chinese.

The grammar is the ideal reference source for the learner and user of Chinese. It is suitable either for independent study or for students in schools, colleges, universities and adult classes of all types.

The book sets out the complexities of Chinese in short, readable sections. Explanations are clear and free from jargon. Throughout, the emphasis is on Chinese as used by native speakers today.

Features include:

- copious examples to illustrate language points
- detailed contents list and index for easy access to information
- two glossaries: one of grammatical terms and one of Chinese characters

Yip Po-Ching is Lecturer in Chinese Studies at the University of Leeds. **Don Rimmington** is Professor of East Asian Studies and Head of the East Asian Studies Department at the University of Leeds.

Titles of related interest

Colloquial Chinese
Kan Qian

Colloquial Cantonese
Keith S. T. Ting and Gregory James

Cantonese: A Comprehensive Grammar
Stephen Matthews and Virginia Yip

Forthcoming

Basic Chinese: A Grammar and Workbook
Yip Po-Ching, Don Rimmington, Zhang Xiaoming and Rachel Henson

Intermediate Chinese: A Grammar and Workbook
Yip Po-Ching, Don Rimmington, Zhang Xiaoming and Rachel Henson

CHINESE:
AN ESSENTIAL
GRAMMAR

Yip Po-Ching and Don Rimmington

London and New York

First published 1997
by Routledge
11 New Fetter Lane, London EC4P 4EE

Simultaneously published in the USA and Canada
by Routledge
29 West 35th Street, New York, NY 10001

© 1997 Yip Po-Ching and Don Rimmington

Typeset in Times by Florencetype Ltd, Stoodleigh, Devon

Printed and bound in Great Britain
by Clays Ltd, St Ives, PLC

British Library Cataloguing in Publication Data
A catalogue record for this book is available from the
British Library

Library of Congress Cataloguing in Publication Data
A catalogue record for this book has been requested

ISBN 0–415–13534–6 (hbk)
      0–415–13535–4 (pbk)

CONTENTS

PREFACE

This book aims to identify the basic features of the grammar of Mandarin Chinese. It should therefore be of use not only to students and teachers of Chinese, but also to those with a general interest in languages and linguistics. While we hope our analysis is based on sound linguistic principles, we have endeavoured to keep technical terminology to a minimum to allow as wide a readership as possible access to the material. Where it has been necessary to use specialist terminology, we have offered explanations which we hope will be intelligible to the general reader. A Glossary of Grammatical Terms is also included (pp. 157–160) for reference.

Our approach has been eclectic: we have used both traditional and modern forms of analysis, and for maximum clarity utilised both syntactic and semantic categories. Our concern has been two-fold. First, we have sought to provide a structural description of Mandarin Chinese, starting with the noun (and its modifiers); moving to the verb and its fundamental characteristics, including pre-verbal adverbials and post-verbal complements; and concluding with the sentence and how it is influenced by word order and sentence particles. Second, we have been conscious of functional needs; we have therefore, where possible, shaped our analysis in the form of meaningful units and provided a wide range of practical vocabulary to illustrate language usage.

The language examples in the book are in most cases provided with both a literal (*lit.*) and a colloquial translation into English. The literal translations include a limited number of grammatical symbols representing functional words as follows:

asp	aspect marker	phon	phonaestheme
int	intensifier	onom	onomatopoeia
mw	measure word	cv	coverb
p	particle	interj	interjection

Two other symbols used in the text are:

| > | meaning 'changes into' |
| * | indicating incorrect usage |

For readers who want to know the Chinese characters for *pinyin* material in the text, we have provided a Glossary of Chinese Characters, listed alphabetically according to the *pinyin* romanisation, with English translations.

We are deeply indebted to Li Quzhen and Zhang Xiaoming for exten-
sive assistance with the production of the Chinese-character glossary, the
addition of tone marks, etc. We also appreciate support given by Simon
Bell, senior editor at Routledge. The contents of the book are, of course,
entirely our responsibility.

Yip Po-Ching and Don Rimmington

INTRODUCTION

THE CHINESE LANGUAGE

The Chinese language, or group of related languages, is spoken by the Hans, who constitute 94 per cent of China's population. One word for the language in Chinese is *Hanyu*, the Han language. Different, non-Han languages are spoken by the remaining 6 per cent of the population, the so-called minority peoples, such as the Mongols and Tibetans.

The Chinese language is divided into eight major dialects (with their numerous sub-dialects). Speakers of different dialects in some cases find each other unintelligible, but dialects are unified by the fact that they share a common script. This book describes the main dialect, which is known by various names: Mandarin, modern standard Chinese, or *Putonghua* ('common speech'). It is spoken in various sub-dialect forms by 70 per cent of Hans across the northern, central and western regions of the country, but its standard pronunciation and grammar are associated with the Beijing region of north China, though not Beijing city itself. The seven other Chinese dialects are Wu (spoken in Jiangsu and Zhejiang, including Shanghai, by 8.4 per cent of Han speakers), Xiang (Hunan, 5 per cent), Cantonese (Guangdong, 5 per cent), Min (Fujian, 4.2 per cent), Hakka (northeast Guangdong and other southern provinces, 4 per cent) and Gan (Jiangxi, 2.4 per cent).

Cantonese, Min and Hakka are widely spoken among overseas Chinese communities. In Taiwan a form of Min dialect is used, though the official language is Mandarin, brought over by the Nationalists in 1949 and called there *Guoyu* ('national language'). Mandarin is also widely used in Singapore, where it is known as *Huayu* ('Chinese language'). The Chinese population of Britain, which comes largely from Hong Kong, uses mainly Cantonese.

Written Chinese employs the character script, which existed virtually unchanged in China for over two thousand years, until a range of simplified forms began to be introduced by the mainland Chinese government in the 1950s. Words in Chinese are made up of one or more syllables, each of which is represented by a character in the written script. Since the last century, Chinese has also been transcribed into Western alphabetic scripts, and this book makes use of the standard romanisation *pinyin*.

Note: Mandarin is China's official language, transmitted nationally by radio and television, and therefore understood by virtually everyone in the country.

MANDARIN PRONUNCIATION

Syllables can be divided into initials (consonants) and finals (vowels or vowels followed by **-n** or **-ng**). Below is a full list of initials and finals, with some guidance to pronunciation. Where possible, the closest equivalents in English pronunication have been given, but care should be taken with these and confirmation sought, if necessary, from a native Chinese speaker.

Initials

f, **l**, **m**, **n**, **s**, **(w)** and **(y)** – similar to English
p, **t** and **k** – pronounced with a slight puff of air, like the initials in *pop*, *top* and *cop*
h like *ch* in the Scottish *loch,* with a little friction in the throat
b, **d** and **g** – not voiced as in English, but closer to *p* in *spout*, *t* in *stout*, and *c* in *scout*, than to *b* in *bout*, *d* in *doubt* and *g* in *gout*.

j like *j* in *jeep*
q like *ch* in *cheap*
x like *sh* in *sheep*
The three above are pronounced with the lips spread as in a smile

ch like *ch* in *church*
sh like *sh* in *shirt*
zh like *j* in *judge*
r like *r* in *rung*
The four above are pronounced with the tip of the tongue curled back

c like *ts* in *bits*
z like *ds* in *bids* (but not voiced)

Finals

a as in *father*
ai as in *aisle*
an as in *ran*
ang as in *rang*, with the *a* slightly lengthened as in *ah*
ao like *ou* in *out*

e as in *her, the*
ei as in *eight*
en as in *open*
eng like **en** + *g*
er like *err*, but with the tongue curled back and the sound coming from the back of the throat

i – with initials **b, d, j, l, m, n, p, q, t** and **x**, as in *machine*, or like *ee* in *see* (but prónounced differently with other initials, see below)
ia – **i** followed by **a**, like *ya* in *yard*
ian – similar to *yen*
iang – **i** followed by **ang**
iao – **i** followed by **ao**, like *yow* in *yowl*
ie like *ye* in *yes*
in as in *thin*
ing as in *thing*
iong – **i** merged with *ong*
iu like *yo* in *yoga*

i – with initials **c, r, s, z, ʿch, sh** and **zh**, somewhat like *i* in *sir, bird* (but pronounced differently with other initials, see above)

o as in *more*
ou as in *dough*, or like *oa* in *boat*
ong like *ung* in *lung*, but with lips rounded

u as in *rule*, or like *oo* in *boot*
ua – **u** followed by **a**
uai – **u** followed by **ai**, like *wi* in *wild*
uan – **u** followed by **an**
uang – **u** followed by **ang**, like *wang* in *twang*
ueng – **u** followed by **eng**, which exists only with zero initial as **weng**
ui – **u** followed by **ei**, similar to *way*
un – **u** followed by **en**, like *uan* in *truant*
uo – **u** followed by **o**, similar to *war*

u/ü – with initials **j, q** and **x** (as u) and with initials **l** and **n** (as ü) like *i* in *machine*, pronounced with rounded lips, and similar to *u* in French *une* or *ü* in German *über*
uan – **u/ü** followed by **an**, only with initials j, q and x
ue or **üe** – with initials **j, q** and **x** (as ue) and with initials **l** and **n** (as üe), **u/ü** followed by **e** as above
un – **u/ü** with **n**, like French **une**, only with initials j, q and x
Most finals can be used without an initial (zero initial), and finals beginning with **i** (as in *machine*) and **u/ü** (like the French *une*) are written in the *pinyin* romanisation with **y** as the first letter, and those beginning with **u** (as in *rule*) with **w** as the first letter:

-i	>	yi	-ie	>	ye
-ia	>	ya	-in	>	yin
-ian	>	yan	-ing	>	ying
-iang	>	yang	-iong	>	yong
-iao	>	yao	-iu	>	you

-u/ü	>	yu		-ue/üe	>	yue
-uan	>	yuan		-un	>	yun
-u	>	wu		-uang	>	wang
-ua	>	wa		-ui	>	wei
-uai	>	wai		-un	>	wen
-uan	>	wan		-uo	>	wo

Note the vowel changes with -iu (> you), -ui (> wei) and -un (> wen).

Note: Strictly speaking, in the *pinyin* system the hand-written form 'ɑ' is used instead of the printed version 'a', but this book has adopted 'a' throughout.

Tones

In Chinese each syllable (or character) has a tone, and in Mandarin there are four tones. In the *pinyin* romanisation, the mark above a syllable indicates its tone: ˉ first tone, ´ second tone, ˇ third tone and ` fourth tone. Some words have unstressed syllables which are toneless and therefore are not given tone marks. Structural words like particles are also often unstressed and are similarly unmarked.

First tone   high, level pitch; constant volume
Second tone   rising quite quickly from middle register and increasing in volume
Third tone   starting low and falling lower before rising again; louder at the beginning and end than in the middle
Fourth tone   starting high, falling rapidly in pitch and decreasing in volume

In speech, when a third tone precedes another third tone it changes to a second tone. Also, the pronunciation of yī 'one' and bù 'not' varies according to their context. Yi 'one' is first tone in counting but otherwise is fourth tone yì, except if followed by a fourth tone when it changes to second tone yí. Similarly, bù 'not' is fourth tone but changes to second tone bú when it comes before a fourth tone. However, since these tonal adjustments are all rule-governed, they will not be indicated in our example sentences. That is to say, yī will always be shown as first tone and bù as fourth tone.

THE CHINESE VOCABULARY

A large number of words in everyday vocabulary are of one syllable:

wǒ 'I', nǐ 'you', tā 'he/she/it', tiān 'sky', hǎi 'sea', jiē 'street', pǎo 'run', mǎi 'buy'

Structural particles are also almost always monosyllabic:

le aspect marker and sentence particle
de indicator of attributives, adverbials or complements
ma signifier of general questions

In general, however, the vocabulary is full of disyllabic words or expressions which combine monosyllables in one way or another. These words or expressions derive their meaning explicitly or implicitly from the words or syllables that make them up:

diàn 'electricity' + **tī** 'ladder'	= **diàntī** 'lift'; 'elevator'
hǎi 'sea' + **yáng** 'ocean'	= **hǎiyáng** 'ocean'
dà 'big' + **jiā** 'family'	= **dàjiā** 'everybody'
dǎ 'to hit' + **duàn** 'to break'	= **dǎduàn** 'to interrupt' or 'to break in two'
fáng 'house' + **zi** suffix	= **fángzi** 'house'
wán 'to play' + **r** suffix	= **wánr** 'to have fun'; 'to enjoy oneself'
zǒu 'to walk' + **lù** 'road'	= **zǒulù** 'to go on foot'
pǎo 'to run' + **bù** 'step'	= **pǎobù** 'to run'; 'to jog'
tiào 'to jump' + **gāo** 'high'	= **tiàogāo** 'high jump'
sǎo 'to sweep' + **xìng** 'interest'	= **sǎoxìng** 'to disappoint'
tóu 'to throw' + **zī** 'funds'	= **tóuzī** 'to invest (money)'
hòu 'behind' + **lái** 'to come'	= **hòulái** 'afterwards'
guó 'nation' + **jiā** 'family'	= **guójiā** 'nation'
huǒ 'fire' + **chē** 'vehicle'	= **huǒchē** 'train'
shǒu 'head' + **dū** 'capital'	= **shǒudū** 'capital (of a country)'

Words or expressions of three or more syllables can also be formed:

yóu 'postal' + **dì** 'to pass on' + **yuán** 'person'	= **yóudìyuán** 'postman'
kēxué 'science' + **jiā** 'expert'	= **kēxuéjiā** 'scientist'
dǎ 'to hit' + **diànhuà** 'telephone'	= **dǎ diànhuà** 'to make a telephone call'
míng 'open' + **xìn** 'letter' + **piàn** 'piece'	= **míngxìnpiàn** 'postcard'
zì 'self' + **xíng** 'to walk' + **chē** 'vehicle'	= **zìxíngchē** 'bicycle'
shèng 'saint' + **dàn** 'birth' + **jié** 'festival'	= **Shèngdànjié** 'Christmas'
chūzū 'to hire out' + **qìchē** 'car'	= **chūzū qìchē** 'taxi'
bǎihuò 'hundred goods' + **shāngdiàn** 'shop'	= **bǎihuò shāngdiàn** 'department store'

The lists above show how the majority of Chinese words are constructed in accordance with grammatical principles. Chinese word-formation is therefore in a sense Chinese syntax in miniature. For example:

1 **huā** 'flower' + **yuán** 'plot (of land)' = **huāyuán** 'garden' is a *modifier + modified* structure

2 **tóu** 'head' + **tòng** 'to be painful' = **tóutòng** 'headache' is a *subject + verb* structure

3 **xué** 'to learn' + **xí** 'to practise' = **xuéxí** 'to study' is a *juxtapositional* structure where two synonymous items are placed side by side

4 **chàng** 'to sing' + **gē** 'song' = **chànggē** 'sing' is a *verb + object* structure

5 **chǎo** 'to make a noise' + **xǐng** 'to wake up' = **chǎoxǐng** 'to wake (somebody) up (by making a noise)' is a *verb + complement* structure.

I   NOUNS

INTRODUCTION

In this section we discuss nouns and pronouns in Chinese. In particular we will look at the different types of nouns and those elements closely associated with them: numerals, demonstratives, measure words and attributives.

Nouns in Chinese generally have one or two syllables. A few have three syllables, but four-syllable nouns are quite rare. Some nouns are identifiable by the suffixes **-zi**, **-(e)r** or **-tou** but most are not obviously distinguishable from other word classes.

Nouns do not change for number. An unqualified noun can therefore be singular or plural, though out of context it is likely to be plural. The plural suffix **-men** is used with pronouns, and in particular circumstances with human nouns.

Numerals are placed before nouns to specify number, but a measure word must be inserted between the numeral and the noun. Similarly, a measure word must be placed between a demonstrative and a noun. There is a general measure word **gè**, but most measure words are specific to particular nouns or sets of nouns.

Adjectives or other qualifying elements also come before the nouns they qualify. If the qualifier is monosyllabic, it is usually placed directly before the noun. If the qualifier is of two or more syllables, the particle **de** will come after the qualifier and before the noun.

Definite and indefinite reference for Chinese nouns is not signified by articles like English *the* or *a(n)*; though the demonstratives and the numeral **yī** 'one' when used with a noun (with a measure) may indicate respectively definiteness and indefiniteness. Perhaps more important is the location of the noun in the sentence, since a pre-verbal position is normally definite and a post-verbal position indefinite.

Pronouns are naturally of definite reference. The third person pronoun **tā**, in its spoken form, may signify any of the three genders: masculine, feminine or neuter. However, **tā** as a third person neuter pronoun indicating an inanimate entity is rarely present as the subject or object of a sentence, since its sense is usually understood from the context or cotext.

1 NOUNS

1.1 In Chinese *nouns* may consist of one or more syllables, each syllable being represented by a written character. Nouns with two syllables are by far the most numerous in the vocabulary, though in everyday speech mono-syllabic nouns are likely to be as frequent as disyllabic ones. A noun of more than one syllable is usually formed by building meaning-related sylla-bles around a headword. For example:

bǐ	pen	
qiānbǐ	pencil	(*lit.* lead-pen)
máobǐ	writing brush	(*lit.* hair-pen)
yuánzhūbǐ	biro; ball-point pen	(*lit.* round-pearl-pen)
bǐmíng	pen name; pseudonym	(*lit.* pen-name)
bǐshì	written examination	(*lit.* pen-examination)
bǐjì	notes	(*lit.* pen-note)
bǐjìběn	notebook	(*lit.* pen-note-book)

Nouns do not change for number or case. That is, they remain the same whether they are singular or plural (the distinction usually indicated by context or, more obviously, by use of numbers), and whether they are the subject or the object of a verb. For example:

yī zhī *bǐ*	one/a *pen*
hěn duō *bǐ*	a lot of *pens*
Bǐ zài zhèr.	*The pen* is here.
Wǒ yǒu *bǐ*.	I have got a pen.

Nouns may be divided into the following categories:

(a) Proper nouns: **Zhōngguó**, China; **Chángchéng,** The Great Wall; **Shèngdànjié,** Christmas

(b) Common nouns: **zúqiú**, soccer; **huǒchē**, train; **cídiǎn**, dictionary

(c) Abstract nouns: **yìnxiàng**, impression; **yìjiàn**, opinion; **nénglì**, ability

(d) Material nouns: **shuǐ**, water; **sùliào**, plastics; **méiqì**, gas

(e) Collective nouns: **chēliàng**, vehicles; **rénkǒu**, population; **xìnjiàn** correspondence (letters)

1.2 *Proper nouns* are names of people, places, institutions, etc. Contrary to English practice, the names of individuals in Chinese are in the order of first surname, which is usually one syllable, and then chosen name, which can be either one or two syllables.

Lǐ Huìmíng, in which **Lǐ** is the surname and **Huìmíng** the chosen name

Zhāng Lán in which **Zhāng** is the surname and **Lán** the chosen name

Note: There is a relatively small number of surnames in Chinese; some of the most common, as well as **Lǐ** and **Zhāng**, are **Wáng**, **Huáng**, **Zhào**, **Sūn**, **Mǎ**, **Wú**, **Hú**, **Qián**, **Xú**

In forms of address, nouns denoting title or status follow the surname:

Wáng xiānsheng	Mr Wang
Lǐ xiǎojie	Miss Li
Zhōu zǒnglǐ	Prime Minister Zhou
Gāo xiàozhǎng	Headmaster Gao
Zhào jīnglǐ	Manager Zhao

Note: People are addressed in Chinese by their occupational title far more than in English. It would therefore be normal to address someone as Headmaster Gāo, Manager Zhào, etc.

The names of places can also be followed by a status noun such as **xiàn** 'county', **zhèn** 'town', **shì** 'city', **dìqū** 'district' or **shěng** 'province'. For example,

Běijīngshì	the City of Beijing
Héběishěng	Hebei Province
Shùndéxiàn	Shunde County

Similarly, in the names of institutions the place name is followed by a noun indicating institutional function:

Shànghǎi Shīfàn Dàxué	Shanghai Normal University
Guǎngdōngshěng Gōng'ānjú	Guangdong Provincial Public Security Bureau

In the case of postal addresses, the sequence of wording is the opposite of English with the largest entity coming first and the smallest last:

Zhōngguó	Mr Ming Li
Shāndōng(shěng) Jǐnán(shì)	Department of Chinese
Jǐnán Dàxué	Jinan University
Zhōngwénxì	Jinan
Lǐ Míng xiānsheng shōu	Shandong Province, CHINA

A direct translation of the Chinese address would be:

CHINA
Shandong (province) Jinan (city)
Jinan University
Department of Chinese
Li Ming Mr to receive

Note: *Shōu* 'to receive' is conventionally added after e name of the recipient.

This principle of the large coming before the small is applied elsewhere in Chinese. Dates, for instance, are in the order year, month and day. (See 10.2.1)

1.3 *Common nouns* make up a large part of the language's vocabulary. Some incorporate conventional monosyllabic suffixes such as: **-zi, -(e)r,** or **-tou;** others have more meaningful monosyllabic suffixes such as: **-yuán** 'person with specific skills or duties', **-zhě** 'person concerned with an activity', **-jiā** 'specialist', etc. For example,

háiz*i*	child	**píng**z*i*	bottle
niǎor	bird	**huā**r	flower
zhuānt*ou*	brick	**mán**t*ou*	bun

yùndòngy*uán*	athlete	**jiàshǐ**y*uán*	pilot/driver
jìz*hě*	journalist	**xué**z*hě*	scholar
zuòj*iā*	writer	**huà**j*iā*	painter

Common nouns by themselves, unless specified, can be either singular or indefinite plural:

shū	a book or books	**bǐ**	a pen or pens
xuésheng	a student or students	**lǎoshī**	a teacher or teachers

1.3.1 Human nouns can be followed by the *plural suffix -men*; they then take on definite reference. Compare:

xuésheng	a student or students	**xuésheng**m*en*	*the* students
háizi	a child or children	**háizi**m*en*	*the* children

There is usually some implication of familiarity when **-men** is used; it often occurs when groups of people are addressed:

Xiānshengm*en*, **nǚshì**m*en* ...	Ladies and gentlemen ...
Péngyoum*en* **hǎo!**	How are you, my friends?

However, **-men** cannot be used with a number:

	liǎng gè xuésheng	two students
NOT:	****liǎng gè xuésheng**m*en*	

Neither can **-men** be used as a plural suffix for non-human nouns:

****shūmen**	**(lit.* book + plural suffix)
****māomen**	**(lit.* cat + plural suffix)

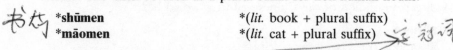

1.3.2 There are no definite or indefinite articles like *the* or *a(n)* in Chinese. Definite or indefinite reference is usually determined by the positioning of the noun before or after the verb. A pre-verbal position normally denotes definite reference, and a post-verbal position indefinite reference. Take, for example, **māo** 'cat(s)' in the following sentences:

Māo zài nǎr?	Tā xǐhuan *māo.*
(*lit.* cat be-at where)	(*lit.* s/he like cat)
Where is/are *the cat(s)*?	S/he likes *cats.*

1.4 Two or more nouns may be joined together by the conjunctions **hé** 'and' or **huò** 'or':

dāo *hé* chā	knives *and* forks
bǐ *hé* zhǐ	pen *and* paper
Lǐ Huìmíng *hé* Zhāng Lán	Li Huiming *and* Zhang Lan
xìnzhǐ, xìnfēng *hé* yóupiào	letter-paper, envelopes *and* stamps
yágāo, yáshuā, máojīn *hé* féizào	toothpaste, toothbrush, towel *and* soap
māo *huò* gǒu	cats *or* dogs
xiànjīn *huò* zhīpiào	cash *or* cheque
Xiǎo Lǐ *huò* Lǎo Wáng	Little Li *or* Old Wang

Note 1: There are other words in Chinese for 'and' used in a similar way to **hé**, e.g. **gēn**, **tóng** and, more formally, **yǔ**: **luóbo *gēn* báicài** 'turnips and cabbage', **jiějie *tóng* mèimei** 'elder sisters and younger sisters', **gōngyè *yǔ* nóngyè** 'industry *and* agriculture'.

Note 2: In familiar speech **xiǎo** 'little' and **lǎo** 'old' are prefixed to surnames or sometimes given names. **Xiǎo** generally indicates that the addressee is younger than the speaker, and **lǎo** the reverse.

Note 3: The conjunctions **hé** (**gēn**, **tóng** and **yǔ**) 'and' and **huò** 'or' may only be used to join words or expressions and NOT clauses:

**Tā xǐhuan māo, *hé* wǒ xǐhuan gǒu.*
*(lit. s/he likes cats, *and* I like dogs)

1.5 One feature of common nouns is that they can be counted. This involves the use not only of numbers (see Chapter 2) but also measure words (see Chapter 3).

2 NUMERALS AND NOUNS

2.1 *Cardinal numbers* one to ten:

yī	one	**liù**	six
èr/liǎng	two	**qī**	seven
sān	three	**bā**	eight
sì	four	**jiǔ**	nine
wǔ	five	**shí**	ten

Numbers ranging from eleven to ninety-nine are combinations of members of the basic set one to ten:

shí yī	eleven	**sānshí**	thirty
shí èr	twelve	**sìshí yī**	forty-one
èrshí	twenty	**jiǔshí jiǔ**	ninety-nine

The system extends itself beyond the basic set with the following:

bǎi	hundred
qiān	thousand
wàn	ten thousand
yì	hundred million

For example:

sān*bǎi* liùshí bā	368
jiǔ*qiān* sì*bǎi* èrshí qī	9,427
wǔ*wàn* bā*qiān* liù*bǎi* sānshí yī	58,631
èrshísānyì sìqiānwǔbǎiliùshíqī*wàn* bā*qiān* jiǔ*bǎi* èrshí yī	2,345,678,921

Care must be taken with large numbers, since the English number sets a thousand and a million differ from the Chinese **wàn** 'ten thousand' and **yì** 'hundred million'. A million in Chinese is **yībǎiwàn**; ten thousand is **yīwàn**, NOT *shíqián.

If there is a nought (or noughts) in a figure, **líng** 'zero' must be added as a filler. For example,

sānbǎi *líng* wǔ	305
sānqiān *líng* wǔ	3,005
sānqiān *líng* wǔshí	3,050

2.1.1   There are two forms of the number two in Chinese: **èr** and **liǎng**. **Èr** is used in counting, or in telephone, room, bus numbers, etc.:

yī, èr, sān, sì ...	one, two, three, four ...
èr hào	no. two (house, room, etc)
èr hào chē	no. two bus
bā jiǔ èr sān sān liù	892336 (telephone number)

Èr occurs in compound numbers: **shí èr** 'twelve', **èrshí èr** 'twenty two', **èrbǎi** 'two hundred', etc. (though **liǎng** can also be used with **bǎi**, **qiān**, **wàn** and **yì**). **Liǎng** is almost always used with measures (see Chapter 3):

liǎng *gè* rén	two people (*lit.* two *mw* person)
NOT: *èr gè rén	

2.2 *Ordinal numbers* in Chinese are formed simply by placing **dì** before the cardinals. For example,

yī	one	>	**dì yī**	first
èr	two	>	**dì èr**	second
sān	three	>	**dì sān**	third
jiǔshí qī	ninety-seven	>	**dì jiǔshí qī**	ninety-seventh
yībǎi	hundred	>	**dì yībǎi**	hundredth

When used with nouns, ordinals, like cardinals, need to be followed by measure words (see Chapter 3).

Note: In the following cases Chinese uses ordinal numbers where English employs cardinals:

(1) dates:	**sān yuè *yī hào***	March *1st*
	wǔ yuè *liù hào*	May *6th*
(2) floors/storeys:	**èr lóu**	(American English) the second floor;
		(British English) the first floor
	sān lóu	(American English) the third floor;
		(British English) the second floor

Whereas the British convention is to number floors ground, first, second, etc., in Chinese the ground floor is **dìxià** (or less commonly **yī lóu**) and the floors above are second, third, etc. This means that 'first floor' in British English is **èr lóu** (*lit.* two floor) in Chinese, 'second floor' is **sān lóu**, etc.

(3) years of study (at an educational institution):

yī niánjí	first year
sān niánjí	third year

2.3 Bàn 'half' functions as a number and therefore requires a measure word. **Bàn** may also come after the measure word when it follows a whole number:

bàn **gè píngguǒ**	half an apple
bàn **bēi píjiǔ**	half a glass of beer
yī gè *bàn* **lí**	one and half pears

2.4 *Other forms of numbers* in Chinese are:

(1) Fractions:	**sān *fēn zhī* èr** 2/3	**bā *fēn zhī* wǔ** 5/8
	(*lit.* three *parts'* two)	(*lit.* eight *parts'* five)
(2) Percentages:	**bǎi *fēn zhī* yī** 1%	**bǎi *fēn zhī* liùshí** 60%
	(*lit.* hundred *parts'* one)	(*lit.* hundred *parts'* sixty)
(3) Decimals:	**líng *diǎn* wǔ** 0.5	**yī *diǎn* sì** 1.4
	(*lit.* nought *point* five)	(*lit.* one *point* four)
(4) Multiples:	**liǎng *bèi*** 2 times	**shí èr *bèi*** 12 times
(5) The inclusive **měi** 'every':		
	měi gè rén everyone	**měi tiān** every day

2.5 *Approximation* in Chinese may take the following forms:

(1) **Jǐ** 'several':	*jǐ* **gè píngguǒ**	a few apples
	jǐ **gè jùzi**	a few sentences
	jǐ **gè shēngcí**	a few new words
	jǐ **shí gè péngyou**	a few dozen friends (*lit.* a few tens friends)
	jǐ **qiān gè jǐngchá**	a few thousand policemen

Jǐ can also mean 'or so, and more', when used after **shí** 'ten' or its multiples:

shí *jǐ* gè rén	a dozen or so people
sān shí *jǐ* gè píngzi	thirty or so bottles

(2) **Lái** 'or so' and **duō** 'just over', placed like **jǐ** after **shí** 'ten' or its multiples. However, while **duō** may also occur after **bǎi** 'hundred', **qiān** 'thousand', or **wàn** 'ten thousand', **lái** is used only after **bǎi**:

shí *lái* gè lǎoshī	ten teachers or so
èr shí *duō* gè xuésheng	over twenty students
bǎi *lái/duō* gè gōngrén	a hundred and more workmen
liǎng qiān *duō* gè rén	over two thousand people

Note 1: All these expressions of approximation with **jǐ, lái** and **duō** require measure words when used with nouns (see Chapter 3).

Note 2: **Duō** must come after the measure when the number is not ten or a multiple of ten. This is notably the case in expressions relating to age, distance, height, weight, money, etc.

wǔ *suì duō*	over 5 (years old)
shí liù *gōngjīn duō*	over 16 kilo(gram)s
sān *Yīnglǐ duō*	over 3 miles

(3) two consecutive numbers (from one to nine) in increasing order, either alone or as part of larger numbers:

sì *wǔ* gè kèren	4 or 5 guests
sì *wǔ shí* ge nán háizi	40 to 50 boys
shí *qī bā* gè nǚ háizi	17 to 18 girls
wǔ *liù bǎi* gè rén	5 to 6 hundred people

(4) **(Da)yuè** 'about; around' and **zuǒyòu** 'more or less', used with any numbers and any of the above forms of approximation:

(a) **dàyuē** is placed before the 'numeral + measure word + noun' phrase:

dàyuē shí wǔ gè dàren	about/around fifteen adults
dàyuē sānshí lái/duō gè láibīn	about thirty or so visitors

(b) **Zuǒyòu** comes after the 'numeral + measure word + noun' phrase:

èrshí gè háizi *zuǒyòu*	roughly twenty children

Note: **Shàngxià** functions in a similar way to **zuǒyòu**, but its use is limited to approximation about age, height and weight: e.g. **sānshí suì** *shàngxià* 'around thirty years of age'.

3 MEASURES FOR NOUNS

3.1 When in Chinese a number is used with a noun, a *measure word* must be placed between the number and the noun. This contrasts with English where nouns can be divided into countables and uncountables, the former being used directly with numbers and the latter requiring a measure phrase after the number, e.g. *three students* (countable) and *three loaves of bread* (uncountable). Chinese nouns on the other hand all take measure words:

sān *gè* xuésheng	three students
sān *gè* miànbāo	three loaves of bread

Note: Measure words are sometimes also called classifiers.

Gè is by far the commonest measure and can be used with almost all nouns, including abstract nouns:

yī gè rén	one/a person
liǎng gè jiějie	two elder sisters
sān gè shǒubiǎo	three watches
yī gè huāyuán	one/a garden
sìshí gè zì	forty Chinese characters
wǔ gè yuè	five months
měi gè lǚkè	every passenger
yī gè yìnxiàng	an impression

3.2 In addition to **gè**, there is a wide range of commonly used measure words, which can be divided roughly into the categories below. (In the examples, the numeral **yī** 'one' is used, though any number could appear in its place.)

(1) Shapes: The shape measure words are perhaps the most interesting because they evoke images of their associated nouns.

(a) **tiáo** (long and flexible):

yī tiáo shé	a snake
yī tiáo hé	a river

Other nouns used with **tiáo** include: **qúnzi** 'skirt', **kùzi** 'trousers', **xiàn** 'thread', **shéngzi** 'rope; string', **jiē** 'street', etc.

(b) **zhī** (long and slender):

yī zhī bǐ	a pen
yī zhī (xiāng)yān	a cigarette

Also with **zhī**: **yágāo** '(tube of) toothpaste', **qiāng** 'pistol; rifle', etc.

(c) **gēn** (slender):

yī gēn xiāngjiāo	a banana
yī gēn xiāngcháng	a sausage

Also with **gēn**: **tóufa** 'hair', **tiěsī** 'wire', **zhēn** 'needle', etc.

(d) **zhāng** (flat):　　　　**yī zhāng zhǐ**　　a piece of paper

yī zhāng piào　a ticket

Also with **zhāng**: **bàozhǐ** 'newspaper', **yóupiào** 'stamp', **zhīpiào** 'cheque', **míngpiàn** 'name card', **míngxìnpiàn** 'postcard', **dìtú** 'map', **zhàopiàn** 'photograph', **chàngpiàn** 'gramophone record', **chuáng** 'bed', **zhuōzi** 'table', etc.

(e) **kē** (small and round)　　**yī kē zhēnzhū**　a pearl

yī kē xīng　　a star

Also with **kē** : **táng** 'sweets', **xīn** 'heart', etc.

(f) **lì** (round and smaller than **kē**) **yī lì mǐ**　　a grain of rice

yī lì shā　　a grain of sand

Also with **lì** : **zǐdàn** 'bullet', **huāshēng** 'peanut', etc.

(2) Associated actions:

(a) **bǎ** (to handle)　　**yī bǎ dāo**　　a knife

yī bǎ yáshuā　a toothbrush

Also with **bǎ** : **shūzi** 'comb', **yǐzi** 'chair', **suǒ** 'lock', **yàoshi** 'key', **chǐ** 'ruler', **sǎn** 'umbrella', etc.

(b) **fēng** (to seal)　　　**yī fēng xìn**　　a letter

(3) Particular sets:

(a) **běn** (for books, etc.)　　**yī běn cídiǎn**　a dictionary

yī běn zázhì　a magazine

(b) **zhī** (for animals, birds and insects):

yī zhī gǒu　　a dog

yī zhī niǎo　　a bird

yī zhī cāngying　a fly

There are alternative measure words for some common animals: **yī tóu niú** 'an ox', **yī pǐ mǎ** 'a horse', **yī tiáo gǒu** 'a dog'.

(for utensils):　　　　**yī zhī xiāngzi**　a box/suitcase

yī zhī wǎn　　a bowl

Also with: **bēizi** 'cup'; 'glass'; 'mug', etc.

(c) **kē** (for certain plants):　　**yī kē cài**　　a vegetable

yī kē cǎo　　a tuft of grass

Also with: **shù** 'tree', etc.

(d) **liàng** (for vehicles);　　**yī liàng qìchē**　a car

yī liàng huǒchē　a train

�架 (e) **jià** (for planes):   **yī jià fēijī**   a(n) (aero)plane
                              yī jià hōngzhàjī   a bomber
                              yī jià pēnqìjī   a jet plane

台 (f) **tái** (for machines):   **yī tái jīqì**   a machine
                               yī tái diànshìjī   a television

        Also with: **féngrènjī** 'sewing-machine', etc.

件 (g) **jiàn** (for shirts, coats, etc.):   **yī jiàn chènshān** a shirt
                                           yī jiàn dàyī   an overcoat

間 (h) **jiān** (for rooms, etc.):   **yī jiān wūzi**   a room
                                   yī jiān wòshì   a bedroom

所 (i) **suǒ** (for houses, institutions):   **yī suǒ fángzi**   a house
                                           yī suǒ xuéxiào   a school

        Also with: **yīyuàn** 'hospital', etc.

座 (j) **zuò** (for buildings, mountains, etc.)

                              yī zuò gōngdiàn a palace
                              yī zuò shān   a hill/mountain

        Also with: **qiáo** 'bridge', **chéngshì** 'city', etc.

場 (k) **chǎng** (for activities, etc.):   **yī chǎng diànyǐng**   a film
                                        yī chǎng zúqiú(sài) a soccer match

Note: The measures associated with particular sets of nouns are too numerous to list.
They include: **yī** *duǒ* **huār** 'a flower', **yī** *dǐng* **màozi** 'a hat/cap', **yī** *chū* **xì** 'a play', **yī** *shǒu*
gē 'a song', etc.

(4) Containers:

yī bēi kāfēi   a cup of coffee
yī wǎn fàn   a bowl of rice

Other containers include: **píng** 'bottle', **pán** 'plate', **guàn** 'tin; can', **hé** 'small box', **bāo**
'packet', etc.

Note: Cultural artefacts can sometimes dictate different sets of container measures.
Take the case of **bēi** 'cup'; 'glass'; 'mug':

yī bēi chá   a cup of tea
yī bēi píjiǔ   a glass of beer

(5) Standard measures:

公斤 **yī gōngjīn píngguǒ**   a kilo(gram) of apples
      yī mǎ bù   a yard of cloth

Other standard measures include: **Yīnglǐ** 'mile', **gōnglǐ** 'kilometre', **mǐ** 'metre', **bàng** 'pound', **àngsī** 'ounce', and the Chinese measures **jīn** 'catty', **liǎng** 'tael', **chǐ** 'foot', **cùn** ' inch'.

(6) Collections:

yī qún rén	a crowd of people
yī tào kèběn	a set of textbooks

Other collection measures include: **chuàn** 'cluster', **duī** 'pile'/'heap', **dá** 'dozen', **pī** 'batch', etc.

Note 1: The collection measure **qún** 'group'/'crowd' in Chinese is matched in English by a range of measures used with different nouns: **yī qún mìfēng** 'a swarm of bees', **yī qún niú** 'a herd of cows', **yī qún láng** 'a pack of wolves', **yī qún yáng** 'a flock of sheep', etc.

Note 2: The notion of *pair* is usually expressed in Chinese by **duì**, **shuāng** or **fù**: **yī shuāng xié** 'a pair of shoes', **yī shuāng kuàizi** 'a pair of chopsticks', **yī duì ěrhuán** 'a pair of ear-rings', **yī fù yǎnjìng** 'a pair of spectacles/glasses', **yī fù shǒutào** 'a pair of gloves', etc.

However: a pair of trousers **yī *tiáo* kùzi**, a pair of scissors **yī *bǎ* jiǎndāo**.

(7) Portion:

yī kuài dàngāo	a piece of cake
yī piàn miànbāo	a slice of bread
yī dī shuǐ	a drop of water

Note: **kuài** is also used for **féizào** 'soap', **dì** 'land', etc.; **piàn** for **yèzi** 'leaf', etc; **dī** for **xiě** '(drop of) blood', etc.

(8) Indefinite small numbers or amounts (**yī xiē** 'some'; **yī diǎnr** 'a little'):

yī xiē shū	some books
yī xiē shíjiān	some time
yī diǎnr miànfěn	a little flour

Note 1: **Xiē** can only be used with the numeral **yī** 'one' and with demonstratives (see 4.3).

Note 2: **Yī xiē** occurs with both common nouns (e.g. books) and material nouns (e.g. water), but **yī diǎnr** only with material nouns (e.g. flour). (See also 3.4 below)

3.3 *Abstract nouns* in Chinese also take measure words. For example,

yī *tiáo* xiāoxi	a piece of news
yī *gè* zhǔyi/zhǔzhāng	an idea/a proposal
yī *jiàn* shì	a matter
yī *sī* xiàoróng	a smile

The measure word **zhǒng** 'kind, type' is regularly found with abstract nouns:

yī zhǒng nénglì	a skill
yī zhǒng fāngfǎ	a method
yī zhǒng sīxiǎng	a kind of thinking

Abstract nouns may always be used with the indefinite small amount measures **yī xiē** or **yī diǎn** 'some':

| **yī xiē/diǎnr jiànyì** | some suggestions |
| **yī xiē/diǎnr yìnxiàng** | some impression |

3.4 *Material nouns* in Chinese, on the other hand, may only occur with standard measures, container measures, portion measures and indefinite small amount measures:

yī jīn mǐ	a **jīn** (i.e. half a kilogram) of rice (standard)
yī píng jiǔ	a bottle of wine/spirit (container)
yī kuài bù	a piece of cloth (portion)
yī xiē shuǐ	some water
yī diǎnr shuǐ	a little water

3.5 *Collective nouns* are generally formed by attaching a measure word as a kind of suffix to their related nouns. For example,

yī zhī chuán	a ship	>	**chuán***zhī*	shipping, ships
yī běn shū	a book	>	**shū***běn*	books
sì kǒu rén	a family of four	>	**rén***kǒu*	population

Note 1: Other collective nouns include: **chēliàng** 'vehicles', **xìnjiàn** 'correspondence (letters)', **mǎpǐ** 'horses', **zhǐzhāng** 'paper', etc.

Note 2: **Kǒu** is used as a measure word for the number of people in a family.

Collective nouns, since they are notionally plural, cannot be used with numerals and measure words. The only excepion is: **liǎngqiānwàn rénkǒu** 'a population of twenty million' (no measure word is required).

4 PRONOUNS

4.1 *Personal pronouns* in Chinese are as follows:

	singular			*plural*	
1st person	**wǒ**	I		**wǒmen**	we
2nd person	**nǐ**	you		**nǐmen**	you
3rd person	**tā**	he, she, it		**tāmen**	they

As for nouns, there is no case inflection for pronouns; they remain the same whether they are the subject or the object:

Wǒ xǐhuan tā.	I like him/her.
Tā xǐhuan wǒ.	S/he likes me.
Wǒmen bù xǐhuan tāmen.	We don't like them.
Tāmen bù xǐhuan wǒmen.	They don't like us.

The spoken form of the third person singular is the same for masculine, feminine and neuter genders. In other words, **tā** may mean he/she/it or him/her/it.

Note: In the modern written form different characters are used for third person masculine, feminine and neuter pronouns (see Glossary of Chinese Characters).

Two other personal pronouns are widely used. The first, **nín** is a polite form of second person singular:

Nǐ hǎo!	(*lit.* you good)	Hello; how are you?
Nín hǎo!	(*lit.* polite: you good)	How do you do?

Note: There is no corresponding polite form for the second person plural: *****nínmen**. To address a group politely one can use the phrase: **nín jǐ wèi**, where **jǐ** means 'several' and **wèi** is a polite measure word for *people*.

The second, **zánmen** meaning 'we'/'us' is used where the speaker intends to include the listener(s) in what is said:

    Zánmen zǒu ba!   (*lit.* we [you and I] leave p)   Let's go!

Note: **Ba** is a sentence particle indicating a suggestion (see 8.6).

Zánmen is particularly used by speakers from northern China. However, the distinction between **zánmen** and **wǒmen** seems to be growing increasingly blurred, and **wǒmen zǒu ba** 'let's go' is now common among northern as well as southern speakers.

The use of these personal pronouns is generally analogous to English. However, the neuter third person singular or plural occurs only rarely, particularly when the reference is to (an) inanimate object(s). In the sentence below, for example, there is no pronoun in the second clause:

    Zhèi gè xiǎoshuō hěn cháng, kěshì wǒ hěn xǐhuan.
    (*lit.* this mw novel very long, but I very like)
    This novel is very long, but I like *it* very much.

Note: The neuter third person singular or plural form must still be used in a **bǎ**-structure (see last example under 20.1(2)).

In contrast, when a person is referred to, the personal pronoun must be used:

Nèi gè rén hěn jiāo'ào, kěshì wǒ hěn xǐhuan tā.
(*lit.* that mw person very proud, but I very like him/her)
That person is very proud but I [still] like *him/her* very much.

When an animal is referred to, the pronoun may be included or omitted. For example,

Wǒ yǒu yī zhī māo, (tā) hěn kě'ài, wǒ hěn xǐhuan (tā).
(*lit.* I have one mw cat, (it) very lovely, I very like (it))
I have a cat. *It* is a lovely cat. I like *it* very much.

Chinese, unlike English, does not use the third person neuter pronoun in expressions about time, distance, the weather, etc. (e.g. it's late, it's a long way); instead it employs a relevant noun.

Shíjiān bù zǎo le.	**Lù hěn jìn.**
(*lit.* time not early p)	(*lit.* way very near)
It's late.	It's quite near.
Tiān qíng le.	**Zuótiān tiānqì hěn hǎo.**
(*lit.* sky turn-fine p)	(*lit.* yesterday weather very good)
It's cleared up.	It was fine yesterday.

Note: See Chapter 16 for further discusssion of **le** at the end of a sentence.

4.2   The *possessive forms* of these personal pronouns in Chinese, whether adjectives (e.g. my, your, our, etc.) or pronouns (e.g. mine, yours, ours, etc.) are all formed by adding the suffix **de:**

	singular		plural	
1st person	**wǒde**	my/mine	**wǒmende**	our/ours
			zánmende	our/ours
2nd person	**nǐde**	your/yours		
	nǐnde (polite)	your/yours	**nǐmende**	your/yours
3rd person	**tāde**	his/her(s)/its	**tāmende**	their/theirs

For example,

wǒde shū	my book
Shū shì wǒde.	The book is mine.

Note: **De** may be omitted when the reference is to relatives or close friends: e.g.

wǒ māma	my mother
nǐ nǚ péngyou	your girl-friend
tā gēge	his/her elder brother

4.3 The two *demonstrative pronouns* in Chinese are **zhè** 'this' and **nà** 'that':

Zhè shì wǒde.	This is mine.
Nà shì nǐde chēpiào.	That is your train/coach ticket.
Nà bù xíng.	That won't do.

Zhè and **nà** can also modify nouns as *demonstrative adjectives*, but like numerals they must normally be followed by a measure. With measures regularly **zhè** becomes **zhèi** and **nà** becomes **nèi**.

Nèi gè rén shì wǒ bàba.
(*lit.* that mw person be my father)
That man is my father.

Wǒ yào mǎi *zhèi* zhāng dìtú.
(*lit.* I want buy this mw map)
I want to buy this map.

Note: Where the context is sufficient (i.e. when the noun has already been identified), the noun may be omitted:

Nèi gè shì tāde.	That one is his/hers.
Wǒ xǐhuān *zhèi gè*.	I like this one.
Zhèi wèi shì wǒmende lǎoshī.	This (polite form) is our teacher.

Plurals of the demonstratives can be formed by using the measure **xiē** (cf. 3.2 (8)): **zhèi xiē** 'these' and **nèi xiē** 'those':

Zhèi xiē shì wǒmende.	These are ours.
Nèi xiē shì nǐmende.	Those are yours.
Zhèi xiē xiāngzi shì wǒde.	These suitcases are mine.
Nèi xiē yīfu shì tāde.	Those clothes are his/hers.
Zhèi xiē qián shì tāde.	This money is his/hers.

When demonstratives are used with numbers, the word order is demonstrative, number, measure, noun:

Zhè/Zhèi sān zhāng piào shì nínde.	These three tickets are yours (polite).
Nà/Nèi liǎng fēng xìn shì nǐde.	Those two letters are yours.

4.4 The main *interrogative pronouns* in Chinese are:

shéi/shuí	who(m)
shéide/shuíde	whose
nǎ/něi (+ measure word + noun)	which
nǎ/něi + xiē (+ noun)	which (plural)
shénme	what

When interrogative pronouns are used, the word order of the sentence does not change from that of statement. In other words, the interrogative word comes at the point in the sentence where the answer word is expected:

Q: **Nèi gè rén shì *shéi*?**
(*lit.* that mw person be who)
Who is that person?

A: **Nèi gè rén shì *wǒ bàba*.**
(*lit.* that mw person be my father)
That person is my father.

Q: **Zhèi zhī qiānbǐ shì *shéide*?**
(*lit.* this mw pencil be whose)
Whose pencil is this?

A: **Zhèi zhī qiānbǐ shì *tāde*.**
(*lit.* this mw pencil be his/hers)
This pencil is his/hers.

Q: **Nǐ xǐhuan *nǎ/něi* fú huàr?**
(*lit.* you like which mw painting)
Which painting do you like?

A: **Wǒ xǐhuan *zhèi* fú huàr.**
(*lit.* I like this mw painting)
I like this painting.

Q: **Nǐ rènshi *nǎ/něi* liǎng gè rén?**
(*lit.* you know which two mw people)
Which two people do you know?

A: **Wǒ rènshi *zhè/zhèi* liǎng gè rén.**
(*lit.* I know this two mw people)
I know these two people.

Q: **Nǐ rènshi nǎ/*něi* xiē zì?**
(*lit.* you know which mw character)
Which characters do you know?

A: **Wǒ rènshi *zhèi* xiē zì.**
(*lit.* I know these mw character)
I know these characters.

Q: **Nǐ zhǎo *shénme*?**
(*lit.* you look-for what)
What are you looking for?

A: **Wǒ zhǎo *wǒde qiánbāo*.**
(*lit.* I look-for my purse/wallet)
I'm looking for my purse/wallet.

4.5 Other *miscellaneous pronouns* include:

dàjiā	everybody (used before and after the verb)
rénjiā	the other person (occurring before and after the verb)
shéi/shuí	everybody (placed before the verb and *always* with **dōu** 'all' or **yě** 'also')
shénme	everything (likewise placed before the verb and *always* with **dōu** 'all' or **yě** 'also')

Dàjiā **dōu zhīdào zhèi jiàn shì.**
(*lit.* everybody all know this mw matter)
Everybody knows this.

Tā rènshi *dàjiā*
(*lit.* s/he recognise everybody)
S/he knows everybody.

Rénjiā **bù lǐ tā.**
(*lit.* others not bother-with him/her)
The others ignored him/her.

Tā bù lǐ *rénjiā.*
(*lit.* s/he not bother-with others)
S/he ignored the others.

Shéi **dōu/yě xǐhuan tā.**
(*lit.* everybody all/also like him/her)
Everybody likes him/her.

Shéi **yě bù xǐhuan tā.**
(*lit.* everybody also not like him/her)
Nobody likes him/her.

Tā *shéi* **dōu/yě bù xǐhuan.**
(*lit.* s/he everybody all/also not like)
S/he doesn't like anybody.

Tā *shénme* **dōu/yě chī.**
(*lit.* s/he everything all/also eat)
S/he eats everything.

Tā *shénme* **dōu/yě bù chī.**
(*lit.* s/he everything all/also not eat)
S/he doesn't eat anything.

Note 1: **Dōu** 'all' and **yě** 'also' are referential adverbs used to reinforce the idea of 'every-body'. Their use is discussed in full in 14.3. A discussion of the joint occurrence of both subject and topic in a pre-verbal position (e.g. **Tā** *shéi* **dōu/yě bù lǐ** 's/he ignores everybody') is found in 18.4 and 18.5.

Note 2: To express 'each other' or 'one another' the adverb **hùxiāng** 'mutually' is placed after the subject: e.g. **Tāmen** *hùxiāng* **bāngzhù.** 'They help each other/one another.'

4.6 Pronouns, like nouns, may be linked by conjunctions, such as **hé** (**gēn**, **tóng** and **yǔ**) 'and' and **huò** 'or': (See 1.4)

nǐ *hé* **wǒ**   you and me
zhèi gè *huò* **nèi gè**   this one or that one

5   ADJECTIVES AND ATTRIBUTIVES

5.1   *Attributives* are words or expressions used to qualify nouns. They may either describe or delimit them. In Chinese, all attributives precede the word they qualify. This contrasts with English where many attributives, e.g. relative clauses, prepositional and participial phrases, follow the noun.

5.2 When *adjectives* are used as attributives in Chinese, a distinction can be made between monosyllabic adjectives and adjectives with more than one syllable.

5.2.1 Monosyllabic adjectives are placed directly before the nouns they qualify:

jiù shū	*old* books
hǎo péngyou	*good* friends
yī tiáo *hóng* qúnzi	a *red* skirt
yī gè *dà* jiātíng	a *big* family
Zhè shì *zhēn* pí.	This is *real* leather.
Nà shì yī gè *xīn* shǒubiǎo.	That is a *new* watch.

Note: A monosyllabic adjective attached to a noun may often become an established word or expression and take on a distinctive meaning of its own: **dàren** 'adult'(*lit.* big person), **xiǎofèi** 'tip, gratuity' (*lit.* small fee), **gōngyuán** 'park' (*lit.* public garden), **sīrén** 'personal, private' (*lit.* private person), etc.

5.2.2 If the adjective has more than one syllable, the particle **de** is generally used between the adjective and the noun it qualifies:

piàoliàng de yīfu	*beautiful* clothes
niánqīng de gūniang	*young* girls
yī gè *cuòwù de* juédìng	a *wrong* decision
ruǎnmiánmiān de dìtǎn	*soft* carpet

The same general principle applies when a monosyllabic adjective is preceded by an adverb of degree:

hěn xīn de yīfu	very new clothes
yī gè *shífēn zhòng de* bāoguǒ	a very heavy parcel
yī suǒ *jí dà de* fángzi	an extremely big house

5.2.3 However, a limited number of common two-syllable adjectives are used *without* **de**. Idiomatic phrases such as **hěn duō** 'many' and **bù shǎo** 'quite a few' may be included with them:

cǎisè diànshì	colour television
gēnběn yuánzé	fundamental principles
hěn duō rén	a lot of people
bù shǎo shì	quite a few matters
bù shǎo shíjiān	quite some time

Note 1: Other disyllabic adjectives which do not usually require **de** are: **yīqiè** 'all', **gèbié** 'specific', **xīnshì** 'new-style' 'modern', **zhǔyào** 'primary', etc.

Note 2: Disyllabic attributives without **de** may often be used with disyllabic nouns to form idiomatic expressions: **lǚxíng zhīpiào** 'traveller's cheque', **shèngdàn lǐwù** 'Christmas present', **bǎihuò shāngdiàn** 'department store' (*lit.* hundred-goods shop)', **diànshì jiémù** 'television programme', etc.

5.3 Nouns may also act as *nominal attributives*. Whether monosyllabic or polysyllabic, they do not generally require the particle **de**. In some cases the resulting expressions have become established terms in the language, as in the first three examples below:

shū jià	>	**shūjià**	*book*shelf
diànyǐng yuàn	>	**diànyǐngyuàn**	cinema (*lit. film* house)
shíjiān biǎo	>	**shíjiānbiǎo**	*time*table
yǔfǎ shū			*grammar* book
diànhuà hàomǎ			*telephone* number
shí bàng fákuǎn			*ten pound* fine
liǎng Yīnglǐ lù			*two miles* distance

Note: Material nouns are often used as nominal attributives: **yī shàn *tiě* mén** 'an iron gate', **yī dǔ *zhuān* qiáng** 'a brick wall', **yī tiáo *jīn* xiàngliàn** 'a gold necklace', **yī jiàn *pí* jiākè** 'a leather jacket', etc.

5.3.1 The particle **de** may be used between a nominal attributive and the noun it qualifies, but in these cases it indicates either possession or close association:

bàba de **lǐngdài**	father's tie
xuéxiào de **yùndòngchǎng**	the school's sportsfield

Note: Compare this with the use of **de** in possessive pronouns: **wǒde xié** 'my shoes', **tāde wàzi** 'his/her socks/stockings', etc.

5.4 *Prepositional phrases* (e.g. *kào* **chuáng** 'against the bed', see Chapter 19) and *postpositional phrases* (e.g. **zhuōzi** *xià* 'under the table', see Chapter 11), when used as attributives, always require **de**:

(1) Prepositional phrases:

kào qiáng de **zhuōzi**	the desk/table against the wall
yán lù de **shāngdiàn**	the shops along the road

(2) Postpositional phrases:

wūzi lǐ de **jiājù**	furniture in the room
qiáng shàng de **biāoyǔ**	slogans on the wall

5.5 Attributives in Chinese become more complex when they contain verbs. Below are some examples of verbal phrase or clause attributives. They always require the use of the particle **de**:

(1) Verbal phrases:

mài bàozhǐ de **shāngdiàn**	a shop *that sells newspapers*
xīn lái de **mìshū**	the secretary *who has just come*
yǒu qián de **jiātíng**	families *which have money*

> **yào xǐ de yīfu**   clothes *which need washing*

(2) Verbal clauses:

> **nǐ yào fù de qián**   the money *you will have to pay*
> **nǐ jiào de cài**   the dish(es) *you have ordered*
> **tāmen qù Zhōngguó de nèi**   the day *they went to China*
> **(yī) tiān**
> **gémìng kāishǐ de dìfang**   the place *where the revolution started*

5.6 Where attributives of various types (adjectival, nominal or verbal) occur in one sentence, they must follow one of the following sequences:

(1) An adjectival attributive will always precede a nominal attributive:

> **hēi pí xié**   *black leather* shoes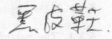
> **huīsè de róng dàyī**   [a] *grey felt* coat

(2) An adjectival attributive with **de** always comes before an adjectival attributive without **de**:

> **gānjìng de xiǎo fángjiān**   [a] *clean, small* room
> **hěn gāo de bái fángzi**   [a] *very high white* house

(3) A verbal attributive invariably precedes all other attributives:

> **huì huà huàr de xīn tóngxué** [a] *new* coursemate *who can draw/*
>   *paint*
> **dài yǎnjìng de nǚ lǎoshī**   [the] *woman* teacher *who wears glasses*

5.7 Demonstrative and numeral phrases precede all attributives:

> **zhè/zhèi liǎng tiáo hóng qúnzi**   *these two red* skirts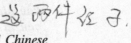
> **nà/nèi xiē kàn Zhōngwén zázhì**   *those* people *who read Chinese*
> **de rén**   *magazines*
> **nà/nèi zhī nǐ xǐhuan de xiǎo**   *that little tabby* cat *(which) you like*
> **huā māo**

Note: The only exception is that with verbal attributives the demonstrative/numeral phrase may come after the attributive:

> **kàn Zhōngwén zázhì de nèi xiē rén**   *those* people *who read Chinese magazines*
> **nǐ xǐhuan de nèi zhī xiǎo huā māo**   *that little tabby* cat *(which) you like*

5.8 A possessive pronoun will precede all qualifying phrases (e.g. demonstrative/numeral phrase and attributives):

wǒde sān gè hǎo **péngyou**
my three good friends

nǐde nèi jiàn xīn mǎi de pí **jiǎkè**
that newly-bought leather jacket *of yours*

5.9   When two similar adjectives qualify the same noun, they are usually joined together by the conjunction **ér** 'as well as':

(yī gè) niánqīng *ér* **piàoliang de gūniang**
(a) young, beautiful girl

(yī jiān) gānjìng *ér* **zhěngqí de fángjiān**
(a) clean and tidy room

5.10   If the context makes it clear, the noun following the attributive can be omitted, though in these cases **de** must always be retained:

Wǒ xǐhuan nèi gè *xīn de.*
(*lit.* I like that mw new p)
I like that new one.

Zhè shì *wǒ zuótiān mǎi de.*
(*lit.* this be I yesterday buy p)
This is what I bought yesterday.

5.11   Finally, in Chinese any grammatical category or construction may be attached without **de** to a following noun headword to become a word or idiom in the language:

*yǎnglǎo*jīn	old-age pension	(*lit.* support-old-money)
*qīngyīn*yuè	light music	(*lit.* light-music)
*lǚxíng*shè	travel agent	(*lit.* travel-society)
*shuāngrén*chuáng	double bed	(*lit.* two-people-bed)
*lùyīn*jī	tape recorder	(*lit.* record-sound-machine)

Note: The italics mark out the attributives from the (non-italicised) headwords.

II VERBS

是有. 了过着. 在.
能

INTRODUCTION

Verbs in Chinese (as in English) may be divided into three major categories: the verb **shì** 'to be', the verb **yǒu** 'to have' and a broad set of verbs that may be loosely called action verbs. **Shì** 'to be' is used to introduce nominal predicates. It does not occur with adjectival predicates, which come directly after the (pro)nominal subject without any copula, usually with the reinforcement of a degree adverb. Many such adjectives, if followed by the particle **le**, can acquire a function similar to verbs; we have called these state verbs, since they signify state rather than action. **Yǒu** 'to have', as well as indicating possession, may express existence, providing the structure for introductory phrases like 'there is/are' in English. Action verbs embrace a wide range of semantic groups including motion verbs, modal verbs, attitudinal verbs, intentional verbs, dative verbs, causative verbs, etc. Analysis of these groups enables the characterisation of many verbal constructions and their functions.

One feature common to all verbs in Chinese is that they do not conjugate for tense. The time of the action specified by the verb is normally indicated by placing a time expression before the verb or at the beginning of the sentence. Chinese verbs do have to be related to aspect, however, in that there needs to be some indication of whether the action has been completed, is on-going, or is part of past experience. This is achieved by introducing an aspect marker **le**, **guo**, or **zhe** as a suffix to the verb, or **zài** directly before the verb. Action verbs without aspect markers usually express habitual action or intention.

Expressions indicating location, like time expressions, come before the verb. This means that the action of a verb is always expressed against a previously established setting of time and place.

Everything that comes after the verb (apart from the object) we have put in the category of complement. The various types of complement, indicating duration, frequency, result, direction, manner, consequential state, etc., follow logically from the action of the verb. One interesting feature of result and direction complements is that they can be converted into potential complements. Such potential complements have a slightly different emphasis from **néng** 'to be able', which is one of a substantial number of modal verbs in Chinese.

Chinese, as a verb-oriented language, encodes most ideas in terms of verbs (instead of prepositions, abstract nouns, long attributives, etc.). It is therefore important to understand the central role of verbs in Chinese sentences and the various syntactic elements associated with them.

6   ADJECTIVAL AND NOMINAL PREDICATES; THE VERB SHÌ

6.1 In this chapter we deal with predicates which describe or define the subject. In English such predicates would normally use the verb 'to be' as a *copula* or *link verb*. In Chinese they are slightly more complex, particularly in the case of adjectival predicates.

6.2 In an adjectival predicate the verb 'to be' is not used. This is a distinctive feature of Chinese:

Tā *hěn* gāo.
(*lit*. s/he very tall)
S/he is (very) tall.

Zhèi suǒ fángzi de zūjīn *hěn* guì.
(*lit*. this mw house p rent very expensive)
The rent of this house is (very) expensive.

6.2.1 The adjective used in such an adjectival predicate must always be modified by a *degree adverb*, most commonly **hěn** 'very'. **Hěn** is often unstressed, when it carries little meaning:

Wǒ *hěn* nánguò.
(*lit*. I very sad)
I am (very) sad.

Zhèi jiàn shì *hěn* qíguài.
(*lit*. this mw matter very strange)
This matter is (very) strange.

Nèi gè rén *hěn* kěkào.
(*lit*. that mw person very reliable)
That person is (very) reliable.

Other degree adverbs, unlike **hěn**, are normally stressed. The most common are **zhēn** 'really', **xiāngdāng** 'fairly', **fēicháng** or **shífēn** 'extremely':

Nèi suǒ xuéxiào *zhēn* dà.	That school is *really* big.
Nèi gè háizi *xiāngdāng* cōngmíng.	That child is *fairly* clever.
Zhèi gè lǐtáng *fēicháng* kuānchang.	This hall is *extremely* spacious.
Zhèi tiáo jiē *shífēn* fánmáng.	This street is *extremely* busy.

Note: If a degree adverb is not used with an adjectival predicate, a contrast is implied:

Zhèi běn shū *yǒuyòng.*   This book is useful (but that one isn't).
Zuótiān *liángkuài.*   Yesterday was cool (but today isn't).

6.2.2 However, there is no need for a degree adverb when the adjectival predicate is negated by **bù** 'not':

Zhèi gè wèntí *bù* **zhòngyào.**
(*lit.* this mw problem not important)
This problem is not important.

Nèi bǎ yǐzi *bù* **shūfu.**
(*lit.* that mw chair not comfortable)
That chair is not comfortable.

If both **hěn** and **bù** are present, the word order becomes important to the meaning:

Zhèi gè wèntí *bù hěn* **zhòngyào.**
(*lit.* this mw problem not very important)
This problem is not very important.

Nèi bǎ yǐzi *hěn bù* **shūfu.**
(*lit.* that mw chair very not comfortable)
That chair is very uncomfortable.

6.2.3 Adjectival predicates are often followed by a verb (phrase) to indicate the area in which the quality or property expressed in the adjective applies:

Zhèi gè cài *hěn hǎochī.*
(*lit.* this mw dish very good-eat)
This dish is delicious.

Tāde Yīngwén *hěn nán dǒng.*
(*lit.* his/her English very difficult-understand)
His/her English is difficult to understand.

Zhōngwén yǔfǎ *hěn róngyì xué.*
(*lit.* Chinese grammar very easy learn)
Chinese grammar is easy to learn.

Note: **hǎo** 'good', as in the first example, may be followed by a number of verbs to form established words or expressions: **hǎotīng** 'pleasant to the ear', **hǎokàn** 'good-looking', **hǎowán** 'enjoyable', etc. **nán** 'difficult' can be used similarly to convey the opposite meaning: **nán chī** 'unpleasant to the taste', **nánkàn** 'ugly', **nán tīng** 'unpleasant to the ear', etc.

6.3 In the examples above, the adjectives may be described as *gradable* in that they can be modified by degree adverbs. Adjectives which have a more definite either-or quality (e.g. **nán** 'male', **nǚ** 'female', **zhēn** 'true',

jiǎ 'false', etc.) and are therefore not so readily modified, may be called *non-gradable* adjectives. These non-gradable adjectives, when functioning as adjectival predicates, commonly require the use of the copula **shì** in conjunction with the particle **de:**

Zhè *shì* **zhēn** *de.*
(*lit.* this be true p)
This is true.

Tāde huà *shì* **jiǎ** *de.*
(*lit.* his words be false p)
What he said is untrue.

Zhèi xiē fúzhuāng *shì* **xīnshì** *de.*
(*lit.* these clothes be new-type p)
These clothes are fashionable.

Most non-gradable adjectives exist in complementary pairs, either as antonyms (e.g. **zhèngquè** 'correct' and **cuòwù** 'false') or as positives and negatives (e.g. **zhèngshì** 'formal' and **fēi zhèngshì** 'informal').

Note: Other common non-gradable adjectives and adjectival idioms are: **sǐ** 'dead', **huó** 'alive'; **cí** 'female' (animal), **xióng** 'male' (animal); **tiānrán** 'natural', **rénzào** 'man-made' 'artificial'; **(yǒu) kěnéng** 'possible', **bù kěnéng** 'impossible', etc.

6.3.1 *Terms of shape, colour or material* similarly tend to indicate an absolute either-or quality or property and as adjectival predicates follow the same ... **shì** ... **de** format:

Nèi zhāng zhuōzi *shì* **yuán** *de.*
(*lit.* that mw table be round p)
That table is round.

Tāde chènshān *shì* **bái** *de.*
(*lit.* his/her shirt/blouse be white p)
His/her shirt/blouse is white.

Zhèi tiáo qúnzi *shì* **bù** *de.*
(*lit.* this mw skirt be cloth p)
This skirt is made of cloth.

Note 1: Other terms in this category include: (shape) **fāng** 'square', **biǎn** 'flat', **chángfāngxíng** 'oblong'; (colour) **hóng** 'red', **lán** 'blue', **huáng** 'yellow', **zǐ** 'purple', **hēi** 'black', **hèsè/kāfēisè** 'brown', **huīsè** 'grey'; (material) **jīn** 'gold', **yín** 'silver', **sùliào** 'plastic', **nílóng** 'nylon', **pí** 'leather', **mù** 'wood', **tiě** 'iron', **gāng** 'steel', **cí** 'porcelain'.

Note 2: Regarding terms of colour and shape, it is possible to have different degrees of, for example, 'redness' or 'roundness'; it is therefore possible to say:

Zhèi duǒ huā *hěn hóng.*   This flower is very red.
Nèi gè pánzi *bù tài yuán*.   That plate is not quite round.

6.4 Nouns and pronouns can also act as *nominal and pronominal predicates*, where they generally require the use of the copula or link verb **shì** 'to be':

Tā *shì* wǒde bǐyǒu.
(*lit.* s/he be my pen-friend)
S/he is my pen-friend.

Zhè *shì* Wáng xiānsheng.
(*lit.* this be Wang mister)
This is Mr Wang. (as in an introduction)

Wǒ měi gè yuè de shōurù *shì* yī qiān duō bàng.
(*lit.* I every mw month p income be one thousand more pound)
My monthly income is over a thousand pounds.

Zhèi gè chéngshì de shìzhǎng *shì* shéi?
(*lit.* this mw city p mayor be who)
Who is the mayor of this town?

Zhè *shì* shénme?
(*lit.* this be what)
What is this?

Jīnnián *shì* zhū nián.
(*lit.* this-year be pig year)
This is the year of the pig.

Note: In the Chinese lunar calendar, the years are divided into cycles of twelve years, with each year named after a particular animal, real or imaginary: i.e. rat, ox, tiger, rabbit, dragon, snake, horse, sheep, monkey, rooster, dog, pig. Someone born in the year of the pig, for example, may say **Wǒ shǔ zhū** 'I belong to the pig'.

Wǒde àihào *shì* pá shān.
(*lit.* my hobby be climbing-hills)
My hobby is hill-walking/mountain-climbing.

Wǒ(de) fùqīn shì dàifu.
(*lit.* my father be doctor)
My father is a (medical) doctor.

Zhèr *shì* pàichūsuǒ/jǐngchájú.
(*lit.* here be police-station)
This is the police station.

Note 1: **Pàichūsuǒ** (*lit.* dispatch-out-unit) and **gōng'ānjú** (*lit.* public-security bureau) are used in mainland China for 'police station', and **jǐngchájú** (*lit.* police bureau) in Chinese communities outside mainland China.

Note 2: It will be apparent from the above examples that **shì**, in contrast with other verbs, may be followed by a noun which is of either definite or indefinite reference. Where **shì** is defining something (or someone), the reference is indefinite; where it is locating something (or someone) the reference is definite. Compare:

Zhè shì (yī gè) túshūguǎn.	This is a library.
Zhè shì túshūguǎn.	This is the library (you're looking for).

6.4.1 A number of verbs can be said to resemble the copula **shì**:

Wǒ *xìng* **Lǐ**.
(*lit*. I surname Li)
My surname is Li.

Wǒ *jiào* **Àilíng**.
(*lit*. I call Ailing)
My name is Ailing.

Zhèi gè háizi *xiàng* **tā māma, bù** *xiàng* **tā bàba**.
(*lit*. this mw child resemble his/her mother, not resemble his/her father)
This child is like his/her mother, not his/her father.

Wǒ *shǔ* **lóng**.
(*lit*. I belong dragon)
I was born in the year of the dragon. (See note under 6.4)

6.4.2 However, nouns indicating nationality, personal characteristics, age, or dates, price, etc., may be used as nominal predicates without a copula or link verb:

Wǒ *Yīngguó rén*.
(*lit*. I England person)
I am from Britain.

Wǒ mèimei *jīn tóufa*.
(*lit*. my younger-sister golden hair)
My younger sister is a blonde.

Wǒ *èrshí yī suì*.
(*lit*. I twenty-one years-of-age)
I am twenty-one.

Jīntiān xīngqī yī.
(*lit*. today Monday)
Today is Monday.

Zhèi shuāng xié *shí èr bàng*.
(*lit*. this pair shoes twelve pound)
This pair of shoes costs twelve pounds.

6.5 In the negative form of a non-gradable adjectival predicate (6.3 and 6.3.1) or a nominal/pronominal predicate (6.4 and 6.4.1), the copula **shì** is always present with **bù** placed immediately before it:

Tāde kùzi *bù shì* **hēi de.**
(*lit.* his trousers not be black p)
His/her trousers are not black.

Zhèi xiē chuānglián *bù shì* **chóu de.**
(*lit.* this mw curtain not be silk p)
These curtains are not made of silk.

Jīntiān *bù shì* **xīngqī sān.**
(*lit.* today not be week three)
Today is not Wednesday.

Tā *bù shì* **Měiguórén.**
(*lit.* s/he not be American)
S/he is not American.

Note: **Shì** may also be used as an *intensifier* for emphatic statements. This is discussed in detail in Chapter 22.

7 THE VERB YǑU; COMPARISONS

7.1 The verb **yǒu** has a number of functions. Primarily it indicates possession or existence (the latter is discussed in 11.5), but it also appears in expressions of comparisons.

7.1.1 We start here with **yǒu** as a verb of possession meaning 'to have':

Wǒ *yǒu* **(yī) gè dìdi.**
(*lit.* I have one mw younger-brother)
I have a younger brother.

Tā *yǒu* **hěn duō qián.**
(lit. s/he have very much money)
S/he has a lot of money.

Zhīzhū *yǒu* **bā zhī jiǎo.**
(lit. spider have eight mw foot)
Spiders have eight legs.

Zhèi gè guìzi *yǒu* **wǔ gè chōuti.**
(lit. this mw cabinet have five mw drawer)
This cabinet has five drawers.

Míngtiān wǒ *yǒu* **(yī) gè yuēhuì.**
(lit. tomorrow I have one mw appointment)
I have an appointment tomorrow.

7.1.2 Yǒu is negated by placing **méi** (NOT **bù**) before it:

Wǒ *méi yǒu* zìxíngchē.
(*lit.* I not have bicycle)
I haven't got a bicycle.

Tāmen *méi yǒu* diànshìjī.
(*lit.* they not have television-set)
They don't have a television.

Note: In a negative sentence, the object of **yǒu** is not normally qualified by the 'numeral **yī** (+ measure word)', because in Chinese there is no need to quantify what one doesn't possess:

*Wǒ méi yǒu **yī** *liàng* zìxíngchē.
(*lit.* *I not have one mw bicycle)

Méi yǒu may often be abbreviated to **méi** in speech:

Wǒ xiànzài méi gōngzuò.
(*lit.* I now not-have work)
I haven't got a job at the moment.

7.1.3   Yǒu often takes modified or unmodified verbal objects to indicate change or development:

Tāde Zhōngwén *yǒu jìnbù*.
(*lit.* his/her Chinese have progress)
S/he has made progress in his/her Chinese.

Tā jiā de shēnghuó shuǐpíng *yǒu* hěn dà de *tígāo*.
(*lit.* his/her family p living standard have very big p rise)
The living standard of his/her family has greatly improved.

Yīngguó de jīngjì zuìjìn *yǒu* yī xiē *fāzhǎn*.
(*lit.* Britain p economy recently have some develop)
There has been some development in Britain's economy recently.

Zhèr de qíngkuàng *yǒu* bù shǎo *biànhuà*.
(*lit.* here p situation have not-few change)
There have been quite a few changes in the situation over here.

Tāde shōurù *yǒu* yī xiē *zēngjiā*.
(*lit.* his/her income have some increase)
There has been some increase in his/her income.

7.1.4   Yǒu often takes abstract noun objects to form idiomatic expressions, which may be equivalent to English adjectives. These regularly function as gradable adjectival predicates and can be modified by adverbs of degree:

Zhèi běn xiǎoshuō *hěn yǒu yìsi*.
(*lit.* this mw novel very have meaning)
This novel is very interesting.

Nèi gè yǎnyuán *fēicháng yǒu míng.*
(*lit.* that mw actor/actress extremely have name)
That actor/actress is extremely famous.

These expressions must be negated by **méi(yǒu)**:

Wǒ jīntiān wǎnshang *méi(yǒu) kòng.*
(*lit.* I today evening not-have leisure)
I am busy tonight.

Nèi gè niánqīng rén zhēn *méi(yǒu) lǐmào.*
(*lit.* that mw young person really not-have politeness)
That young person is really impolite.

Note: Other commonly used idioms with **yǒu** are **yǒu qián** 'rich', **yǒu xuéwèn** 'learned', **yǒu jīngyàn** 'experienced'. For example,

Nèi gè shāngrén hěn *yǒu qián.*
That business-man is (very) rich.

Nèi gè jiàoshòu hěn *yǒu xuéwèn.*
That professor is very learned.

Zhèi gè lǎo rén fēicháng *yǒu jīngyàn.*
This old man is extremely experienced.

7.1.5 Yǒu may also be used to introduce an adjectival predicate which incorporates a number:

Zhèi zhuàng lóufáng *yǒu èrshí mǐ gāo.*
(*lit.* this mw storey-building have twenty metre high)
This building is twenty metres high.

Nèi tiáo lù *yǒu liǎng bǎi Yīnglǐ cháng.*
(*lit.* that mw road have two hundred mile long)
That road is two hundred miles long.

By extension **yǒu** may be followed by **duō** (how) and an adjective to express questions about age, time, distance, and so on:

Nǐ dìdi *yǒu duō gāo?*
(*lit.* you(r) younger-brother have how tall)
How tall is your younger brother?

Nǐ mèimei *yǒu duō dà?*
(*lit.* you(r) younger-sister have how big)
How old is your younger sister?

Nǐ jiā *yǒu duō yuǎn?*
(*lit.* you(r) home have how far)
How far is your home from here?

7.2 *Comparison* in Chinese may be expressed in a number of ways. The most common makes use of the preposition **bǐ** 'compared with', and follows the pattern X **bǐ** Y + gradable adjective. (We noted in 6.2.1 that a gradable adjective unmodified by a degree adverb implies a contrast or comparison.)

Wǒ bàba *bǐ* **wǒ māma** *shòu.*
(*lit.* my father compare my mother thin)
My father is thinner than my mother.

Zhōngwén *bǐ* **Yīngwén** *nán.*
(*lit.* Chinese compare English difficult)
Chinese is more difficult than English.

Láihuípiào *bǐ* **dānchéngpiào** *hésuàn.*
(*lit.* return-ticket compare single-journey-ticket fit-calculation)
A return ticket is more economical than a single.

The adjective in a comparison cannot be modified by degree adverbs such as **hěn** 'very', **fēicháng, shífēn** 'extremely', etc., and it would be wrong to say:

*****Zhōngwén bǐ Yīngwén** *hěn* **nán.**
(*lit.**Chinese compare English very difficult.)

7.2.1 The degree of comparison may be made clear, however, either by using the adverbs **gèng** or **hái** meaning 'even more':

Jīntiān bǐ zuótiān *gèng* **lěng.**
(*lit.* today compare yesterday even-more cold)
Today is *even* colder than yesterday.

Zhèr bǐ nár *hái* **ānjìng.**
(*lit.* here compare there even-more quiet)
It is *even* quieter here than there.

or by tagging various kinds of *degree complements* to the adjectives:

Zhōngwén bǐ Yīngwén nán *de duō.*
(*lit.* Chinese compare English difficult p much)
Chinese is *much* more difficult than English.

Wǒ mèimei bǐ wǒ jiějie gāo *yī diǎnr.*
(*lit.* my younger-sister compare my elder-sister tall one bit)
My younger sister is *slightly/a bit* taller than my elder sister.

Wǒ gēge bǐ wǒ dà *liǎng suì.*
(*lit.* my elder-brother compare me big two years-of-age)
My elder brother is *two years* older than I am.

Note: For further discussion of degree complements see 13.6.

7.2.2 A negative comparison can be expressed in two ways:

(1) By placing **bù** before **bǐ** (i.e. X is not more ... than Y):

Jīntiān *bù bǐ* zuótiān *lěng*.
(*lit.* today not compare yesterday cold)
Today is not colder than yesterday.

Zhèi tiáo lù *bǔ bǐ* nèi tiáo *jìn*.
(*lit.* this mw road not compare that mw near)
This is not a shorter way than that.

(2) By using the formulation X **méi** (**yǒu**) Y (**nàme/zhème** 'so') adjective
(i.e. X is not so ... as Y):

**Jīntiān de tiānqì *méi(yǒu)* zuótiān (nàme/zhème)
nuǎnhuo/liángkuài.**
(*lit.* today p weather not-have yesterday (so) warm/cool)
It's not so warm/cool today as it was yesterday.

Wǒde wéijīn *méi(yǒu)* nǐde (nàme/zhème) *hǎokàn*.
(*lit.* my scarf not-have your (so) good-to-look-at)
My scarf doesn't look as nice as yours

Note 1: As illustrated in the first example under (2), Chinese like English can concentrate
on the contrasting attributive rather than expressing the comparison in full, i.e. it is not
necessary to say **zuótiān de tiānqì**.

Note 2: This formulation with **yǒu** may be used in a positive sentence when a question is
asked:

Zhèi gè *yǒu* nèi gè *piányi* ma?
(*lit.* this mw have that mw cheap p)
Is this as cheap as that?

Shuō Rìyǔ *yǒu* shuō Hànyǔ nàme *róngyì* ma?
(*lit.* speak Japanese have speak Chinese so easy p)
Is speaking Japanese as easy as speaking Chinese?

In fact these questions are asking about 'equivalence'; their meaning overlaps with that of
the **yīyàng** structure (see 7.2.3).

7.2.3 Equivalence or similarity is conveyed by use of the adjective **yīyàng**
'the same' (*lit.* one kind) in the formulation X **gēn** Y **yīyàng** (i.e. X is the
same as Y):

Wǒde *gēn* nǐde *yīyàng*.
(*lit* my and your one-kind)
Mine is the same as yours.

This structure can be extended by the addition of a further adjective·

Nèi jiàn xínglǐ *gēn* zhèi jiàn *yīyàng qīng*.
(*lit.* that mw luggage and this mw same light)
That piece of luggage is as light as this one.

Wǒ *hé* nǐ *yīyàng lèi*.
(*lit.* I and you same tired)
I am just as tired as you are.

Note: We have seen earlier that **gēn**, **hé**, **tóng**, and **yǔ** 'and' may be used interchangeably (see 1.4)

7.3   Where only one item is mentioned in a comparison, a simple comparative or superlative expression like **bǐjiào** 'comparatively' or **zuì** 'most' is placed before the adjective:

Zhèi gè páizi de mìtáng *bǐjiào* piányi.
(*lit.* this mw brand p honey comparatively cheap)
This brand of honey is (relatively) cheaper.

Nèi gè gōngyuán *zuì* měilì.
(*lit.* that mw park most beautiful)
That park is the most beautiful [of all].

8   VERBS AND ASPECT MARKERS

8.1   Having discussed **shì** 'to be' and **yǒu** 'to have', we will now look at action verbs, state verbs and dative verbs.

8.2   *Action verbs* signify movement or action (e.g. **dǎ** 'hit'; 'strike'; 'beat'; **pǎo** 'run'; **hē** 'drink'). Apart from being used in imperatives (see 8.6), they are generally employed for narrative purposes. One of the most prominent features of action verbs in narration is that they are almost always used in conjunction with an *aspect marker*, **le**, **guo** or **zhe** (suffixed to the verb), or **zài** (preceding the verb). However, action verbs may also occur without any marker, when they describe one of the following:

(1)   *Habitual action*:

Háizimen tiāntiān *kàn* diànshì.
(*lit.* children day-day see television)
The children watch television every day.

Mǎ *chī* cǎo.
(*lit.* horse eat grass)
Horses eat grass.

(2) *Permanent or long-term characteristics*:

Wǒ yī jiǔ sān wǔ nián *chūshì*.
(*lit*. I one-nine-three-five year come-out-into-world)
I was born in 1935.

Wǒ *xìn* **Jīdūjiào.**
(*lit*. I believe Christ-religion)
I am a Christian.

Note: Other religions (branches of religion): **Fójiào** 'Buddhism', **Tiānzhǔjiào** 'Catholicism', **Yīsīlánjiào** 'Islam', **Dàojiào** 'Taoism', etc.

(3) *Intended action*:

Wǒ xiànzài *qù* **bàngōngshì.**
(*lit*. I now go office)
I am going to the office now.

Jīntiān wǒ *qǐngkè*.
(*lit*. today I invite-guest)
It'll be on me today.

8.3 The aspect markers **le, guo, zhe** and **zài**:

8.3.1 Le indicates the *'completion of an action'*:

Wǒ *xiěle* **sān fēng xìn.**
(*lit*. I write asp three mw letter)
I wrote three letters..

Wǒ *xǐle* **yī gè zǎo.**
(*lit*. I wash asp one mw bath)
I took a bath.

Wǒ *mǎile* **liǎng zhāng láihuí piào.**
(*lit*. I buy asp two mw come-return ticket)
I bought two return tickets.

As in these three examples, the object of a verb with **le** is usually something specified or defined. If the object is a single unmodified noun, the sentence is generally felt to be incomplete:

*Wǒ *chīle* **fàn.**
(*lit*. * I eat asp cooked-rice)

This problem is resolved if the object is specified or the sentence is extended:

Wǒ *chīle* **liǎng wǎn fàn.**
(*lit*. I eat asp two bowl rice)
I have eaten two bowls of rice.

Wǒ *chīle* **fàn** *jiù huí jiā.*
(*lit.* I eat asp rice-meal then return home)
I'll go home as soon as I finish the meal.

Note: For a full discussion of composite sentences like this last extended sentence, see Chapter 24.

It must be stressed that aspect markers are NOT indicators of tense. Whereas in English the form of the verb changes to indicate tense, in Chinese time expressions specify the time of the action of the verb (compare Chapter 10).

Wǒ *zuótiān* **kàn xiǎoshuō,** *jīntiān* **xiě xìn,** *míngtiān* **shōushí fángzi.**
(*lit.* I yesterday read novel, today write letter, tomorrow tidy-up house)
Yesterday I read a novel, today I'm writing letters and tomorrow I will tidy the house.

A completed action with **le** may take place in the past or future.

Wǒ *zuótiān xiàle* **kè yǐhòu qù kàn diànyǐng.**
(*lit.* I yesterday finish asp lesson after-that go see film)
Yesterday when I'd finished class, I went to see a film.

Wǒ *míngtiān xiàle* **kè yǐhòu qù kàn diànyǐng.**
(*lit.* I tomorrow finish asp lesson after-that go see film)
Tomorrow when I finish class, I'll go and see a film.

To express the negative of completed action, i.e. to say what did not happen in the past or has not happened, **méi(yǒu)** is used, WITHOUT **le**:

Tā *méi(yǒu)* **qù Ōuzhōu.**
(*lit.* s/he not(-have) go Europe)
S/he did not go to Europe.

Shéi *méi(yǒu)* **tīng zuótiān de guǎngbō?**
(*lit.* who not(-have) listen yesterday p broadcast)
Who didn't listen to yesterday's broadcast?

Note: However, **bù** is used for a habitual action, whether in the past, present or future:

Tā yǐqián *bù chōuyān.*
(*lit.* s/he before not inhale-smoke)
S/he did not smoke before.

8.3.2 **Guo** denotes that an action is a *'past experience'*:

Wǒ *kànguo* **Jīngjù.**
(*lit.* I see asp Beijing-drama)
I have seen Peking opera. (I therefore know what it is.)

Wǒ *hēguo* **Máotái (jiǔ).**
(*lit.* I drink asp Maotai (wine/spirit))
I have tried Maotai. (I therefore know what it tastes like.)

To illustrate the difference between **le** and **guo**, consider the following:

Wǒmen *chīguo* **Běijīng kǎoyā.**
(*lit.* we eat asp Beijing roast-duck)
We have tried Beijing duck before.

Nèi tiān wǒmen *chīle* **Běijīng kǎoyā.**
(*lit.* that day we eat asp Beijing roast-duck)
We had Beijing duck that day.

Tāmen jīnnián *qùguo* **Táiwān.**
(*lit.* they this-year go asp Taiwan)
They went to Taiwan this year (but they are back now).

Tāmen jīnnián *qùle* **Táiwān.**
(*lit.* they this-year go asp Taiwan)
They went to Taiwan this year (and they are still there).

The sentence **Tāmen jīnnián qùguo Táiwān** shows that **guo** can be used to indicate experience within a defined period of time, **jīnnián** 'this year' (as well as experience up to the present). The defined period can of course be any period including the immediate past. Hence the colloquial enquiry **Nǐ chīguo fàn méiyǒu** 'Have you eaten' is acceptable because the speaker has subconsciously in mind the immediate meal-time.

Méi(yǒu) also functions as the negative in a past experience sentence, but in this construction **guo** is retained:

Tā *méi(yǒu)* *qùguo* **Fēizhōu.**
(*lit.* he not go asp Africa)
He has never been to Africa.

Shéi *méi(yǒu)* *hēguo* **Máotái?**
(*lit.* who not(-have) drink asp Maotai)
Who has not tried Maotai?

8.3.3 **Zài**, which is placed before the verb, indicates an '*action in progress*':

Jiāoxiǎng yuètuán *zài yǎnzòu* **Bēiduōfēn de yuèqǔ.**
(*lit.* join-sound music-group asp: in-the-process-of play Beethoven p
   music-song)
The symphony orchestra is playing Beethoven's music.

Jiějie *zài niàn* **dàxué.**
(*lit.* elder-sister asp: in-the-process-of read university)
Elder sister is studying at the university.

Note: The use of **zài** in this construction appears to derive from its function as a preposition (coverb). The fact that the sentences **tā zài xuéxí** and **tā zài nàr xuéxí** can be seen to be identical in meaning 's/he is (there) studying', would seem to confirm this point. The **nàr** in the second sentence, in fact, provides no precise indication of place.

Zhèng 'just' is regularly used with **zài** and makes the sentence slightly more emphatic:

Tāmen *zhèng zài* **dǎ pīngpāngqiú.**
(*lit.* they just asp: in-the-process-of beat pingpong-ball)
They are just playing pingpong/table tennis.

The sentence particle **ne** may be added to 'action-in-progress' sentences to introduce a tone of mild assertion:

Tā (zhèng) zài shōushí kètīng *ne.*
(*lit.* s/he (just) asp: in-the-process-of tidy-up lounge p)
S/he is just tidying up the lounge.

Note: It is possible to express action in progress without **zài**, employing **zhèng** and **ne**:

Tāmen zhèng xiūxi ne.
(*lit.* they just rest p)
They are just having a rest.

Zài can refer to defined periods of time other than the immediate present:

Nǐ jìnlái zài zuò shénme?
(*lit.* you recently asp: in-the-process-of do what)
What have you been doing recently?

Tā qùnián zài xué qí mǎ.
(*lit.* s/he last-year asp: in-the-process-of learn ride-horse)
S/he was learning to ride (a horse) last year.

With a frequency adverb, it can also express continuing or persistent 'action in progress':

Tāmen *tiāntiān zài* **chǎojià.**
(*lit.* they day-day asp: in-the-process-of quarrel)
They are quarrelling every day.

Tā yǐqián *méi tiān wǎnshàng* **dōu zài hē jiǔ.**
(*lit.* s/he before every-day evening all in-the-process-of drink wine)
S/he used to be drinking every night.

In negative 'action-in-progress' sentences, which rarely occur, the negator **bù** comes before **zài**:

Wǒ bù zài gēn nǐ shuō, wǒ zài gēn tā shuō.
(*lit.* I not asp: in-the-process-of with you talk, I asp: in-the-process-of with him/her talk)
I am not talking to you, (but) I am talking to him/her.

8.3.4 **Zhe** implies either that the action is an '*accompaniment to another action*':

Lǎoshī *xiàozhe* **shuō, 'Xièxie!'**
(*lit*. teacher smile asp say: thank-thank)
The teacher smiling/with a smile said, 'Thanks!'

Tāmen *zhànzhe* **liáotiān.**
(*lit*. they stand asp chat)
They stood chatting.

or a '*state resulting from an action*':

Mèimei *chuānzhe* **yī tiáo bái qúnzi.**
(*lit*. younger-sister wear asp one mw white skirt)
Younger sister is wearing a white skirt.

Mén *guānzhe.*
(*lit*. door closed asp)
The door is closed.

Chuāng *kāizhe.*
(*lit*. window open asp)
The window is open.

Mén shàng *tiēzhe* **yī fù duìlián.**
(*lit*. door-on paste asp one mw couplet)
On the door was posted/pasted a couplet.

Note: Most verbs expressing the wearing of articles of clothing may be suffixed with **zhe**: **chuānzhe píxíe/wàzi** 'wearing leather shoes/socks', **dàizhe màozi/shǒutào** 'wearing a hat/gloves', **dǎzhe lǐngdài** 'wearing a tie', **wéizhe wéijīn** 'wearing a scarf', etc.

(Zhèng) zài and **zhe** have similar meanings, but the following sentences illustrate the difference between them:

Tā (*zhèng***)***zài* **chuān dàyī.**   **Tā** *chuānzhe* **dàyī.**
(*lit*. s/he right-now put-on big-coat) (*lit*. s/he wear asp big-coat)
S/he is putting on an overcoat.   S/he is wearing an overcoat.

Note: There is some similarity between the use of **zài** and **zhe** when a verb-**zhe** phrase is modified by an adverbial expression:

Tāmen gāogao xìngxìng de chàng*zhe* **gē.**
(*lit*. they high-spirited p sing asp song)

Tāmen gāogao xìngxìng de *zài* **chànggē.**
(*lit*. they high-spirited p asp: in-the-process-of sing-song)

Both the above sentences mean 'they are/were singing happily'. If there is any distinction, the first emphasises a persistent state while the second implies an ongoing action.

It is also possible for **zhe** to be used in action-in-progress sentences:

Tāmen zhèng zài tǎolùnzhe nèi gè wèntí.
(*lit.* they just asp: in-the-process-of discuss asp that mw question)
They are just discussing that question.

8.4 The aspect marker **le** may be used with adjectival predicates (see Chapter 6) to create *state verbs*. Whereas adjectives indicate existing or permanent properties, state verbs express changed or changing features. Compare the following pairs:

State verb	*Adjective*
Wǒ *zhòngle* liǎng gōngjīn.	**Zhèi gè xiāngzi zhēn *zhòng*.**
(*lit.* I heavy asp two kilo)	(*lit.* this mw box/suitcase really heavy)
I have put on two kilos (of weight).	This box/suitcase is really heavy.
Tiān *hēile*.	**Tiān hěn *hēi*.**
(*lit.* sky black asp/p)	(*lit.* sky very black)
It has gone dark.	It is (very) dark.
Nǐ *pàngle*.	**Tā hěn *pàng*.**
(*lit.* you fat asp/p)	(*lit.* s/he very fat)
You've put on weight.	S/he is very fat.

Note 1: This use of **le** at the end of a sentence is linked with the function of **le** as sentence particle (see Chapter 16).

Note 2: To say **nǐ pàngle** in a Chinese context is a compliment since it implies that the person you are addressing looks to be in good health.

8.5 There are a few *dative verbs* which take two objects in the order *indirect object* followed by *direct object*.

Jiějie *gěi* mèimei yī hé táng.	Elder sister gave younger sister a box of sweets.
Tā *sòng* wǒ yī zhī gāngbǐ.	S/he gave me a pen [as a gift].
Wǒ *huán* tā liǎng bàng qián.	I gave him back [his] two pounds.

Certain action verbs with **gěi** 'to give' as a suffix follow the same pattern:

Tā *jiāo gěi* wǒ yī piān zuòwén.	S/he handed in a composition to me.
Wǒ *dì gěi* tā liǎng fēng xìn.	I passed him two letters.
Tāmen *dài gěi* wǒ yī shù huā.	They brought me a bouquet of flowers.

This dative construction may be reversed with the subject of the verb becoming the recipient:

Wǒ *shōudào* tā yī fēng xìn.
(*lit.* I receive him/her one mw letter)
I received a letter from him/her.

Wǒ *dédào* tāmen hěnduō bāngzhù.
(*lit.* I get them very much help)
I got a lot of help from them.

8.5.1 Some verbs relating to spoken activity may also be used in a dative construction:

Tāmen *jiào* wǒ Lǎo Lǐ.	They call me Old Li.
Tā *gàosù* wǒ yī jiàn shì.	S/he told me something.
Lǎoshī *wèn* wǒ yī gè wèntí.	The teacher asked me a question.

Note: An idiom with **wèn** in the dative construction is **Wǒ bàba wèn nǐ hǎo**. 'My father sends you his regards'.

8.5.2 The aspect markers **le, guo** and occasionally **(zhèng) zài** may occur with dative verbs but not **zhe**.

Tā *jièguo* nǐ qián méi yǒu?
(*lit.* s/he borrow asp you money not-have)
Has s/he ever borrowed money from you?

Tāmen *sòngle* wǒ yī gè jǐngtàilán huāpíng.
(*lit.* they give asp me one mw cloisonné vase)
They gave me a cloisonne vase.

Tā *(zhèng) zài* jiāo wǒmen Yīngyǔ.
(*lit.* s/he (just) asp: in-the-process-of teach us English)
S/he is teaching us English now.

Note: For a further discussion of dative constructions, see 21.4.

8.6 Action verbs and dative verbs may also be used in *imperatives*. In these sentences the subject (apart from **zánmen** 'we' inclusive or **wǒmen** 'we') is generally omitted, and the particle **ba** is often added at the end to connote suggestion:

Chī (yī) diǎnr rǔlào *ba*.
(*lit.* eat (a) little cheese p)
Have a bit of cheese.   (*action verb*)

Zánmen *dǎ* (yī) cháng lánqiú *ba*.
(*lit.* we hit (a) game basket-ball p)
Let's have a game of basket-ball.   (*action verb*)

Gěi **wǒ yī bēi júzishuǐ** *ba.*
(*lit.* give me one glass orange-juice p)
Give me a glass of orange juice.   (*dative verb*)

Sòng **tā yī píng jiǔ** *ba.*
(*lit.* give-as-a-gift him/her one bottle wine/spirit p)
Give him/her a bottle of wine/spirit.   (*dative verb*)

Without the particle **ba**, imperatives are more like commands:

Guò lái!   **Zhàn qǐlái!**
(*lit.* across come)   (*lit.* stand up-come)
Come (over) here!   Stand up!

8.6.1 Polite requests may be expressed by using **qǐng** 'please' at the beginning of the imperative with or without the second person pronoun and the particle **ba** (see 21.5.1):

Qǐng **(nǐ) shuō Yīngwén (ba).**   *Qǐng* **gēn wǒ lái.**
(*lit.* please (you) speak English (p))   (*lit.* please follow me come)
Please speak English.   Please follow me.

Qǐng **(nǐ) yuánliàng.**
(*lit.* please (you) excuse)
Please forgive me.

8.6.2 The aspect marker **zhe** (not **le, guo** or **zài**) may be used in imperatives to imply that the action is expected to be continued in some way. In these cases the verb is generally monosyllabic:

Fàng*zhe* **ba.**   **Dài***zhe* **ba.**   *Qǐng* **děng***zhe.*
(*lit.* put asp p)   (*lit.* carry asp p)   (*lit.* please wait asp)
Keep it.   Bring [it] with you.   Please wait.

9 MOTION VERBS AND DIRECTION INDICATORS

9.1 There are a number of common *motion verbs* in Chinese, which express not only motion but also direction. They may be used *transitively* or *intransitively* and they fall naturally into two groups:

(1) The first group consists of the two basic verbs **lái** 'come' and **qù** 'go':

Wǒ lái.   I'll come.
Tāmen bù lái.   They won't come.
Wǒ bù qù.   I won't go.
Tāmen qù.   They'll go.

Used transitively, these can take location objects:

Tā *lái wǒ zhèr.*	S/he'll come to my place.
Wǒmen *qù Běijīng.*	We are going to Beijing.

(2) The second group comprises a number of verbs which regularly precede **lái** and **qù** to express movement in particular directions. Linked with **lái** they indicate movement towards the speaker, and with **qù** movement away from the speaker:

(a) **shàng** 'upwards':

Tā *shàng lái* **le.**	S/he came up.
Tā *shàng qù* **le.**	S/he went up.

If used transitively, the location object is always placed between the verb and **lái** or **qù**:

Tā *shàng* **lóu** *lái* **le.**	S/he came upstairs.
Tā *shàng* **lóu** *qù* **le.**	S/he went upstairs.

Note: The particle **le** which comes at the end of these sentences has the simultaneous functions of aspect marker and sentence particle (see 16.2.2).

(b) **xia** 'downwards':

Tāmen *xià lái* **le.**	They came down.
Tāmen *xià qù* **le.**	They went down.

Tāmen *xià* **lóu** *lái* **le.**	They came downstairs.
Tāmen *xià* **lóu** *qù* **le.**	They went downstairs.

(c) **guò** 'across or over a distance':

Qǐng *guò lái.*	Please come over (here).
Qǐng *guò qù.*	Please go over (there).

Qìchē *guò* **qiáo** *lái* **le.**	The car has come over the bridge.
Chuán *guò* **hé** *qù* **le.**	The boat has gone across to the other side of the river.

(d) **huí** 'returning to a place':

Māma *huí lái* **le.**	Mother has come back.
Yéye *huí qù* **le.**	Grandfather has gone back.

Bàba *huí* jiā *lái* **le.**	Father has come home.
Dàshǐ *huí* **Lúndūn** *qù* **le.**	The ambassador has gone back to London.

(e) **jìn** 'entering':

Qǐng *jìn lái.*	Please come in.
Qǐng *jìn qù.*	Please go in.

Kèren *jìn* **wūzi** *lái* **le.**	The guest(s) came into the room.
Nǎinai *jìn* **chéng** *qù* **le.**	Grandmother has gone to town.

(f) **chū** 'exiting':

Nǚ zhǔren *chū lái* **le.**	The hostess came out.
Lǎobǎn *chū qù* **le.**	The boss has gone out.

Note: **chū** is seldom used transitively with **lái** or **qù**, but there are established phrases such as:

Tā *chu* **mén** *qù* **le.**   (*lit.* S/he out door go p)   S/he is away.

(g) **qǐ** 'directly upwards':

Dìdi *qǐ lái* **le.**	My younger brother has got up.

Note: **Qǐ** does not occur with **qù** in spoken Chinese. It is also rarely used transitively with an object.

9.2 These motion verbs not only function as independent verbal expressions, but also serve as *direction indicators* for other *action verbs*. Again, **lái** or **qù** imply motion towards or away from the speaker, and their partner verbs **shàng**, **xià**, **guò**, **huí**, **jìn**, **chū** and **qǐ** express more precise directions.

Gōnggòng qìchē *kāi* **guòlái lái le.**
(*lit.* public car drive across come p)
The bus drove up.

Jǐngchá *pǎo guòqù* **le.**
(*lit.* policeman/policewoman run across go p)
The policeman/policewoman hurried across (away from the speaker).

Hǎi'ōu *fēi huílái* **le.**
(*lit.* gull fly back p)
The gulls flew back (to where the speaker is).

If the action verb is used transitively, the object may be placed either after the whole verb phrase or before **lái** or **qù**:

Tāmen *dài lái* **le yī bāo yān.**   or, **Tāmen** *dài* **le yī bāo yān** *lái.*
They have brought a packet of cigarettes.

Tā *ná chūlái* **yī zhī yān.**   or, **Tā** *ná chū* **yī zhī yān** *lái.*
S/he took out a cigarette.

However, if the object is a location, it must go between the first part of the direction indicator and *lái* or *qù*:

Tā *pǎo shàng* **lóu** *qù* **le.**   S/he ran upstairs.
NOT, *Tā *pǎo shàngqù* **lóu le.**

Further examples:

(1) intransitive:

Tàiyáng zhèngzài *shēng qǐlái*.	The sun is rising.
Kèrenmen dōu *zuò xiàlái* **le.**	The guests all sat down.
Yīshēng *zǒu guòlái* **le.**	The doctor came over.
Yùndòngyuán *pǎo chūlái* **le.**	The athlete ran out (towards the speaker).
Xiǎo māo *pá shàngqù* **le.**	The kitten has climbed up (away from the speaker).
Qìchē *kāi guòqù* **le.**	The car has gone past.

(2) transitive:

Māma *mǎi huí* **yī tiáo yú** *lái*.	Mum has bought a fish. (*lit.* bought and come back with a fish)
Yóudìyuán *dì guò* **jǐ fēng xìn** *lái*.	The postman handed over a few letters.
Bàba *tiào xià* **chuáng** *lái*.	Father jumped out of bed.
Jiějie *zǒu jìn* **shāngdiàn** *qù* **le.**	Elder sister walked into a shop.
Jīnglǐ *pǎo huí* **gōngsī** *qù* **le.**	The manager has gone (or hurried) back to the company.
Xíngrén *héng guò* **mǎlù** *qù* **le.**	The pedestrian has crossed the road (to the other side).
Hùshi *zǒu chū* **jiùhùchē** *lái*.	The nurse came out of the ambulance.
Qìqiú *piāo shàng* **tiānkōng** *qù* **le.**	The balloon floated up into the sky.

9.3 Motion verb expressions may carry meanings beyond simply physical movement. For example:

(1) The motion verb **guò qù** may indicate the passsage of time:

Chūntiān *guò qù* **le.**	Spring has passed.

(2) The direction indicators **qǐlái**, **xiàlái** and **xiàqù**, which can be used with both state and action verbs, may convey various meanings:

    (a) **qǐlái** (i) mentioning or recollecting something:

Tā *tí qǐ* **zhèi jiàn shì** *lái*.	S/he brought this matter up.
Tā *xiǎng qǐ* **nèi jiàn shì** *lái*.	S/he recalled that incident.

    (b) **qǐlái** (ii) initiating an action or a state:

Tā *chàng qǐ* **gē** *lái*.	S/he started singing.
Háizi *kū qǐlái* **le.**	The child started to cry.
Tiānqì *nuǎnhuo qǐlái* **le.**	The weather is getting warmer.

(c) **xiàlái**   gradual diminishing of an action or state:

Qìchē *tíng xiàlái* **le.**   The car has gradually come to a stop.
Dàjiā dōu *jìng xiàlái* **le.**   Everybody became quiet.

(d) **xiàqù** continuation or resumption of an action:

Qǐng *shuō xiàqù*.   Please go on (with what you are saying).
Jiānchí *xiàqù*!   Stick it out/keep at it.

9.4   **shàng**, **xià**, **chū** and **guò** may occur alone with action verbs, i.e. without **lái** or **qù**. They then have specific meanings, depending on the verbs they are associated with. Some of the most common usages are:

(1) **shàng**
(a) putting on the body or the surface of something:

Tā *chuān shàng* **yī jiàn lán chènshān.**
S/he put on a blue shirt/blouse.

Lǎo jiàoshòu *dài shàng* **tāde yǎnjìng.**
The old professor put on his/her glasses.

Tā *tiē shàng* **liǎng zhāng yóupiào.**
S/he stuck two stamps on [the envelope].

(b) closing something:

Tā *bì shàng* **le yǎnjing.**   S/he closed her/his eyes.
Tā *guān shàng* **le chuānghù.**   S/he closed the window.

(c) implying success:

Tā *kǎo shàng* **dàxué le.**   S/he has passed [to get into] university.

(d) making an addition:

Qǐng *jiā shàng* **sān ge.**   Please add three more.
Suàn shàng wǒ.   Count me in.

(2) **xià**
(a) removing, detaching:

Tā *tuō xià* **máoyī.**   S/he took off her/his sweater.
Tā *zhāi xià* **yī duǒ huār.**   S/he plucked a flower.

(b) noting down:

Tā *jì xià* **le zhèi jù huà.**   S/he made a note of these words.

(3) **chū**
revealing:

Tā *shuō chū* le zhè jiàn shì.   S/he revealed this matter.
Tā *xiǎng chū* le yī gè hǎo bànfǎ.   S/he came up with a good plan.

(4) **guò**
doing in excess: 生过去了.

Tā *zuò guò* zhàn le.   S/he went past the stop/station.

10 VERBS AND TIME

10.1 We have seen in Chapter 8 the importance of time expressions in the Chinese sentence, in that they provide a time reference or context for the action of the verb, which does not change tense. The following sentences illustrate the point:

Wǒ *zuótiān* jìn chéng qù.   **Wǒ *míngtiān* jìn chéng qù.**
(*lit*. I yesterday into city go.)   (*lit*. I tomorrow into city go.)
I went to town *yesterday*.   I'll go to town *tomorrow*.

Wǒ *chángcháng* jìn chéng qù.
(*lit*. I often into city go.)
I *often* go to town.

Because of their significance, time expressions invariably occur in an early position before the verb, often at the beginning of the sentence. In the mind of the Chinese speaker, the time reference has to be made clear before the action is stated. This means that the word order of a Chinese sentence is likely to contrast with its English translation, which will almost certainly have the time reference towards the end of the sentence:

Xīngqī sì jiàn.
(*lit*. Thursday see)
See [you] on Thursday.

Wǒmen *míngtiān xiàwǔ* qù Dōngjīng.
(*lit*. we tomorrow afternoon go Tokyo)
We are going to Tokyo tomorrow afternoon.

10.2 Time expressions indicating a *point of time* for an action can be placed either in front of the subject or after it:

Míngnián wǒ shàng Běijīng qù.   or, **Wǒ *míngnián* shàng Běijīng qù.**
(*lit*. next-year I up-to Beijing go.)   (*lit*. I next-year up-to Beijing go.)
I am going to Beijing next year.   I am going to Beijing next year.

If the time expression is more specific, it is likely to come after the subject:

Wǒ zǎoshàng qī diǎn (zhōng) qǐ chuáng.
(*lit.* I morning seven hour (clock) get-up bed)
I get up at seven in the morning.

Note: The following are examples of some of the most common point-of-time expressions, which normally appear before the verb:

Year
qùnián, last year; **jīnnián,** this year; **míngnián,** next year; **qiánnián,** the year before last; **sān nián qián,** three years ago; **yī nián hòu,** a year later; **yī jiǔ jiǔ wǔ nián,** (in) 1995.

Wǒ *jīnnián* **shíjiǔ suì.**	I'm nineteen *this year*.
Wǒ yéye *sān nián qián* **qùshì le.**	My grandpa died *three years ago*.
Tā *yī jiǔ jiǔ wǔ nián* **bìyè.**	S/he graduated *in 1995*.

Season
chūntiān, spring; **xiàtiān,** summer; **qiūtiān,** autumn; **dōngtiān,** winter; **qùnián chūntiān,** spring last year.

Qùnián chūntiān **wǒ qù Zhōngguó.**	I went to China *in the spring of last year*.

Month
The months in Chinese are formed simply by placing the cardinal numbers one to twelve before **yuè** 'month'/'moon': **yīyuè** (also **zhēngyuè**), January; **èryuè**, February; **sānyuè**, March; etc.

Wǒ fùmǔ *sānyuè* **lái.**	My parents are coming in March.

For days of the month **hào,** or more formally **rì,** follows the number: **shíyuè èr hào/rì,** 2nd October.

Tāmen *shíyuè èr hào* **lái wǒ jiā.**	They will come to my place on the second of October.

Other expressions include: **shàng gè yuè,** last month; **zhèi gè yuè,** this month; **xià gè yuè,** next month; **liǎng gè yuè qián,** two months ago; **sān gè yuè hòu,** three months later/in three months; **qùnián yīyuè,** in January last year; **jīnnián èryuè,** in February this year; **míngnián sānyuè,** in March next year.

Wǒ *shàng gè yuè* **mǎi le yī liàng xīn qìchē.**
I bought a new car *last month*.

Tā *sān gè yuè hòu* **jiéhūn.**
S/he's getting married in three months' time.

Wǒ *jīnnián èryuè* **líkāi zhèr.**
I'll leave this place *in February this year*.

Week
Shàng (gè) xīngqī, last week; **zhèi (gè) xīngqī,** this week; **xià (gè) xīngqī,** next week; **liǎng gè xīngqī (yǐ)qián,** two weeks ago; **sān gè xīngqī (yǐ)hòu,** three weeks later/in three weeks.

Wǒmen *xià gè xīngqī* **kǎoshì.**
We'll have an examination *next week*.

Zhāng tàitai *liǎng gè xīngqī* **(yǐ)qián láiguo zhèr.**
Mrs Zhang was here *two weeks ago*.

Days

For days of the week apart from Sunday the cardinal numbers one to six are placed after **xīngqī** or **lǐbài** 'week', and for Sunday either **tiān** or **rì** is used instead of a number: **xīngqī yī**, Monday; **xīngqī èr**, Tuesday; **xīngqī sān**, Wednesday; **xīngqī rì/xīngqī tiān**, Sunday; **shàng (gè) xīngqī yī**, last Monday (*lit.* Monday last week); **zhèi gè xīngqī èr**, this Tuesday; **xià xīngqī sān**, next Wednesday (*lit.* Wednesday next week).

Wǒmen *xīngqī sān* **kāihuì.**	We are holding a meeting on Wednesday.

Other expressions for days include: **zuótiān**, yesterday; **qiántiān**, the day before yesterday; **jīntiān**, today; **míngtiān**, tomorrow; **hòutiān**, the day after tomorrow; **bā tiān (yǐ)qián**, eight days ago; **jiǔ tiān (yǐ)hòu**, nine days later/in nine days.

Tā *qiántiān* **húi lái.**	S/he came back *the day before yesterday.*
Wǒ *hòutiān* **xiūxi.**	I'll take a day off *the day after tomorrow.*

Time of day

Zǎoshàng, (in) the morning; **shàngwǔ**, (in) the morning (i.e. forenoon); **xiàwǔ**, (in) the afternoon; **zhōngwǔ**, (at) noon; **wǎnshàng**, (in) the evening; **yèlǐ**, (at) night; **bànyè**, midnight/in the middle of the night.

Zǎoshàng **tiānqì bù cuò.**	The weather wasn't bad *in the morning.*
Xiàwǔ **tiānqì biàn le.**	The weather changed *in the afternoon.*
Tā *bànyè* **xǐng lái.**	S/he woke up i*n the middle of the night.*

Liǎng diǎn (zhōng), two o'clock; **liǎng diǎn bàn**, half past two; **liǎng diǎn yī kè**, a quarter past two; **liǎng diǎn sān kè**, (*lit.* two hour three quarters) a quarter to three; **yī diǎn líng wǔ fēn**, five minutes past one; **sì diǎn èrshí wǔ fēn**, 25 minutes past four; **yī diǎn chà wǔ fēn**, five minutes to one; **zǎoshàng jiǔ diǎn (zhōng)**, nine o'clock in the morning.

Wǒ *liǎng diǎn bàn* **xiàbān.**
I came off work *at half past two.*

Tāmen *yī diǎn chà wǔ fēn* **chī wǔfàn.**
They have lunch *at five to one.*

Wǒmen *zǎoshàng jiǔ diǎn (zhōng)* **chūfā.**
We'll set out *at nine in the morning.*

General

Shàng (yī) cì, last time; **xià (yī) cì**, next time; **(zài) sì diǎn yǔ sì diǎn bàn** *zhījiān, between* four and four thirty; **(zài) jiàqī lǐ,** *during* the holidays; **zhōumò**, (over) the weekend; **sì tiān nèi**, *within* four days.

Wǒ *xià cì* **zài lái kàn nǐ.**	I'll come and see you again *next time.*
Jiàqī lǐ wǒ qù lǚxíng.	I went travelling *during the holidays.*

10.2.1 In detailed time expressions giving years, months, dates, etc., the larger always precede smaller. For example, 2.35 pm on 31 August, 1995 is:

yī jiǔ jiǔ wǔ nián bā yuè sānshí yī hào xiàwǔ liǎng diǎn sānshí wǔ fēn
(*lit.* 1995 year 8 month 31 day afternoon 2 hour 35 minute)

Note 1: Lengthy expressions of time and date are more likely to be placed at the beginning of a sentence before the subject.

Note 2: The descending order of scale for these time expressions is similar to that for location expressions, e.g. addresses (see Chapter 1).

10.3 More complex point-of-time expressions in the form of verb phrases also go before the main verb. In these phrases the verb is followed by **de shíhou** or **shí** 'when/while', **yǐhòu** or **zhīhòu** 'after', or **yǐqián** or **zhīqián** 'before':

Wǒmen *shàngkè (de) shí(hou)*, lǎoshī shuō ...
(*lit.* we have-class p time, teacher say)
When we were in class, the teacher said ...

Wǒ *xià le bān yǐhou* jiù qù tī zúqiú le.
(*lit.* I finish asp work-shift after immediately go kick football p)
After I came off work, I went to play football.

***Huí jiā yǐqián* tā lái zhǎo wǒ.**
(*lit.* return home before s/he come look-for me)
Before s/he went home, s/he came to see me.

The last two examples illustrate that if the time phrase and the main verb have the same subject, the subject may go before either verb.

Note 1: The adverb **jiù** 'then' is regularly found in the second clause of such sentences. It is placed immediately before the verb (and after the subject, if there is one). (See Chapter 24.)

Note 2: These time expressions may be preceded by the preposition **zài** 'in/during'. Expressions with **(de) shí(hou)** may also be linkèd with the preposition **dāng** 'when' if a subject is present:

zài xǐzǎo yǐqián	before having a bath
dāng wǒ qǐchuáng (de) shí(hou)	while I was getting up
not, **dāng* qǐchuáng (de) shí(hou)	

Note 3: Other complex point-of-time expressions are:

zài Zhōngguó dòuliú *qījiān*	*while* staying in China
zài Yīngguó fǎngwèn *qījiān*	*while* visiting England

Wǒ *zài Zhōngguó dòuliú qījiān* bìng le.
I fell ill *during my stay in China.*

10.4 Adverbs expressing *imprecise points of time* are generally placed after the subject:

Tā *yǐjing* bìyè le.	S/he has *already* graduated.
Jiùhuǒchē *lìkè* dào le.	The fire engine arrived *at once.*
Tā *xiān* hē tāng.	S/he drank the soup *first.*

One cannot say:

Yǐjing tā bìyè le.
Lìkè jiùhuǒchē dào le.

Note 1: Common adverbs of this kind include: **mǎshàng**, immediately; **chángcháng**, often; **zǒng/lǎo**, always; **cóng(lái) bù**, never; **yīzhí (dōu)**, all along.

Wǒ *mǎshàng* jiù lái.
I'll be with you *immediately*.

Tā *lǎo* tí qǐ zhèi huí shì.
S/he's *always* bringing up this matter.

Wǒ *cónglái bù* chōuyān.
I have *never* smokèd.

Tā *yīzhí dōu* zài bāngzhù wǒ.
S/he's been helping me *all along*.

Note 2: There are however some adverbs which can occur both before and after the subject: **jiānglái/yǐhòu**, in future; **xiànzài**, now; **guòqù**, in the past; **qǐchū**, at first; **shǒuxiān**, first of all; **yǐqián**, formerly; **hòulái**, later/afterwards; **jiēzhe**, next; **zuìhòu**, finally/in the end; **zuìjìn**, lately; **jìnlái**, recently/lately.

Wǒ *xiànzài* qù yínháng.	I'm going to the bank *now*.
Qǐchū wǒ bù xiāngxìn tā.	*At first* I didn't believe him/her.
Wǒ *hòulái* qù Àodàlìyā le.	I went to Australia *later on*.
Zuìhòu tā tóngyì le.	S/he *finally* agreed [to it].
Nǐ *jìnlái* zěnme yàng?	How have you been *lately*?

10.5 Phrases indicating *indefinite point of time* (often with **yǒu**) are invariably placed at the beginning of a sentence, as they set the time for a narrative:

Yī tiān wǒ qù tā jiā.   One day I went to his place.
Yǒu yī nián nàr xià dà xuě.   One year that place had a heavy snowfall.

Note: Many expressions of this type can be formulated. For example, (**yǒu**) **yī gè xīngqī tiān**, one Sunday; (**yǒu**) **yī gè xīngqī tiān wǎnshàng**, one Sunday evening.

Yǒu (yī) gè xīngqī tiān wǒmen qù pá shān.
One Sunday we went mountain-climbing.

10.6 Frequency expressions with **měi** 'every' may be placed before or after the subject. They are usually followed by the adverb **dōu** 'all' :

Wǒ *měi tiān dōu* duànliàn shēntǐ.
(*lit.* I every day all temper body)
I do physical exercises every day.

Tā *měi cì dōu* mǎshàng huí xìn.
(*lit.* s/he every time all immediately reply-to letter)
S/he replies immediately to letters every time.

Měi (gè) xīngqī liù zǎoshàng wǒ dōu qù shìchǎng mǎi dōngxi.
(*lit.* every mw Saturday morning I all go market buy things)
I go shopping in the market every Saturday morning.

10.7 Time expressions may also introduce existence sentences with **yǒu** 'there is/are' in the pattern: time expression + **yǒu** + (qualifier) + noun. In contrast, parallel English sentences usually begin with 'there is/are'.

Jīn(tiān) wǎn(shàng) yǒu yī gè yīnyuèhuì.
(*lit.* today evening there-is one mw concert)
There will be a concert this evening.

Xià xīngqī liù yě yǒu yǔmáoqiú bǐsài ma?
(*lit.* next Saturday also there-is badminton contest p)
Is there a basket-ball match next Saturday too?

Míngtiān méi(yǒu) gōnggòng qìchē dào chéng lǐ qù.
(*lit.* tomorrow there-isn't public car to town-in go)
There aren't any buses to town tomorrow.

Note: For similar use of location phrases, see 11.5.

10.7.1 Time expressions can also introduce emergence or disappearance sentences in which the verb is marked by the aspect marker **le:**

Gānggāng zǒule yī liàng huǒchē.
(*lit.* just-now leave asp one mw train)
A train left just now.

Mǎshàng láile yī liàng jiùhùchē.
(*lit.* immediately come asp one mw ambulance)
An ambulance arrived immediately.

Note: Location phrases occur in a similar construction. See 11.6.

11 VERBS AND LOCATION

11.1 Like the time expressions described in Chapter 10, *location phrases*, that identify the locus of an action or event, always precede the verb. Place and time have to be made clear before the verb is expressed to establish the context for the action.

Tāmen *zài Xī'ān* **gōngzuò.**	They are working *in Xi'an.*
Qǐng *zài zhèr* **děng wǒ.**	Please wait for me *here.*

Where a location phrase and a time phrase are both present, the time phrase normally precedes the location phrase; it may come right at the beginning of the sentence, that is before the subject:

Tāmen *zuótiān zài túshūguǎn* **xuéxí.**
(*lit.* they yesterday at library study)
They were studying at the library yesterday.

***Qùnián* wǒ** *zài Xiānggǎng* **zuò shēngyi.**
(*lit.* last-year I at Hong Kong do business)
Last year I was doing business in Hong Kong.

As illustrated in the above examples, *location phrases* may take the form of **zài** 'in, at' with a simple *location pronoun* (**zhèr** 'here', **nàr** 'there' or **nǎr** 'where') or with a place name or *location noun* (**Xi'ān**, **Xiānggǎng** 'Hong Kong', **túshūguǎn** 'library').

11.2 Another, perhaps more common form of location phrase uses **zài** with what we will call a *postpositional phrase*, which consists of a noun followed by a *postposition*:

Postposition		Postpositional phrase	
lǐ	in(side)	**wūzi** *lǐ*	in the room
wài	out(side)	**chéng** *wài*	outside the town
shàng	on, above, over	**zhuōzi** *shàng*	on the table
xià	under, below	**shù** *xià*	under the tree
qián	in front of	**mén** *qián*	in front of the door
hòu	at the back of/behind	**shāfā** *hòu*	behind the sofa
biān/pángbiān	by the side of	**lù** *biān*	by the side of the road
zhōng/zhōngjiān	in the middle of	**dàtīng** *zhōngjiān*	in the middle of the hall
duìmiàn	opposite	**xuéxiào** *duìmiàn*	opposite the school
nàr/zhèr	at a place (where sb or sth is)	**lǜshī** *nàr*	at the lawyer's place

Note 1: Other postpositional phrases include: **dǐxia** 'underneath', **zhī jiān** 'between'; 'among', **sìzhōu** 'around', **fùjìn** 'nearby', **gébì** 'next door to', etc.

Note 2: Inevitably there are some idiomatic differences between Chinese postpositions and English prepositions, e.g. **yàoshi zài mén shàng** (*lit.* key be-at door-on) 'the key is in the door'; **bào shàng** (*lit.* newspaper-on) 'in the newspaper'; **tàiyáng xià sànbù** (*lit.* sun under stroll) 'stroll in the sun'.

11.2.1 **lǐ, wài, shàng, xià, qián** and **hòu** take the suffixes **-miàn, -bian** or more colloquially **-tou** to form disyllabic postpositions.

-miàn	-bian	-tou	
lǐmiàn	lǐbian	lǐtou	in(side)
wàimiàn	wàibian	wàitou	out(side)
shàngmiàn	shàngbian	shàngtou	on, above, over
xiàmiàn	xiàbian	xiàtou	under, below
qiánmiàn	qiánbian	qiántou	in front (of)
hòumiàn	hòubian	hòutou	at the back (of)

Note: Other disyllabic postpositions with **-miàn** or **-bian** are:

zuǒmiàn/zuǒbian	to the left (of)
yòumiàn/yòubian	to the right (of)
dōngmiàn/dōngbian	to the east (of)
nánmiàn/nánbian	to the south (of)
xīmiàn/xībian	to the west (of)
běimiàn/běibian	to the north (of)

Such disyllabic postpositions usually follow disyllabic nouns to maintain a matching rhythm:

chuānghu qiánmiàn/qiánbian	in front of the window
dàmén hòumiàn/hòubian	behind the door/gate
mǎlù pángbiān	by the side of the road
huāyuán zhōngjiān	in the middle of the garden

Note: There is also a tendency to match monosyllabic elements, e.g. the first three of the above examples could be reformulated **chuáng qián, mén hòu, lù biān**. However, this should not be taken as a hard and fast rule.

11.2.2 Disyllabic postpositions can also act as location pronouns and form location phrases with **zài**:

zài hòubian	at the back
zài lǐtou	inside
zài shàngmiàn	on top

11.3 Simple location sentences are formed by using the verb **zài** 'to be in/at' followed by a location noun or pronoun, or a postpositional phrase:

Cèsuǒ *zài* **èr lóu.**	The toilet is on the first floor.
Nǐ de zuòwèi *zài* **dìsān pái.**	Your seat is in the third row.
Zuì jìn de yóutǒng *zài* **nǎr?**	Where is the nearest pillar-box?
Háizi dōu *zài* **wàitou.**	The children are all outside.

Shūfáng *zài* **zhōngjiān.**	The study is in the middle.
Tā *zài* **huāyuán lǐ.**	S/he is in the garden.
Shū *zài* **shūjià shàng.**	The book is on the bookshelf.
Wǒ jiā *zài* **Hǎidé gōngyuán fùjìn.**	My home is near Hyde Park.

Postpositions should not be attached to place names:

Tā zài Zhōngguó.	He (or she) is in China.
NOT: *Tā zài Zhōngguó lǐ.	

Wǒ péngyou zài Běijīng.	My friend is in Beijing.
NOT: *Wǒ péngyou zài Běijīng lǐ.	

With nouns indicating location, rather than objects, the postposition **lǐ** 'in' is optional:

Wǒ zài túshūguǎn.   or, **Wǒ zài túshūguǎn lǐ.**
I was in the library.

Note: It must be made clear that **zài** has two functions: (1) location verb 'to be in/at' and (2) a location preposition (coverb) 'in'/'at' (see 11.4 below).

11.4 As illustrated by the first set of simple sentences in 11.1, in a location phrase used adverbially to modify the main verb of the sentence, **zài** functions as a preposition meaning 'in' or 'at'. (For further discussion of **zài** and other similar prepositions, see Chapter 19 on coverbs.)

Tā *zài* **huāyuán lǐ gē cǎo.**
(*lit.* s/he at garden in cut grass)
S/he is cutting the grass *in the garden.*

Wǒmen *zài* **hǎitān shàng shài tàiyáng.**
(*lit.* we at beach on bask sun)
We were sunbathing *on the beach.*

Tāmen *zài* **kètīng lǐ tīng yīnyuè.**
(*lit.* they at lounge in listen music)
They listened to music *in the sitting-room.*

Māma *zài* **shìchǎng mǎi cài.**
(*lit.* mother at market buy food)
Mum is buying food *at the market.*

Nǐ *zài* **dàxué xué shénme kēmù?**
(*lit.* you at university study what subject)
What subjects are you studying *at the University?*

Wǒ *zài* **yínháng kāi le yī gè zhànghù.**
(*lit.* I at bank open asp one mw account)
I have opened an account *at the bank.*

Jiějie *zài wàimiàn* liàng yīfu.
(*lit.* elder-sister at outside take-out-to-dry clothes)
My elder sister was hanging *out* clothes to dry (*outside*).

Tā *zài cǎodì shàng* tǎngzhe.
(*lit.* s/he at grass-land on lie asp)
S/he was lying *on the grass*.

Note: In the last example above, **tǎng** must have the aspect marker **zhe**, since the verb in narrative sentences of this type must have more than one syllable.

11.5 Sentences expressing the *existence* of someone or something in a particular locality usually have a phrase indicating location plus the verb **yǒu** 'there is/are' as follows: phrase indicating location + **yǒu** + (qualifier) + noun(s).

This construction is similar to the time expression existence sentences discussed in 10.7. Again, there is a contrast with English in which parallel sentences usually begin with 'There is/are . . .':

Jìngzi pángbiān *yǒu* yī pén huār.
(*lit.* mirror beside have one mw pot flower)
There is a pot of flowers beside the mirror.

Sōngshù dǐxia *yǒu* yī zhī tùzi.
(*lit.* pine-tree under there-is one mw hare [or rabbit])
There is a hare under the pine tree.

Wǔtái shàng zhǐ *yǒu* liǎng gè yǎnyuán.
(*lit.* stage on only there-are two mw actor)
There are only two actors on the stage.

Zhèr fùjìn *yǒu* xǐyīdiàn ma?
(*lit.* here nearby there-is laundry p)
Is there a laundry near here?

Nǎr *yǒu* cèsuǒ?
(*lit.* where there-is toilet)
Where is there a toilet?

Lǐbian *yǒu* rén.
(*lit.* inside there-are people)
There is somebody inside.

Note: We have already pointed out (see Chapter 1) that the subject of a verb tends to be of definite reference. The last two examples could therefore be rephrased as:

Cèsuǒ zài nǎr?	Where is *the* toilet?
Rén zài lǐbian.	*The* person/people (or, colloquially 's/he'/'they') is/are inside.

As illustrated by the above examples, the noun following **yǒu** is always of indefinite reference. It would not be natural to say:

*Dòngwùyuán lǐ *yǒu* **nèi tóu xióngmāo.**
(*lit.* *zoo in there-is that mw panda)
*There is that panda in the zoo.

11.5.1 The verb **shì** may also be used in existence sentences which start with a phrase indicating location. The function of **shì** in these sentences is more complex than that of **yǒu**. When the emphasis is on 'defining' what exists at a location, **shì** is followed by a noun of indefinite reference:

Shìzhèngtīng gébì shì yī gè zhǎnlǎnguǎn.
(*lit.* town-hall next-door be one mw exhibition-hall)
Next door to the town hall is *an* exhibition hall.

When the emphasis is on 'locating' where something is, the noun after **shì** is of definite reference:

Kètīng duìmiàn shì wòshì.
(*lit.* guest-hall opposite be bedroom)
Opposite the sitting room is *the* bedroom.

Note: See also the last note under 6.4.

Shì can also be modified by **dōu** or **quán** 'all' to mean that a location is filled or covered with identified objects or people:

Bīngxiāng lǐbian *dōu shì* **shuǐguǒ.**
(*lit.* ice-box inside all be fruit)
Inside the fridge there was nothing but fruit.

Dì shàng *quán shì* **shuǐ.**
(*lit.* floor/ground on all be water)
There is water all over the floor/ground.

11.5.2 Like **yǒu** and **shì**, action verbs suffixed with the aspect marker **zhe** may be used in location-related existence sentences. As in 8.3.4, these verbs indicate a 'state resulting from an action':

Qiáng shàng *guàzhe* **yī fú huà.**
(*lit.* wall on hang asp one mw painting)
There is a painting hanging on the wall.

Zhuōzi shàng *fàngzhe* **liǎng bēi chá.**
(*lit.* table on put asp two mw:cup tea)
There are two cups of tea (placed) on the table.

Fángzi lǐ *zhùzhe* **bù shǎo rén.**
(*lit.* house in live asp not few person)
There are quite a lot of people living in the house.

Xìyuàn rùkǒuchù *páizhe* **yī duì rén.**
(*lit.* theatre entrance queue asp one mw:queue people)
There was a line of people queuing at the entrance to the theatre.

Note: Some nouns (e.g. **rùkǒuchù**) themselves may indicate location (without any post-position).

If the action verb denotes persistent activity, **(zhèng)zài** is used instead of **zhe:**

Tǐyùguǎn lǐ (*zhèng***)zài** *jìnxíng* **tǐcāo bǐsài.**
(*lit.* gymnasium in (just) asp: in-the-process-of conduct gymnastics competition)
A gymnastics contest is going on in the gymnasium.

11.6 In the same way, a phrase indicating location may be followed by a verb with the aspect marker **le** to express the *emergence* or *disappearance* of something or somebody at or from that location. The pattern is: phrase indicating location + action verb + **le** + (qualifier) + noun(s).
For example,

Wǒ jiā *láile* **hěn duō kèren.**
(*lit.* my house come asp very many guest)
Many guests came to/turned up at my place.

Túshūguǎn *diūle* **bù shǎo shū.**
(*lit.* library lost asp not few book)
The library has lost quite a few books.

Note: Compare the similar structure for time expressions (10.7.1)

11.7 Where a location phrase and a time phrase occur in an existence or an emergence/disappearance sentence, either phrase may come first. (This differs from the adverbial use of location and time phrases, discussed in 11.1 in which the time expression must come first). For instance:

***Zuótiān wǎnshàng chéng lǐ* yǒu yī gè shìwēi yóuxíng.**
(*lit.* yesterday evening town-in there-was one mw demonstration parade)

or, ***Chéng lǐ zuótiān wǎnshàng* yǒu yī gè shìwēi yóuxíng.**
(*lit.* town in yesterday evening there-was one mw demonstration parade)
There was a demonstration in (the) town yesterday evening.

12 VERBS: DURATION AND FREQUENCY

12.1 Unlike defined point-of-time expressions, duration and frequency expressions usually come after the verb. As observed above, in a Chinese sentence setting in time and space is established before the action of the verb is expressed; duration and frequency on the other hand, as consequences of the verb, are delineated after the action of the verb has been described.

Duration expressions naturally take the form of a numeral followed by a time word. In some cases the time word requires a measure (e.g. **yuè** 'month', **zhōngtóu** 'hour', **lǐbài** 'week', which take **gè**). In other cases the time word is itself a measure word, and numerals may therefore be placed immediately before it (e.g. **yī nián** 'one year', **sì tiān** 'four days'). With **xiǎoshí** 'hour' and **xīngqī** 'week' the measure **gè** is optional. Other more general duration expressions are **hěn jiǔ/hěn cháng shíjiān** 'a long time'.

Note: Since numerals up to twelve are used with **yuè** to denote the calendar months (see Chapter 10 above), care must be taken to distinguish, for example **sān yuè** 'March' and **sān gè yuè** 'three months'.

Wǒ zài Yīngguó zhùle *liǎng nián*.
(*lit.* I at Britain live asp two year)
I lived in Britain for two years.

Wǒ zhǔnbèi zài Yīngguó dāi *liù gè yuè*.
(*lit.* I prepare at Britain stay six mw month)
I am preparing/intend to stay in Britain for six months.

Wǒ shuìle *bā gè xiǎoshí/zhōngtóu*.
(*lit.* I sleep asp eight mw hour)
I (have) slept for eight hours.

Wǒmen tánle *hěn jiǔ*.
(*lit.* we talk asp very long)
We talked for a long time.

12.1.1 If the verb in the sentence has a noun object as well as a duration phrase, the duration phrase is placed between the verb and the noun:

Wǒ xuéguo *sì gè duō yuè* Zhōngwén.
(*lit.* I study asp four mw more month Chinese)
I studied Chinese for more than four months (at one stage).

Wǒ dǎle *bàn gè zhōngtóu* yǔmáoqiú.
(*lit.* I hit asp half mw hour badminton)
I played badminton for half an hour.

The duration phrase may also be regarded as attributive and used with **de**:

Wǒ xuéguo *sì gè yuè de* Zhōngwén.
(*lit.* I study asp four mw month p Chinese)
I studied Chinese for four months (at one stage).

Wǒ míngtiān xiàwǔ yào jiǎng *liǎng gè zhōngtóu de* kè.
(*lit.* I tomorrow afternoon will talk two mw hour p lesson)
I am going to lecture for two hours tomorrow afternoon.

12.1.2 An alternative pattern when a noun object is present is to repeat the verb after the object and then place the duration phrase after the repeated verb:

Wǒ *xué* Zhōngwén *xuéle sì nián*.
(*lit.* I study Chinese study asp four year)
I studied Chinese for four years.

Tāmen *liáotiān liáole yī gè wǎnshàng*.
(*lit.* they chat chat asp one mw evening)
They chatted the whole evening.

In this construction the repeated verb is usually one of completed action with aspect marker **le**.

12.1.3 When there is a pronoun object, the duration phrase always follows the pronoun:

Wǒ děngle *tā bàn gè duō zhōngtóu*.
(*lit.* I wait asp him/her half mw more hour)
I waited for him for over half an hour.

12.1.4 If the duration expression alludes to a period of time in the past within which something has or has not happened, it then takes on definite reference and is placed, like other time expressions, before the verb. Duration expressions of this type are often followed by **lǐ/nèi** 'within (the last) . . .' or **(yǐ) lái** 'since . . .':

Wǒ *sān gè yuè nèi/lǐ* kànle wǔ cì diànyǐng.
(*lit.* I three mw month within see asp five times film)
I have been to the cinema five times *in the past three months*.

Wǒ *bàn nián* méi qù kàn diànyǐng le.
(*lit.* I half year not go see film p)
I have not been to see a film *for the last six months*.

Wǒ *yī nián (yǐ)lái* dōu zài shíyànshì gōngzuò.
(*lit.* I one year so-far all at laboratory work)
I have been working in the laboratory *for the whole past year*.

Wǒ *Shèngdànjié* **(yǐ)***lái* **dōu méi shàngguo bān.**
(*lit.* I Christmas so-far all not go-on asp shift)
I have not been back to work ever *since Christmas*.

Wǒ *zhèi sān nián lái* **dōu méi jiànguo wǒde biǎo dì.**
(*lit.* I this three year within all not see asp my cousin)
I haven't seen my cousin for the last three years.

Note: In Chinese terms for cousins, like other family relationships, are very precise. On the mother's side they are **biǎo gē**, **biǎo dì**, **biǎo jiě**, **biǎo mèi** and on the father's side **táng gē**, **táng dì**, etc.

12.2 *Brief duration* can be conveyed by repeating the verb, sometimes after **yī** 'one', or by using phrases like **yī xià** 'a moment' or **yī huìr** 'a short while' after the verb:

(1) Repetition of verbs:

    (a) Monosyllabic verbs:

kànkàn	have a look
kàn yī kàn	have a look
kànle kàn	had a look

    (b) Disyllabic verbs (cannot be used with **yī** or **le**):

jièshào jièshào	give a brief introduction
NOT: ****jièshào yī jièshào**	**give a brief introduction
****jièshàole jièshào**	**gave a brief introduction

    (c) Verb object constructions (only the verb is repeated):

xǐ shǒu	wash hands	**xǐ (yī) xǐ shǒu**	wash one's hands
sǎo dì	sweep the floor	**sǎole sǎo dì**	swept the floor (briefly)

    NOT: ****xǐ shǒu xǐ shǒu** or ****sǎo dì sǎo dì**

(2) With **yī xià** or **yī huìr**:

Ràng wǒ *kàn yī xià*.	Let me have a look.
Zànmen *xiū xi yī huìr*.	We'll rest for a while.

Where the verb has an object, brief duration phrases, like other duration phrases, come before the object:

Wǒmen tiàole *yī xià* **wǔ.**	We danced for a while.
Wǒ kànle *yī huìr* **shū.**	I read for a while.

12.2.1 Brief duration may also be expressed by employing an *instrumental object*, often part of the body:

Tā *dǎle* wǒ *yī quán*.
(*lit.* s/he hit asp me one fist)
S/he dealt me a blow.

Wǒ *tīle* tā *yī jiǎo*.
(*lit.* I kick asp him/her one foot)
I gave him/her a kick.

Jiàoliàn *kànle* dàjiā *yī yǎn*.
(*lit.* coach look asp everybody one eye)
The coach cast a glance at everybody.

Wǒmen *jiànguo yī miàn*.
(*lit.* we see asp one face)
We met once.

12.3 *Frequency phrases*, like duration phrases, come after the verb. They consist of a numeral combined with one of a number of common frequency measure words such as **cì**, **biàn**, **huí** and **tàng**. While **cì** simply indicates an occurrence, **biàn** implies 'from beginning to end', **huí** 'to and fro', and **tàng** 'back and forth from a place':

Tāmen láiguo *sān cì*.	They've come/been here three times.
Wǒ niànle *yī biàn*.	I read [it] through once (from beginning to end).
Wǒmen jiànguo tā *liǎng huí*.	We have met him/her twice.
Wǒ qùguo *jǐ tàng*.	I have been [there] several times.

If the verb has a noun object, the frequency phrase is generally placed between the verb and the object.

Wǒ kànguo *liǎng cì* gējù.
(*lit.* I see asp two times opera)
I have been twice to see an opera.

Tā zuòguo *sān tàng* fēijī.
(*lit.* s/he sit asp three trip (air)plane)
S/he has been on a plane three times.

If the object is a location phrase, however, the frequency phrase may be placed either between the verb and the location object or after the location object:

Wǒ qùle *liǎng tàng* Běijīng.   or, **Wǒ qùle Běijīng *liǎng tàng*.**
I went to Beijing twice.

Tā láiguo *yī cì* wǒ jiā.   or, **Tā láiguo wǒ jiā *yī cì*.**
S/he has been to my place once.

As with duration phrases, if the object is a pronoun, the frequency phrase is placed after the pronoun:

Wǒ zhǎoguo tā *yī cì*.   I looked for/visited him once.
NOT: *****Wǒ zhǎoguo *yī cì* tā.**

13 VERBS AND COMPLEMENTS

13.1 As we have seen, Chinese verbs are seldom used without some form of marker or attachment. They are regularly modified (e.g. by time and location expressions) or complemented in some way. *Complements* in Chinese are those elements of a sentence which come after the verb (apart from the object) and which either describe the action of the verb or express its result.

A number of complements which occur with action verbs have already been encountered, for example, aspect markers, direction indicators and duration/frequency markers. Here we introduce a further range of complements, those indicating result, potential, manner, location/destination and degree.

13.2 *Complements of result* are adjectives or verbs which follow immediately after the main verb. They indicate the direct result of an action, either what it achieves or what happens unintentionally. For example, the verb complement **jiàn** 'to see' implies successful seeing or apprehension as in **kàn jiàn** 'to see' (*lit.* look-see) and **tīng jiàn** 'to hear' (*lit.* listen-apprehend), while the adjective complement **cuò** 'wrong' indicates a mistaken result as in **tīng cuò** 'to mishear' (*lit.* listen-wrong) and **kàn cuò** 'to misread' (*lit.* look-wrong). Although most complements of result are monosyllabic, some of the adjectival ones are disyllabic (e.g. **qīngchǔ** 'clear', **gānjìng** 'clean', etc).

(1) Adjectives:

Nǐ *cāi cuò* le.
(*lit.* you guess wrong p)
You have guessed wrong.

Tā *xiū hǎo* le nèi liàng mótuōchē.
(*lit.* s/he repair good asp that mw motorbike)
S/he has repaired that motorbike.

Tā *nòng zāng* le tāde qúnzi.
(*lit.* s/he make dirty asp her skirt)
S/he has dirtied her skirt.

Tā méi *tīng qīngchǔ* wǒde huà.
(*lit.* s/he not listen clear my words)
S/he didn't hear clearly what I said.

(2) Verbs:

Wǒ yǐjing *zuò wán* le wǒde zuòyè.
(*lit*. I already do finish asp my homework/coursework)
I have already done my homework.

Nǐ *tīng dǒng* le ma?
(*lit*. you listen understand asp p)
Did you understand (what was said)?

Nǐ liù diǎn zhōng *jiào xǐng* wǒ.
(*lit*. you six o'clock call wake me)
Wake me up at six.

Tāmen *lā kāi* le liǎng gè zhèngzài dǎjià de rén.
(*lit*. they pull separate asp two mw asp fight p person)
They pulled apart two people who were fighting.

Many verb-and-complement expressions in fact are established terms in the language:

Rénmín de shēnghuo shuǐpíng *tígāo* le.
(*lit*. people p life level raise-high p)
The people's living standards have improved.

Tā *dǎduàn* le wǒde fāyán.
(*lit*. s/he hit-broken-in-two asp my speech)
S/he interrupted my speech.

Note: The most common complements of result, apart from the above, are:

(a) *Adjectives*

huài	bad	**Zhèi gè háizi *nòng huài* le wode diànnǎo.**
		This child has damaged my computer.
duì	right	**Nǐ *cāi duì* le.**
		You guessed right.
bǎo	full (with eating)	**Wǒ *chī bǎo* le.**
		I have eaten my fill/I'm full.
zuì	drunk	**Wǒde péngyou *hē zuì* le.**
		My friend is/was drunk.

(b) *Verbs*

pò	break	**Wǒ *dǎ pò* le yǎnjìng.**
		I broke my glasses.
dào	attain, achieve (purpose)	**Tā *zhǎo dào* le tāde qiánbāo.**
		S/he's found her/his purse/wallet.
diào	drop	**Tā *gǎi diào* le nèi gè huài xíguàn.**
		S/he's dropped that bad habit.
dǎo	fall over	**Yùndòngyuán *shuāi dǎo* le.**
		The athlete fell over.

zhù	stop, make firm	**Jǐngchá** *zhuā zhù* **le xiǎotōu.**
		The policeman (has) caught the thief.
		Jì zhù **zhèi jiàn shì.**
		Try and remember this.

13.3 Ability or inability to do something is regularly expressed by a *potential complement*. This is formed by placing **de** (positive) or **bù** (negative) between a verb and a complement of result. The potential complement, which is a distinctive feature of Chinese, implies that the result of the action can (or cannot) be achieved or happen, that is that the outcome is to some extent dependent on external circumstances beyond the speaker's control. (This contrasts with the use of the modal verb **néng(gòu)** 'can', see 15.2(5).)

(1) Adjectival potential complements:

Tā *chī bù bǎo.*
(*lit.* s/he eat not full)
S/he couldn't eat his/her fill.
(i.e. there wasn't enough food to go round, s/he is such a big eater, etc.)

Nǐ *zhàn de wěn* **ma?**
(*lit.* you stand can stable p)
Can you stand up (without falling)?
(i.e. somebody has had too much to drink, has been ill, etc.)

Zhèi tiáo niúzǎikù *xǐ de gānjìng* **ma?**
(*lit.* this mw jeans wash can clean p)
Can these jeans be washed (clean)?

(2) Verbal potential complements:

Tā *tīng de dǒng* **wǒde huà.**
(*lit.* s/he listen can understand my words)
S/he could understand my words.
(because they were not too profound, not strongly accented, etc.)

Wǒ *zǒu bù liǎo* **le.**
(*lit.* leave not achievable)
I can't (possibly) leave.
(i.e. there are no more trains, the work isn't finished yet, the
   weather is too bad, etc.)

Dàjiā dōu *kàn bù jiàn* **hēibǎn shàng de zì.**
(*lit.* everybody all look not see blackboard-on p words/characters)
Nobody can see the words/characters on the blackboard.
(i.e. the blackboard is too far away, the words/characters are too
   small, etc.)

Wǒ *zǒu bù dòng* le.
(*lit.* I walk not move p)
I can't walk any further.
(i.e. too tired, etc.)

13.3.1 Directional complements (see direction indicators 9.2) can also be used in the potential form:

Wǒ *chī bù xià* le.
(*lit.* I eat not down)
I can't eat any more.
(i.e. too full, having already eaten too much, etc.)

Wǒmen jīntián *bān bù jìnqù*.
(*lit.* we today move not into-go)
We can't move in today (e.g. into a flat, etc.).
(i.e. the flat, etc. has not been vacated yet, etc.)

Shū *yào de huílái* ma.
(*lit.* book get can come-back p)
Can I/you get the books back?
(i.e. someone will or won't return them, etc.)

13.3.2 We have seen in 9.3 that direction indicators/complements may carry meanings beyond simply physical movement. Similar metaphorical usages are found with potential complement of direction:

Zhèi gè lǐtáng *zuò de xià* yī qiān rén.
(*lit.* this mw auditorium sit can contain one thousand person)
This hall can seat one thousand people.

Wǒ *mǎi bù qǐ* zhàoxiàngjī.
(*lit.* I buy not up camera)
I can't afford a camera.

Māma *xiǎng bù qǐ* zhèi jiàn shì.
(*lit.* mother think not up this mw matter)
Mum can't recall this matter.
(i.e. it happened a long time ago, her memory lets her down, etc.)

Tā *shuō bù xiàqù* le.
(*lit.* s/he speak not continue p)
S/he can't carry on talking any more.
(i.e. choked by emotion, having a sore throat, being shouted down, etc.)

13.4 The *complements of manner and of consequential state* involve placing **de** after a verbal or adjectival predicate followed by *either* an adjectival phrase (normally indicating manner) *or* a verbal phrase or clause (usually indicating consequential state). The adjectival phrase in a complement of manner describes the way in which an action is seen to be carried out. (This contrasts with adverbial modifiers which emphasise more the intention or demeanour of the initiator of the action – see 14.1 for further comment on this point.) The complement of consequential state can follow either an adjectival or a verbal predicate. It depicts an observed situation which arises from an action or an ongoing state but which is not necessarily an intended outcome.

13.4.1 In the complement of manner, the adjective in the adjectival phrase, must be either adverbially modified or followed by a degree complement (see 13.6 below):

Tā shuō de *bù tài* **qīngchǔ.**
(*lit.* s/he speak p not too clear)
S/he did not put it too clearly.

Nèi pǐ mǎ pǎo de *bǐjiào/zuì* **kuài.**
(*lit.* that mw horse run p comparatively/most fast)
That horse ran faster [than the others]/ the fastest [of all].

Gēyǒngduì chàng de hǎo *jí le.*
(*lit.* chorus/choir sing p good extreme p)
The chorus/choir sang extremely well.

Wǒ jīntiān qǐ de zǎo *de duō.*
(*lit.* I today get-up p early much-more)
I got up much earlier today.

Zhànshìmen zhàn de *hěn* **zhí.**
(*lit.* soldiers stand p very straight)
The soldiers stood very straight.

Nèi gè gūniang dǎbàn de *hěn* **piàoliang.**
(*lit.* that mw girl dress-up p very beautiful)
That young girl is dressed up very beautifully.

Note: The last two examples illustrate that with some verbs the manner complement borders on expressing consequential state.

13.4.2 The complement of consequential state is either a verbal phrase or a clause:

(1) Verbal phrase:

Tā pǎo de *zhí chuǎnqì.*
(*lit.* s/he run p non-stop pant)
S/he ran till s/he was out of breath.

Tā lěng de *fādǒu le.*
(*lit.* s/he cold p shiver p)
S/he was so cold that s/he began to shiver.

(2) Clause:

Tā zǒu de *jiǎo dōu/yě ruǎn le.*
(*lit.* s/he walk p leg all/also weak p)
S/he walked till her/his legs were very weak.

Tā xiào de *zuǐ dōu/yě hé bù lǒng le.*
(*lit.* s/he smile/laugh p mouth all/also close not together p)
S/he grinned broadly.

Wǒ kùn de *yǎnjing dōu/yě zhēng bù kāi le.*
(*lit.* I tired-and-sleepy p eye both/also open not separate p)
I was so sleepy that my eyes refused to open.

Note: For emphasis these complemental clauses often make use of the adverbs **dōu/yě** 'all'/'also'. In addition, the preposition or coverb **lián** 'even' may precede the subject in the clause. For instance, the second example above may be rewritten as: *Tā xiào de lián zuǐ dōu hé bù lǒng le.*

13.4.3 When a complement of manner or consequential state occurs with a 'verb + object' verb, the verb is repeated after the object and then followed by the complement:

Tā *tiàowǔ tiào de hěn hǎo.*
(*lit.* s/he dance-dances dance p very well)
S/he danced very well.

Tā *dǎzì dǎ de hěn kuài.*
(*lit.* s/he type-words type p very quick)
S/he types very fast.

Wǒ *pǎobù pǎo de húnshēn dōu rè le.*
(*lit.* I run-step run p whole-body all hot p)
I ran (so much) that I was hot all over.

13.4.4 Adjectival complements of manner may express comparison (note the general discussion of comparison, equivalence, etc., in 7.2 and 7.2.3). In such complements the '**bǐ** + (pro)noun', '**gēn** + (pro)noun' and '**méi(yǒu)** + (pro)noun' expressions are placed either before the main verb, or before the adjective in the complement:

Wǒ tiào de *bǐ tā gāo.*
(*lit.* I jump p compare s/he high)
I jump higher than s/he does.

or, **Wǒ *bǐ tā* tiào de gāo.**
(*lit*. I compare s/he jump p high)

Zhèi pǐ mǎ pǎo de *gēn nèi pǐ mǎ* yīyàng kuài.
(*lit*. this mw horse run p and that mw horse same fast)
This horse runs as fast as that one.

or, **Zhèi pǐ mǎ *gēn nèi pǐ mǎ* pǎo de yīyàng kuài.**
(*lit*. this mw horse and that mw horse run p same fast)

Wǒ kǎo de *méi(yǒu)* tā (nàme) hǎo.
(*lit*. I examine p not-have s/he so good)
I did not do as well as s/he did in the examination.

or, **Wǒ *méi(yǒu) tā* kǎo de (nàme) hǎo.**
(*lit*. I not-have s/he examine p so good)

13.4.5 Where the complement-of-manner comparison occurs with a 'verb
+ object' verb, the same rule applies, with the '**bǐ** + (pro)noun', '**gēn** +
(pro)noun' or '**méi(yǒu)** + (pro)noun' phrase located either before the
repeated verb or before the adjective in the complement:

Tā chànggē chàng de *bǐ wǒ* hǎotīng.
(*lit*. s/he sing-songs sing p compare me good-to-hear.)
She sings better than I do.

or, **Tā chànggē *bǐwǒ* chàng de hǎotīng.**
(*lit*. s/he sing-songs compare me sing p good-to-hear.)

Wǒ shuō Zhōngwén shuō de *méi(yǒu)* tā (nàme) liúlì.
(*lit*. I speak Chinese speak p not-have s/he (so) fluent)
I don't speak Chinese as fluently as s/he does.

or, **Wǒ shuō Zhōngwén *méiyǒu tā* shuō de (nàme) liúlì.**
(*lit*. I speak Chinese not-have s/he speak p (so) fluent)

Note: The '**bǐ** + (pro)noun' and other comparative phrases cannot precede the first verb:
e.g. **Tā bǐ wǒ chànggē chàng de hǎotīng.*

13.5 *Complements of location/destination* occur with motion verbs and
indicate the location to which the motion of the verb is heading.

Qìchē *tíng zài chēfáng*.
(*lit*. car stop at garage)
The car was parked at the garage.

Māma *huí dào jiā lǐ*.
(*lit*. mother return to home in)
Mother came home.

It would not be normal to say:

*Tā xuéxí *zài túshūguǎn.*
(*lit.* s/he study at library)

because **xuéxí** 'study' does not express any spatial motion. It would be more natural to use an adverbial modifier before the verb:

Tā *zài túshūguǎn* **xuéxí.**
(*lit.* s/he at library study)
S/he studied at the library.

The location phrase here indicates where the subject was before the action of the verb took place, i.e. one must get to the library before one can settle down to study there. In contrast, the location/destination phrase as complement indicates where the subject finishes up after the action has taken place.
   Compare the following pair of sentences:

Tā zǒu *dào gōngyuán qù.*
(*lit.* s/he walk to park go)
S/he went to the park [on foot].
(i.e. S/he set out with the park as her destination.)

Tā *dào gōngyuán* **qù zǒuzǒu.**
(*lit.* s/he get-to park go walk-walk)
S/he went for a walk in the park.
(i.e. S/he got to the park first and then took a walk there.)

13.6 *Degree complements* follow and intensify adjectives. They are generally stronger in meaning than the degree adverbs and expressions introduced in 6.2.1 (e.g. **hěn** 'very', **tài** 'too', **xiāngdāng** 'rather', **gòu** 'enough', **yǒu diǎnr** 'a bit', etc.). The most common degree complements are:

(1) **de hěn**	very	**lěng de hěn**	very cold
(2) **de duō**	much more	**hǎo de duō**	much better
duō le	much more	**guì duō le**	much more expensive
(3) **jí le**	extremely	**gāoxìng jí le**	extremely happy
(4) **tòu le**	thoroughly	**shī tòu le**	wet through
(5) **sǐ le**	extremely, terribly	**è sǐ le**	terribly hungry
(6) **de yàomìng**	terribly	**rè de yàomìng**	terribly hot
(7) **de bùdeliǎo**	exceedingly	**huài de bùdeliǎo**	exceedingly bad
(8) other **de** + adjective/verb expressions:			
de cìyǎn	eye-dazzling	**liàng de cìyǎn**	dazzlingly bright
de cì'ěr	ear-piercing	**xiǎng de cì'ěr**	ear-piercingly loud

Note: **De** as used throughout this chapter in potential, manner, consequential state and degree complements is different in its written character form from the attributive **de** we have met earlier. The character for the **de** which appears in Chapter 14 in adverbial modifiers is different again (see Glossary of Chinese Characters).

14 VERBS AND ADVERBIALS

14 *Adverbial modifiers* are words or expressions, usually placed immediately before the verb or sometimes at the beginning of a sentence, which give additional information concerning the action or state expressed in the verb. They fall into three main categories: background, manner and attitude indicators. We have already discussed background indicators such as time and location expressions (see Chapters 10 and 11); here the focus is on adverbial modifiers of manner and attitude.

14.1 *Adverbials of manner* consist of adjectives, normally two-syllable, followed by the particle **de:**

Tā *xùnsù de* pǎo guòlái.
(*lit.* s/he speedy p run across)
S/he came over swiftly.

Tā *yúkuài de* xiàole xiào.
(*lit.* s/he happy p smile asp smile)
S/he smiled happily.

The difference between an adverbial of manner and a complement of manner (see 13.4) is that the adverbial is concerned mainly with the 'demeanour', 'intention', etc., of the subject, while the complement is more concerned with the manner and result of the verb as observed by a third party. Compare:

Adverbial	*Complement*
Tā *hěn kuài de* pǎozhe.	**Tā *pǎo de hěn kuài.***
(*lit.* s/he very quick p run asp)	(*lit.* s/he run p very fast)
S/he ran *very fast*. (i.e. s/he was intent on running fast)	S/he ran *very fast*. (i.e. as apparent to an onlooker)
Tā *shífēn chūshén de* tīngzhe.	**Tā *tīng de shífēn chūshén.***
(*lit.* s/he extremely enchanted p listen asp)	(*lit.* s/he listen p extremely enchanted)
S/he listened *with great fascination*. (i.e. s/he was eager to hear)	S/he listened *with great fascination*. (i.e. as could be observed)

14.1.1 A monosyllabic adjective must either be repeated or made disyllabic by the addition of a degree adverb to become an adverbial of manner:

Tā *jìngjìng de* zuòzhe.
(*lit.* s/he quiet-quiet p sit p)
S/he sat (there) quietly.

Tā *hěn kuài de* zhuǎn guò shēn lái.
(*lit.* s/he very quick p turn around body come)
S/he quickly turned round.

Note: Some disyllabic repetitions are established adverbial expressions and do not derive from monosyllabic adjectives:

qiāoqiāo de	quietly	**Tā *qiāoqiāo de* gàosù wǒ ...**
		S/he told me quietly that ...
tōutōu de	furtively	**Tā *tōutōu de* kànle wǒ yī yǎn.**
		S/he stole a glance at me.
mòmò de	silently	**Tā *mòmò de* qiáozhe wǒ.**
		S/he looked at me silently.
jiànjiàn de	gradually	**Tiānqì *jiànjiàn de* nuǎnhuo qǐlái.**
		The weather gradually got warmer.

14.1.2   As in the above sentences illustrating adverbials of manner, the verb preceded by an adverbial modifier usually has to be marked in some way, e.g. by a direction indicator or an aspect marker. In the following examples **zhàn** is marked by **qǐlái** and **xià** by **zhe**.

Wǒ péngyou *mànmàn de* zhàn qǐlái.
(*lit.* my friend slow-slow p stand up)
My friend stood up slowly.

Xuě *fēnfenyángyáng de* xiàzhe.
(*lit.* snow hard-and-fast p fall asp)
The snow came down thick and fast.

14.1.3   Adverbial modifiers may occur with unmarked verbs in expressions such as imperatives. **De** is generally omitted, and the monosyllabic adverbial usually either reduplicated or extended by words such as **diǎnr** or **xiē** 'a bit'/'a little'.

Kuài *diǎnr* lái!
(*lit.* quick a-bit come)
Come here quickly!

Zǎo *xiē* huí lái.
(*lit.* early a-little return-come).
Come back a little earlier.

Hǎohǎo shuì!
(*lit.* good-good sleep)
Go to sleep nicely!
(parent to a child)

Mànmàn lái!
(*lit.* slow-slow come)
Take it easy!

14.1.4 Monosyllabic adverbial modifiers without **de** occur in certain established expressions and imperatives:

màn zǒu	take care	*lit.* slow go (a polite expression when seeing guests off)
kuài qǐlái	up you get	*lit.* quick get-up (waking somebody in the morning)
duō xiè	many thanks	*lit.* much thank (an expression of gratitude)
duō bǎozhòng	look after yourself	*lit.* much take-care (a good wish at parting)

14.1.5 Adverbials of manner are also formed from some particular types of phrase:

(1) Onomatopoeic coinages:

Fēng *hūhū de* chuīzhe.
(*lit.* wind onom p blow asp)
The wind was howling.

Mìfēng zài huāchóng zhōng *wēngwēng de* fēizhe.
(*lit.* bee in flower-cluster middle onom p fly asp)
The bees were humming amongst the flowers.

(2) Phonaesthetic expressions, in which a repeated syllable comes after an adjective, verb or noun to extend its descriptive quality through an association of sound and meaning:

Tā *lǎnyāngyāng de* tǎngzhe.
(*lit.* s/he lazy-phon p lie asp)
S/he *idly* lay there.

Tā *xìngchōngchōng de* zǒu jìnlái.
(*lit.* s/he spirit-phon p walk in)
S/he entered *in high spirits*.

Tā *xiàomīmī de* diǎnle diǎn tóu.
(*lit.* s/he smile-phon p nod asp nod head)
S/he nodded *with a smile*.

(3) Quadrisyllabic idioms:

Tā *wúkě nàihé de* sǒngle sǒng jiān.
(*lit.* s/he without-able-do-what p shrug asp shrug shoulder)
She shrugged her/his shoulders *helplessly*.

Wǒ *qíng bù zì jìn de* tànle (yī) kǒu qì.
(*lit.* I feeling-not-self-forbid p sigh asp one mw:mouthful breath)
I sighed *despite myself.*

Wǒ *bù zhī bù jué de* shuì zháo le.
(*lit.* I not-know-not-feel p sleep achieve p)
I fell asleep *without realising it.*

(4) Parallel constructions:

Tā *yī bù yī bù de* xiàng qián zǒu qù.
(*lit.* s/he one step one step p towards front walk go)
S/he went forward *step by step.*

Tā *yī gè zì yī gè zì de* xiězhe.
(*lit.* s/he one mw character one mw character p write asp)
S/he is writing [it] down *character by character.*

14.2 *Attitudinal adverbial expressions* are words or idioms used by the speaker to bring a tone of judgement or evaluation to the sentence. They occur either immediately after the subject or, if they are phrases, at the beginning of the sentence:

Tā *dāngrán* bù tóngyì.
(*lit.* s/he of-course not agree)
S/he naturally disagreed.

Wǒ *bùyīdìng* qù.
(*lit.* I not-certain go)
I can't say for sure that I will go.

Yī *wǒ kàn,* tā shì duì de.
(*lit.* according-I-see, s/he is right p)
As far as I can see, s/he is right.

Note: Other common expressions of this type include: **shènzhì** 'even', **zǒngsuàn** 'after all', **yěxǔ** 'perhaps', **kěnéng** 'probably', **kěndìng** 'definitely', **duì wǒ lái shuō** 'as far as I am concerned', **zài wǒ kàn lái** 'as I see it', **háowú yíwèn** 'no doubt', **hěn bù xìng** 'unfortunately'.

Wǒmen *zǒngsuàn* xiě wán le.
We've finished writing [it] at last.

Tāmen *yěxǔ* tīng de dǒng Guǎngzhōuhuà.
They can probably understand Cantonese.

14.3 There are a number of monosyllabic adverbs which are placed directly before the main verb and have an important linking function in the meaning of the sentence. Since they refer forwards and/or backwards, we will call them *referential adverbs*. These referential adverbs also function as conjunctives linking clauses or predicates/comments in composite sentences (see Chapter 24), but here we deal with their place in simple sentences. Some are best discussed in pairs:

(1) **Jiù** 'then' and **cái** 'only then': **jiù** emphasises a direct consequence, while **cái** indicates that something ensued only at a particular time or under particular circumstances:

Wǒmen *hěn zǎo jiù* **dào le.**
(*lit.* we very early then arrive p)
We arrived very early.

Tāmen *hěn wǎn cái* **lái.**
(*lit.* they very late only-then come)
They didn't come till very late.

Tāmen *qùnián jiù* **kāishǐ xué Hànyǔ le.**
(*lit.* they last-year then begin learn Chinese p)
They began to study Chinese (as early as) last year.

Tāmen *qùnián cái* **kāishǐ xué Hànyǔ.**
(*lit.* they last-year only-then begin learn Chinese p)
They did not begin to study Chinese until last year.

Note 1: Sentences with **jiù**, as above, regularly end with **le**, since they almost certainly express a change in circumstances (see Chapter 16 for discussion of sentence **le**). **Le** is however not generally used with **cái**- see 16.3 (9).

Note 2: **Biàn** 'then' may be used interchangeably with **jiù** in this sense, particularly in the written language.

Jiù can also emphasise immediacy:

Wǒ *jiù* **lái.**
(*lit.* I immediately come)
I'm coming. (or I'll be right with you.)

Wǒ qùqù *jiù* **huí lái.**
(*lit.* I go-go immediately back-come)
I'll be right back.

(2) **Dōu** 'all' 'both' always refers back to a preceding phrase, e.g. the subject, a posed topic (i.e. object transposed to a pre-verbal position – see 18.4), a frequency expression (e.g. with **měi** 'every'). It never relates to what follows it or follows the verb:

Dàjiā *dōu* **qù chī wǔfàn le.**
(*lit.* everybody all go eat lunch p)
Everybody has gone for lunch.

Tāmen *liǎng gè rén dōu* **huí lái le.**
(*lit.* they two mw people both back-come p)
Both of them have come back.

Zhèr měi nián dōngtiān dōu xià xuě.
(*lit.* here every-year winter all come-down-snow)
It snows here every winter.

Wǒmen *Běijīng, Xī'ān, Shànghǎi dōu* qùguo.
(*lit.* we Beijing, Xi'an, Shanghai all go asp)
We've been to Beijing, Xi'an and Shanghai.

Nèi *liǎng gè diànyǐng* wǒ *dōu* bù xǐhuan.
(*lit.* those two mw film I both not like)
I don't like either of those two films.

(3) **Zhǐ** 'only', in contrast with **dōu**, generally refers to what follows in the sentence:

Wǒ *zhǐ qù Xiānggǎng*.
(*lit.* I only go Hong Kong)
I'm only going to Hong Kong.

Wǒmen *zhǐ tánguo yī cì*.
(*lit.* we only talk asp one time)
We talked [about it] only once.

(4) **Yě** 'also' and **hái** 'additionally' have similar meanings. **Yě** generally refers back to the subject, though it may also point forward to the following verb and/or object:

Tā *yě* fāshāo le.
(*lit.* s/he also start-burn p)
S/he has a fever *too*.

Wǒ *yě* méi (yǒu) qián.
(*lit.* I also not-have money)
I haven't got any money *either*.

Hái, on the other hand, always refers to the following verb or object of that verb, implying an additional action or situation:

Xiǎotōu *hái* tōule *diànshìjī.*
(*lit.* thief in-addition steal asp television-set)
The thief *also* stole the television (i.e. in addition to other things).

Dàxué *hái yǒu Zhōngwénxì*.
(*lit.* university additionally have Chinese-department)
The university has a Chinese Department *as well*.

Note 1: **Hái** also has the meaning 'still':

Tā hái zài zhèr.	**Tāmen hái méi huí jiā.**
(*lit.* s/he still at here)	(*lit.* they still not return home)
S/he is still here.	They haven't gone home yet.

Note 2: In sentences with **shéi** 'everybody'/**shénme** 'everything' as the subject, **yě** can be used interchangeably with **dōu**, and is generally preferred when the sentence is negative:

Zhèi jiàn shì shéi *dōu*/*yě* **zhīdào.**
(*lit.* this mw matter everybody
   all/also know)
Everybody knows this.

Zhèi jiàn shì shéi *yě* **bù zhīdào.**
(*lit.* this mw matter everybody
   also not know)
Nobody knows this.

Note 3: In another construction, **lián** 'even' is used with **dōu** or **yě** in the pattern: subject + **lián** + noun or verb phrase + **dōu** or **yě** + verb (or with '**lián** + noun or verb phrase' preceding the subject):

Tā *lián* **shǒuxiàng** *dōu*/*yě* **rènshi.**
(*lit.* s/he even prime-minister
   all/also know)
S/he even knows the prime
   minister.

Tā *lián* **dòng** *yě* **bù dòng.**
(*lit.* s/he even move also not move)

S/he did not so much as move.

Lián **yī fēn qián tā** *yě* **méi yǒu.**
(*lit.* even one cent money s/he also not have)
S/he doesn't (even) have a cent.

(5) **Zài** and **yòu** both mean 'again', but there is a subtle distinction between them. **Yòu** expresses actual repetition, while **zài** indicates projected repetition. This means that often **yòu** is used in a past or continuous present context, whereas **zài** is used in a future context:

Wǒ míngtiān *zài* **lái.**
(*lit.* I tomorrow again come)
I'll come again tomorrow.

Tāmen zuótiān *yòu* **lái le.**
(*lit.* they yesterday again come p)
They came again yesterday.

Nèi gè háizi *yòu* **zài kàn diànshì le.**
(*lit.* that mw child again asp watch television p)
That child is watching television again.

As an indicator of projected repetition, **zài** may also imply the postponement of an action:

Wǒmen míngtiān *zài* **tán.**
(*lit.* we tomorrow again talk)
We'll discuss [it] tomorrow (i.e. not today).

Zhèi gè wèntí yǐhòu *zài* **kǎolǜ ba.**
(*lit.* this mw question again consider p)
We'll consider this question in future (i.e. not now).

It is possible for **zài** to be used in the past when repetition is anticipated rather than realised. That is why **zài** occurs naturally in negative sentences where the anticipated repetition does not take place:

Hòulái wǒmen bù *zài* **qù zhǎo tāmen le.**
(*lit.* afterwards we not again go look-up them p)
Afterwards we did not go and look them up again.

Tā zǒu le, méi(yǒu) *zài* **huí lái.**
(*lit.* s/he go p, not-have again back-come)
S/he left and did not come back again.

Similarly, **yòu** may occur in future contexts where repetition can be seen as part of a predetermined plan or course of action:

Xià gè yuè wǒmen *yòu* **yào fàngjià le.**
(*lit.* next mw month we again have-to start-holiday p)
Our holiday comes round again next month.

Wǒ hòutiān *yòu* **děi qù jiàn dǎoshī le.**
(*lit.* I day-after-tomorrow again must go see tutor p)
I'll have to go and see my tutor again the day after tomorrow.

(6) **Dào** and **què** both mean 'but', 'however', 'on the other hand', or 'on the contrary'. They are almost interchangeable, though **què** occurs more often in negative sentences:

Xiǎo Lǐ *dào* **gǎnmào le.**
(*lit.* little Li however catch-cold p)
However, Little Li caught a cold.

Xiǎo Lǐ *què* **bù xǐhuan chī shūcài.**
(*lit.* Little Li however not like eat vegetables)
Little Li, however, doesn't like (to eat) vegetables.

14.4 Referential adverbs generally precede the negative adverbs **bù** and **méi(yǒu)**:

Míngtiān wǒ *jiù bù* **lái le.**
(*lit.* tomorrow I then not come p)
I won't come tomorrow then.

Nèi cì yǐhòu tāmen *cái méi(yǒu)* **qù diào yú.**
(*lit* that time after they only-then not-have go fishing)
It was only after that that they did not go fishing again.

14.5 In this chapter and Chapters 10 and 11, we have discussed a whole range of adverbials. Where a number of adverbials occur in sequence before a verb, the general order is: 'attitude', 'time', 'referential', 'manner', 'location'. However, 'time' may change places with 'attitude', and 'location' with 'manner':

> **Tā _hěn kěnéng zhèi_ (_gè_) _shíhou yě rènrenzhēnzhēn de zài bówùguǎn_ kàn zhǎnpǐn ne.**
> (_lit._ s/he very possible this (mw) time also conscientiously at museum see exhibit p)
> It is most likely that at this moment s/he is also looking conscientiously at the exhibits in the museum.

> or, **Tā _zhèi_ (_gè_) _shíhou hěn kěnéng yě zài bówùguǎn rènrenzhēnzhēn de_ kàn zhǎnpǐn ne.**

15 MODAL AND SIMILAR VERBS

15.1 In this chapter we focus on verbs which precede the main verb in a sentence. Chief among these are _modal verbs_ (e.g. **néng** 'can', **yào** 'want', **děi** 'must', etc.). Other verbs of this type are those that express attitude in some way (e.g. **xǐhuan** 'like', **tóngyì** 'agree', etc.), which we refer to loosely as _attitudinal verbs_; there are also _intentional verbs_ (e.g. **dǎsuàn** 'plan', **zhǔnbèi** 'prepare', etc). Modal verbs, attitudinal verbs and most intentional verbs regularly appear with the negator **bù** but never with **méi(yǒu)**. The negator **bù** usually comes before the modal, attitudinal or intentional verb, or occasionally after it, as required by meaning or emphasis:

> **Wǒ jīntiān _bù néng_ lái.**
> (_lit._ I today not can come)
> I can't come today.

> **Wǒ jīntiān _néng bù_ lái ma?**
> (_lit._ I today can not come p)
> Can I not come today?

> **Nǐ _bù néng bù_ lái.**
> (_lit._ you not can not come)
> You must come (you cannot but come).

15.2 _Modal verbs_ express obligation, necessity, permission, possibility, ability, desire, admonition or daring. Note that (1) they can precede any type of verb including attitudinal and intentional verbs, though they occur less commonly with **shì** 'to be' or **yǒu** 'to have'; (2) they are almost never preceded by another verb (see note below); (3) they are never immediately followed by a noun or pronoun object (though **yào** 'want' can be used as a full verb when it may take an object).

Note: Modal verbs may be preceded by verbs expressing hope or aspiration, such as **xīwàng**, **pànwàng**, **kěwàng**, etc.

> **Wǒ** *xīwàng néng* **zài jiàn dào nín.**
> (*lit.* I hope can again see polite:you)
> I hope to see you again.

See also note on **gāoxìng** 'happy' at 15.3.2 below.

(1) **Yīnggāi** or, more colloquially, **gāi** or **děi** indicate *obligation* ('ought to', 'should', 'have to'):

Nǐ *yīnggāi* **qù shuìjiào le!**
(*lit.* you should go sleep p)
You ought to go to bed./It's time you went to bed.

Nǐ bù *yīnggāi* **zài zhèr chōuyān/xīyān.**
(*lit.* you not should at here inhale-smoke)
You shouldn't smoke here.

Wǒ *gāi/děi* **zǒu le.**
(*lit.* I should leave p)
I must be off.

Nǐde xīn shǒubiǎo *děi* **bàoshuì.**
(*lit.* your new watch should report-tax)
You will have to declare your new watch [at customs].

Lǚkè dōu *děi* **tiánxiě zhèi zhāng biǎogé.**
(*lit.* passengers all should fill-write this mw form)
All passengers should fill in this form.

(2) **Bìxū** conveys *necessity* or *compulsion* ('must'):

Nǐ *bìxū* **qù dǎzhēn!**
(*lit.* you must go hit-needle)
You must go and have an injection.

Nǐ *bìxū* **huídá wǒde wèntí.**
(*lit.* you must answer my question)
You must answer my question.

Note: **Bìxū** may be considered an adverb. Like modal verbs it is placed before the verb, but it cannot be used in an affirmative-negative form: **bìxū bù bìxū.

The negation of **bìxū** is **bùyòng** or more formally **bùbì** ('there's no need'):

Nǐ *bùyòng/bùbì* **qù jiē tā.**
(*lit.* you not need go meet him/her)
There's no need for you to go and meet him/her.

Wŏmen *bùyòng* gàosù tāmen.
(*lit.* we not need tell them)
There's no need for us to tell them.

(3) **Kěyĭ** and **néng** express *permission* ('may', 'can'):

Wŏ xiànzài *kěyĭ/néng* zŏu le ma?
(*lit.* I now may/can leave p p)
May I leave now?

Nĭ bù *kěyĭ/néng* zài zhèr tíng chē.
(*lit.* you not may/can at here stop car p)
You may not park your car here.

Wŏ *kěyĭ/néng* kànkàn nĭde jiàshĭ zhízhào ma?
(*lit.* I may/can look-look your driving licence p)
May I have a look at your driving licence?

Wŏ *kěyĭ/néng* tí yī gè wèntí ma?
(*lit.* I may/can raise one mw question)
May I ask a question?

(4) **Huì** indicates either *possibility/probability* ('may', 'is likely to'):

Jīntiān *huì* guā fēng ma?
(*lit.* today likely blow wind p)
Is it likely to be windy today?

Tāmen míngtiān bù *huì* lái.
(*lit.* they tomorrow not likely come)
They won't come tomorrow.

or, *ability* in the sense of an acquired skill (can):

Dǎoyóu *huì* shuō Yīngyǔ.
(*lit.* tourist-guide can speak English)
The tourist guide can speak English.

Wŏ bù *huì* tán gāngqín.
(*lit.* I not can play piano)
I cannot play the piano.

Nĭ *huì* dǎ tàijíquán ma?
(*lit.* you can hit shadow-boxing p)
Can you do shadow-boxing?

(5) **Néng** and **néng(gòu)** also convey *ability* but in the sense of physical strength or capability ('can'):

Wo yī tiān *néng(gòu)* pǎo shí Yīnglĭ lù.
(*lit.* I one day able run ten miles road/way)
I can walk/run ten miles a day.

Jīntiān wǒ bù *néng(gòu)* qù shàngbān.
(*lit.* today I not can go on-shift)
I can't go to work today.

Note: In contrast to the potential complement, **néng(gòu)** tends to imply that personal attitude, capacity or judgement, rather than external circumstances, determine ability (or inability).

(6) **Xiǎng** and **yào** expresses *wish* or *desire* ('want', 'would like to'):

Wǒ *xiǎng* mǎi (yī) xiē shípǐn hé yǐnliào.
(*lit.* I want buy some food and drink)
I'd like to buy some food and drink.

Nǐ xiǎng qù cānguān gōngchǎng ma?
(*lit.* you want go visit factory p)
Do you want to go and visit a factory?

Tā *yào* xué kāi chē.
(*lit.* s/he want learn drive-car)
S/he wants to take driving lessons.

Tā *yào* zài Guǎngzhōu dāi liǎng gè lǐbài.
(*lit.* s/he want at Guangzhou stay two mw week)
S/he wants to stay in Guangzhou for two weeks.

Wǒ *xiǎng* huàn wǔbǎi yuán.
(*lit.* I want change five-hundred yuan)
I would like to change five hundred yuan.

Note: The **yuán** (or more colloquially **kuài**) is the basic unit of Chinese currency. It is divided into 10 **jiǎo** (more colloquially **máo**) and 100 **fēn**.

However, in imperative sentences **yào** and its negative form **bù yào** mean respectively *admonition* ('must') and *prohibition* ('don't'):

Nǐ *yào* xiǎoxīn!
(*lit.* you must small-concern)
You must be careful!

Bù yào dòng!
(*lit.* not must move)
Don't move!

Note 1: With **yào** in this sense the pronoun subject is normally present, but with **bù yào** it is optional.

Note 2: **Yào** may also be used by itself as a transitive verb to mean 'want' or 'need', when it takes a noun or pronoun object:

Wǒ *yào* chá, bù *yào* kāfēi.	I want tea, not coffee.
Zuò chē qù zhǐ *yào* yī gè xiǎoshí.	It takes only an hour to go by car.

Bié can be used as an alternative to **bù yào** for 'don't':

Bié dòng!   Don't move!
Bié xiào wǒ!   Don't laugh at me!
Bié jìn lái!   Don't come in!

(7) **Yuànyi** and **kěn** indicate *willingness* ('be willing'):

Xiàozhǎng *yuànyi* **tuìxiū.**
(*lit.* headmaster willing retire)
The headmaster is willing to retire.

Tā bù *yuànyi* **tán zōngjiào huò zhèngzhì.**
(*lit.* s/he not willing talk religion or politics)
S/he is not willing to talk about religion or politics.

Jīnglǐ bù *kěn* **jiàn wǒ.**
(*lit.* manager not willing see me)
The manager is not willing to see me.

Tā *kěn* **jiāo nǐ ma?**
(*lit.* s/he willing teach you p)
Is s/he willing to teach you?

(8) **Gǎn** indicates either *bravery* or *audacity* ('dare'):

Tā bù *gǎn* **tiào jìn shuǐ lǐ qù.**
(*lit.* s/he not dare jump enter water in go)
S/he did not dare to jump into the water.

Nǐ *gǎn* **mà rén!**
(*lit.* you dare scold people)
How dare you use abusive language (to people)!

Shéi *gǎn* **dǎ tā!**
(*lit.* who dare hit him/her)
Who dares to hit him/her! (i.e. Nobody dares to hit him/her.)

Note: We will see later (18.3.1) that sentences with modal verbs are topic-comment rather than subject-predicate sentences.

15.2.1 Modal verbs do not generally take adverbial modifiers. However, adverbs of degree (e.g. **hěn**, **fēicháng**, etc.) naturally occur with **xiǎng** 'want' and **yuànyi** 'be willing':

Wǒ *hěn* **xiǎng qù dùjià.**
(*lit.* I very want go spend-holiday)
I want very much to go away for a holiday.

Tāmen *fēicháng yuànyi* **bāngzhù nǐ.**
(*lit.* they extremely willing help you)
They are extremely willing to help you.

Also, negative expressions are regularly softened by the addition of **tài/dà** 'too':

Míngtiān bù *dà* **huì xià yǔ.**
(*lit.* tomorrow not too likely fall-rain)
It is not too likely to rain tomorrow.

Tā bù *tài* **yuànyi zhīchí wǒ.**
(*lit.* s/he not too willing support me)
S/he not too willing to support me.

Wǒ bù *dà* **gǎn chī shēng háo.**
(*lit.* I not too dare eat raw-oyster)
I'm a bit of a coward when it comes to eating raw oysters.

15.2.2 Comparisons can be expressed using modal verbs, with the '**bǐ** + (pro)noun' phrase preceding the modal verb (see 7.2 for comparison structures):

Nǐ *bǐ wǒ néng* **chī.**
(*lit.* you compare me can eat)
You can eat more than I can.

Tā *bǐ wǒ huì* **shuōhuà.**
(*lit.* s/he compare me able speak)
S/he was able to speak better than I did.

Tā *bǐ shéi* **dōu** *yuànyi* **bāngzhù wǒ.**
(*lit.* s/he compare anybody all willing help me)
S/he is willing to help me more than anybody else.

15.3 *Attitudinal verbs* may like modal verbs precede verbs, but they can also be followed by nouns or pronouns. Unlike modal verbs, they regularly take adverbial modifiers of degree:

Xīfāngrén *xǐhuan yǎng* **gǒu.**
(*lit.* Westerners like raise dog)
Westerners like keeping dogs.

Xīfāngrén hěn *xǐhuan* **gǒu.**
(*lit.* Westerners very like dog)
Westerners like dogs very much.

Tāmen fēicháng *tǎoyàn mǎi* **dōngxi.**
(*lit.* they extremely hate buy thing)

They really hate shopping.

Tāmen fēicháng *tǎoyàn* **nèi gè rén.**
(*lit.* they extremely hate that mw person)

They really loathe that person.

Wǒ *pà zuò* **lǎnchē.**
(*lit.* I fear sit cable-car)
I am afraid to ride in a cable-car.

Wǒ *pà guǐ.*
(*lit.* I fear ghost)
I am afraid of ghosts.

Wǒ hěn *tóngyì xuǎn* **tā.**
(*lit.* I very agree elect him/her)
I agree to vote for him/her.

Wǒ hěn *tóngyì nǐde yìjiàn.*
(*lit.* I agree your opinion)
I agree to your idea.

Tāmen hěn *fǎnduì chī* **ròu.**
(*lit.* they very oppose eat meat)
They are opposed to eating meat.

Tāmen *fǎnduì zhèi gè tíyì.*
(*lit.* they oppose this mw proposal)
They are opposed to this proposal.

15.3.1 Two commonly used verbs which may be categorised as attitudinal verbs are **wàngle** 'to forget' and **jìde** 'to remember':

Bié *wàngle dài* **yàoshi.**
(*lit.* don't forget asp bring key)
Don't forget to bring [your] keys [with you].

Qǐng *jìde suǒ* **mén.**
(*lit.* please remember lock door)
Please remember to lock the door.

Note: **Wàngle** 'to forget' invariably incorporates the aspect marker **le.**

15.3.2 The adjective **gāoxìng** 'happy' can take on the function of an attitudinal verb and precede another verb:

Wǒ hěn *gāoxìng rènshi* **nín.**
(*lit.* I very happy know polite:you)
I am pleased to meet you.

Wǒmen fēicháng *gāoxìng yǒu* **jīhuì lái zhèr fǎngwèn.**
(*lit.* we extremely happy have opportunity come here visit)
We are extremely happy to have the opportunity of coming here for a visit.

Note: **Gāoxìng** like **xīwàng** 'to hope' may precede a modal verb:

Wǒ hěn gāoxìng néng lái Zhōngguó liúxué.
(*lit.* I very happy can come China study-abroad)
I am very happy to be able to come to study in China.

15.4 *Intentional verbs* are always followed by verbs and do not take adverbial modifiers of degree:

Wǒ *dǎsuàn qù* **lǚxíng.**
(*lit.* I calculate go travel)
I am planning to go travelling.

Wŏmen de gōngchǎng *dǎsuàn zhuāng kōngtiáo.*
(*lit.* our factory calculate install air-conditioning)
Our factory is planning to install air-conditioning.

Tā *zhǔnbèi shēnqǐng yī fèn gōngzuò.*
(*lit.* s/he prepare apply one mw job)
S/he is planning to apply for a job.

Nǐ *juédìng chī shénme?*
(*lit.* you decide eat what)
What have you decided to eat?

Note: Some of these verbs can be followed by nouns (e.g. **Tā zài zhǔnbèi gōngkè** 'S/he is preparing (for) the lesson') but they are then full verbs and carry no meaning of intention.

15.4.1 Negating intentional verbs is slightly more complicated than negating modal or attitudinal verbs. The negator **bù** can come either before or after the intentional verb, without there being any significant difference in meaning. For instance,

Wŏ *bù dǎsuàn* **cānjiā bǐsài.**
(*lit.* I not plan take-part-in contest)
I am not planning to take part in the competition.

Wŏ *dǎsuàn bù* **cānjiā bǐsài.**
(*lit.* I plan not take-part-in contest)
I am planning not to take part in the competition.

Zhǔnbèi, **jìhuà** 'plan', etc., follow this pattern.

Exceptionally, **juédìng** 'decide' can only be followed (not preceded) by the negator **bù**:

Wŏ *juédìng bù* **cānjiā bǐsài.**
(*lit.* I decide not take-part-in contest)
I have decided not to take part in the competition.
NOT * **Wŏ bù juédìng cānjiā bǐsài.**

The negator **méi(yŏu)**, usually preceded by **hái** 'still', can be used before **juédìng**, however. The action verb which follows **juédìng** may then take an affirmative-negative format:

Wŏ hái méi(yŏu) juédìng cān(jiā) bù cānjiā bǐsài.
(*lit.* I still not-have decide take-part-in not take-part-in contest)
I haven't yet decided whether to take part in the competition or not.

III SENTENCES

INTRODUCTION

A distinctive characteristic of many Chinese sentences is the influential role of the particle **le** in their formulation. The addition of **le** at the end of a statement introduces an assertiveness of tone implying change, updating, etc. The presence of **le** may therefore convert a subject-predicate sentence into a topic-comment sentence (see Chapter 18). Other sentence particles, **ma**, **ne**, **ba**, etc., transform statements into various forms of question; imperatives may be signalled by **ba**; and exclamations are indicated by **a** and its variants.

Prepositional or coverbal phrases are a regular feature of Chinese sentences. The location phrases introduced in Part Two are coverbal, and other coverbal phrases provide background information on method, direction, destination, etc. The coverb **bǎ**, which expresses intentional manipulation or unintentional intervention, has the important function of moving an object to a pre-verbal position, leaving the post-verbal space clear for the complement. The coverb **bèi**, rarely used except in narration, introduces the agent in a passive construction. (Passives are more readily formed, however, through topic-comment structures where sentence **le** is generally indispensable.)

Serial constructions occur frequently in Chinese sentences. They bring together verbal elements through meaning relationships such as time-sequence, purpose, etc., rather than through syntax. Composite sentences, on the other hand, consist of more than one clause or predicate/comment, usually linked by conjunctions and/or conjunctives.

As a non-morphological language, Chinese relies heavily on its speakers'/listeners' knowledge of the real world. This makes for not only standard constructions like notional passives in the form of topic-comments but also frequent abbreviations and omissions in sentences so that sense depends on reference to non-linguistic contexts and verbal cotexts.

Emphasis is regularly generated by the use of the intensifier **shì** which can focus stress on almost any element in the sentence. In addition, topicalisation may emphasise an object by transferring it to a topic position in a topic-comment sentence.

The subject-predicate and topic-comment dichotomy we have proposed offers insights into the organisation of Chinese sentences. The shift from subject-predicate to topic-comment through the introduction of sentence particle **le**, modal verbs, the intensifier **shì**, etc., represents a move by the speaker from a narrative to a descriptive, explanatory, or argumentative stance.

16   STATEMENTS AND THE SENTENCE PARTICLE **LE**

16.1 We have earlier discussed the function of **le** as an aspect marker suffixed to a verb of action to indicate the completion of the action (see 8.3.1). A second, important use of **le** is as a *sentence particle* placed at the end of a sentence and influencing its meaning as a whole. By adding **le** to a sentence, the speaker introduces some form of comment on the action or the situation, implying a commitment or involvement on his/her part. The speaker may be suggesting that circumstances have changed or are about to change, that things are not as the listener expects, or that circumstances have reached a particular point. When using **le** in this way, the speaker readily lets his/her enthusiasm, interest and involvement be known. Sentence **le** does occur in written Chinese, especially in letters, but its function makes it particularly common in speech. In effect, adding sentence **le** updates the situation; thus underlying all such statements with **le** is the fundamental notion of change. For example,

Wǒ bù chōuyān.	**Wǒ bù chōuyān** *le.*
(*lit.* I not inhale-cigarette)	(*lit.* I not inhale-cigarette p)
I don't smoke.	I don't smoke any more. (i.e. I have given up smoking.)

The first statement is simply a statement of fact, whereas the second implies a change in habit from 'smoking' to 'non-smoking'.

16.2 In the examples below, sentence **le** conveys to the listener (or reader) a sense of updating, change, reversal, etc. of the previous situation.

(1) Sentences containing result or direction complements which in one way or another signal new situations or conditions:

Tā shuì *zháo* **le.**	**Bàba hē** *zuì* **le.**
(*lit.* s/he sleep achieved p)	(*lit.* father drink intoxicated p)
S/he has fallen asleep.	Father has got drunk.

Tā chū *qù* **le.**	**Tàiyáng shēng** *qǐlái* **le.**
(*lit.* s/he out go p)	(*lit.* sun rise up-come p)
S/he has gone out.	The sun has risen.

(2) Sentences with verbs or indicators which mean 'begin', 'end', 'start', 'finish', 'emerge', 'disappear', 'change', etc., which by definition introduce new circumstances:

Tánpàn *kāishǐ* **le.**
(*lit.* negotiation begin p)
The negotiations have begun.

Huìyì *jiéshù* **le.**
(*lit.* meeting end p)
The meeting has ended.

Tiānqì *biàn* **le.**
(*lit.* weather change p)
The weather (has) changed.

Tā *kū qǐlái* **le.**
(*lit.* s/he cry/weep start p)
S/he (has) started to cry.

Similarly, an adverbial in the sentence may indicate that something is about to take place:

Fēijī *kuài yào* **qǐfēi le.**
(*lit.* plane quick about take-off p)
The plane is about to take off.

Tiān *jiù yào* **xià yǔ le.**
(*lit.* sky soon about fall-rain p)
It is about to rain.

(3) Sentences with a monosyllabic action or state verb which naturally poses a contradiction to a previous action or state:

Huǒchē dào le.
(*lit.* train arrive p)
The train has arrived.

Tā bìng le.
(*lit.* s/he ill p)
S/he has fallen ill.

Tiān liàng le.
(*lit.* sky bright p)
It is light (now).

Huār kāi le.
(*lit.* flower open p)
The flowers have come out.

Dōngxi guì le.
(*lit.* things expensive p)
Things are getting more expensive.

(4) Sentences which have nominal predicates indicating age, height, weight, etc., and register change or updating:

Wǒ jīnnián *liùshí suì* **le.**
(*lit.* I this-year sixty years-old p)
I am sixty (years old) this year.

Xiǎohuǒzi *yī mǐ bā* **le.**
(*lit.* young-man one metre eight p)
The young man is one metre eight tall (now).

Háizi *liù gè yuè* **le.**
(*lit.* child six mw month p)
The child is six months old (now).

Wǒ kuài *qīshí gōngjīn* **le.**
(*lit.* I almost seventy kilogram p)
I am almost seventy kilograms (in weight) (now).

16.2.1 Since the primary function of sentence **le** is to emphasise updating or change of situation, a speaker narrating and commenting on a series of events will tend to delay **le** to the end of the statement, thereby summing up the situation:

Tā bǎ yīfu xǐ gānjìng *le*.
(*lit.* s/he grasp clothes wash clean p)
S/he washed the clothes (clean).

Tā bǎ yīfu xǐ gānjìng, liàng chūqù *le*.
(*lit.* s/he grasp clothes wash clean, hang out p)
S/he washed the clothes and hung them out to dry.

Tā bǎ yīfu xǐ gānjìng, liàng chūqù, ránhòu jì xìn qù *le*.
(*lit.* s/he grasp clothes wash clean, hang out, then post letter go p)
S/he washed the clothes, hung them out to dry and then went to post a letter.

16.2.2 When **le** follows a verb phrase at the end of a sentence, it often functions both as aspect marker indicating completed action and as sentence particle:

Tāmen lái le.
(*lit.* they come asp+p)
They've come.

(i.e. they have arrived [completed action] and they are here now [updating, change of situation, etc.])

Dōngtiān guò qù le.
(*lit.* winter pass go asp+p)
The winter is over.

Tāmen jiéhūn le.
(*lit.* I knot-marriage asp+p)
They have got married.

Note: **Jiéhūn le** could also be expressed as **jiéle hūn le** with the first **le** indicating completed action and the second **le** as a sentence particle.

16.3 Sentence **le** is usually not used where the indication of 'change' is not the speaker's primary concern. For example, in:

(1) Sentences which indicate habitual actions, where the emphasis is more on persistence than change:

Tā chángcháng dǎ *wǎngqiú*.
(*lit.* s/he often-often hit net-ball)
S/he plays tennis very often.

Wǒ tiāntiān *diào yú*.
(*lit.* I day-day hook-fish)
I go fishing every day.

(2) Sentences with verbs marked by a continuous aspect marker or brief duration indicator, where the focus is on the continuity or brevity of the action:

Tā (*zhèng*)*zài tīng guǎngbō*.
(*lit.* s/he (just) asp: in-the-process-of listen broadcast)
S/he is listening to the broadcast.

Tā *diǎnle diǎn* tóu.
(*lit.* s/he nod asp nod head)
S/he nodded.

(3) Sentences with verbs complemented by duration or frequency indicators or used with objects qualified by numeral and measure word phrases, where the interest is in what took place:

Tā xuéle sì nián Zhōngwén.
(*lit.* s/he study asp four year Chinese)
S/he studied Chinese for four years.

Tā qùguo Zhōngguó liǎng cì.
(*lit.* s/he go asp China two times)
S/he has been to China twice.

Tā chīle sān piàn miànbāo.
(*lit.* s/he eat asp three mw bread)
S/he ate three slices of bread.

Note: **Le** can naturally be added to sentences like these where the speaker is providing updated or significantly changed information:

Wǒ xuéle sì nián Zhōngwén *le*.
I have been studying Chinese for four years.

Tā hē le bā bēi píjiǔ *le*.
S/he has drunk eight glasses of beer (and s/he does not look well, should not have done so, etc.).

(4) Sentences with location or manner complements, where attention is usually focused on the resulting location, situation, etc.:

Tā zuò *zài dì shàng*.
(*lit.* s/he sit at land on)
S/he sat on the floor/ground.

Yǔ xià *de hěn dà*.
(*lit*. rain fall p very big)
The rain came down heavily.

(5) Sentences using adjectival predicates, where the interest is in the present state or situation of the subject:

Wǒ *zhēn bèn*.
(*lit*. I really foolish)
I was really stupid./How stupid I was!

Nèi gè zhōngniánrén *hěn pàng*.
(*lit*. that mw middle-aged-person very fat)
That middle-aged man is very fat.

(6) Sentences using the verbs **shì** or **yǒu**, which by definition present a state of affairs:

Tā *shì* huàjiā.
(*lit*. s/he be painter)
S/he is an artist.

Zhèi zhī māo *shì* xióng de.
(*lit*. this mw cat be male p)
This cat is a tom(cat).

Tā *yǒu* hěn duō zhūbǎo.
(*lit*. s/he have very many pearl-jewel)
S/he has got a lot of jewellery.

(7) Sentences expressing existence, emergence or disappearance, where the interest is in the object or entity that exists, emerges or disappears:

Dìtǎn shàng dōu shì huīchén.
(*lit*. carpet-on all be dust)
There is dust all over the carpet.

Huāpíng lǐ chāzhe méiguìhuā.
(*lit*. vase-in insert asp rose)
There are roses in the vase.

Qùnián xiàguo yī cháng dà xuě.
(*lit*. last-year fall asp one mw big snow)
There was a heavy snowfall last year.

Lǐtáng lǐ zuò mǎn le rén.
(*lit*. auditorium-in sit full asp people)
The auditorium is full (of people).

(8) Sentences in which a manner adverb is the centre of interest:

Qìqiú *mànmàn de* **piāo shàng tiānkōng qù.**
(*lit.* balloon slow-slow p float up sky go)
The balloon rose slowly into the sky.

Mǔqīn *jǐnjǐn de* **bào zhù háizi.**
(*lit.* mother tight-tight p embrace firm child)
The mother held the child firmly in her arms.

(9) Sentences with the referential adverb **cái** which emphasise the time or condition referred to:

Tā *hěn wǎn cái* **huí jiā.**
(*lit.* s/he very late until-then return home)
S/he returned home very late.

Tā *hē zuì le cái* **xiě de chū hǎo shī.**
(*lit.* s/he drink intoxicated p only-then write p out good poem)
Only when s/he is drunk can s/he produce good poems.

16.4 Nevertheless, **le** may be used with almost any sentence if the speaker wishes to impart his/her awareness of development or difference in a situation (see note under 16.3 (3) above). Naturally sentence **le** occurs in some circumstances more than others, but it is possible to find it added to unlikely sentences if the situation demands. For example:

Wǒ tiāntiān xǐzǎo le.
(*lit.* I day-day wash-bath p)
I take a bath every day nowadays.
(i.e. I didn't use to, but I have changed my habits, etc.)

Huāyuán lǐ zhòng mǎn le cài le.
(*lit.* garden in grow full asp vegetable p)
The garden is now full of vegetables.
(i.e. it used to be overgrown with weeds, etc.)

Nèi gè rén shì nán de le.
(*lit.* that mw person be male p p)
That person is now a man.
(i.e. he has undergone a sex change, etc.)

17 QUESTIONS

Questions in Chinese take a number of different forms: question-word questions; general questions (with **ma**); surmise questions (with **ba**); affirmative-negative questions; alternative questions; rhetorical questions, etc.

17.1 *Question-word questions* make use of question words or expressions, of which the following are the most obvious examples:

shéi (or shuí)	Who or whom
shéide (or shuíde)	Whose
shénme	What
shénme shíhou (or jǐ shí)	When
jǐ diǎn (zhōng)	What time (of day)
nǎr (or shénme dìfang)	Where
zěnme, zěn(me)yàng	How
nǎ/něi + (numeral) + measure word	Which
wèi shénme	Why

Note: See earlier reference to interrogative pronouns in 4.4.

Question words or expressions occur in the sentence at the point where the answer is expected. There is no change in word order as in English.

Q: **Tā shì** *shéi?*
(*lit.* s/he be who)
Who is s/he?

A: **Tā shì** *wǒ tóngxué.*
(*lit.* s/he be my coursemate)
S/he is my coursemate.

Q: *Shéi* **láiguo?**
(*lit.* who come asp)
Who has been?

A: *Zhāng xiānsheng* **láiguo.**
(*lit.* Zhang Mr come asp)
Mr Zhang has been.

Q: **Nǐ jiàn dào le** *shéi?*
(*lit.* you bump into asp whom)
Who did you bump into?

A: **Wǒ jiàn dào le** *Lǐ xiǎojie.*
(*lit.* I see achieve asp Li Miss)
I bumped into Miss Li.

Q: **Zhè shì** *shéide* **gǒu?**
(*lit.* this be whose dog)
Whose dog is this?

A: **Zhè shì** *wǒ línjū de* **gǒu.**
(*lit.* this be my neighbour p dog)
This is my neighbour's dog.

Q: **Nǐ xiǎng hē (yī) diǎnr** *shénme?*
(*lit.* you want drink a little what)
What would like to drink?

A: **Wǒ xiǎng hē (yì) diǎnr** *kělè.*
(*lit.* I want drink a little coke)
I would like to have some coke.

Q: **Nǐ jīntiān shàng** *shénme* **kè?**
(*lit.* you today attend what class)
What classes do you have today?

A: **Wǒ jīntiān shàng** *wénxué* **kè.**
(*lit.* I today attend literature class)
I have literature classes today.

Q: **Nǐ** *shénme shíhou* **qù Zhōngguó?**
(*lit.* you when go China)
When are you going to China?

A: **Wǒ** *xià gè yuè* **qù Zhōngguó.**
(*lit.* I next month go China)
I'm going to China next month.

Q: **Nǐ** *jǐ diǎn* **(zhōng) huí lái?**
(*lit.* you what time back-come)

What time are you coming back?

A: **Wǒ** *bā diǎn* **(zhōng) zuǒyòu huí lái.**
(*lit.* I eight o'clock about back-come)
I'm coming back around eight.

Q: **Nǐ zài *nǎr* děng wǒ?**
 (*lit.* you at where wait me)
 Where will you wait for me?

A: **Wǒ zài *huǒchēzhàn* děng nǐ.**
 (*lit.* I at train-station wait you)
 I'll wait for you at the (railway)
 station.

Q: **Sìshí yī lù chēzhàn zài *nǎr*?**
 (*lit.* forty one route stop at where)
 Where is the 41 bus stop?

A: **Sìshí yī lù chēzhàn zài *qiánmiàn*.**
 (*lit.* forty one route stop at front)
 The 41 bus stop is just ahead.

Q: **Nǐ zhǔnbèi *zěnme* qù Lúndūn?**
 (*lit.* you plan how go London)
 How are you going to London?

A: **Wǒ zhǔnbèi *zuò chángtú qìchē* qù.**
 (*lit.* I plan sit coach go)
 I am taking a coach.

Note: For discussion of coverbs like **zuò** 'travel by', see Chapter 19.

Q: **Tā *wèi shénme* méi lái?**
 (*lit.* s/he why not come)
 Why didn't s/he turn up?

A: **Tā *yǒu shì* méi lái.**
 (*lit.* s/he have business not come)
 S/he didn't turn up because s/he
 had something to do.

Note: **Wèi shénme** 'why', is asking for an explanation rather than an identification, and the most common responses to it are therefore clauses beginning with **yīnwèi** 'because'. (See Chapter 4.)

Q: **Nǐ juéde zhèi jiàn wàitào
 zěn(me)yàng?**
 (*lit.* you feel this mw jacket how)
 What do you think of this jacket?

A: **Wǒ juéde *hěn hǎo*.**

 (*lit.* I feel very good)
 I think [it is] very nice.

Q: ***Nǎ/něi* běn xiǎoshuō zuì yǒuqù?**
 (*lit.* which mw novel most
  interesting)
 Which novel is the most
 interesting?

A: ***Nà/nèi* běn xiǎoshuō zuì yǒuqù.**
 (*lit.* that mw novel most interesting)
 That novel is the most interesting.

17.1.1 Zěnme yàng 'how' can be used as a predicate by itself without a verb (see also 17.6 below).

Q: **Diànyǐng *zěnmeyàng*?**
 (*lit.* film how/what like)
 How was the film?
 What was the film like?

A: **Diànyǐng *hěn dòngrén*.**
 (*lit.* film very moving)
 The film was very touching.

Q: **Jiàqián *zěnmeyàng*?**
 (*lit.* price how/what like)
 What about the price?

A: **Jiàqián *hěn gōngdào*.**
 (*lit.* price very reasonable)
 The price was very reasonable.

Q: **Kāfēiguǎn de fúwùyuán**
   zěnmeyàng?
   (*lit.* cafe p assistant how/what
   like)
   What are the waiters at the
   cafe like?

A: **Tāmen *hěn yǒuhǎo*.**

   (*lit.* they very friendly)

   They are very friendly.

17.1.2   A number of question expressions are formed with **duō** 'how'; 'to
what extent':

duō jiǔ (or **duō cháng shíjiān**)	how long
duō yuǎn	how far
duō dà	how old
duō + gradable adjective	how + gradable adjective

There is also the common question word **duōshǎo** (*lit.* many-few) 'how
many'/'how much'.

As above, these question expressions are placed in the sentence where
the answer is expected:

Q: **Nǐ xiǎng yào *duōshǎo*?**
   (*lit.* you want have how-many)
   How many do you want?

A: **Wǒ xiǎng yào *liǎng gè*.**
   (*lit.* I want have two mw)
   I would like (to have) two.

Q: **Nǐ yòngle *duōshǎo* qián?**
   (*lit.* you use asp how-much
   money)
   How much (money) did you
   spend?

A: **Wǒ yòngle *sānshíbàng* (qián).**
   (*lit.* I use asp thirty pound money)

   I spent thirty pounds.

Q: **Nǐ děngle *duō jiǔ* le?**
   (*lit.* you wait asp how-long p)
   How long have you been
   waiting?

A: **Wǒ děngle *yī gè xiǎoshí* le.**
   (*lit.* I wait asp one mw hour p)
   I have been waiting (for) an hour.

Q: **Nǐ jiā lí zhèr *duǒ yuǎn*?**
   (*lit.* you home from here
   how-far)
   How far is your home from
   here?

A: **Wǒ jiā lí zhèr *èrshí Yīnglǐ*.**
   (*lit.* my home from here twenty
   mile)
   My home is twenty miles from
   here.

Q: **Nǐ mèimei jīnnián *duǒ dà* le?**
   (*lit.* your younger sister this-
   year how big p)
   How old is your younger sister
   this year?

A: **Tā jīnnián *shí bǎ suì* le.**
   (*lit.* she this-year eighteen years-
   of-age p)
   She is eighteen years old this year.

Q: **Nǐ dìdi _duō gāo_?**
(*lit.* your younger-brother how tall)
How tall is your younger brother?

A: **Tā _yī mǐ qī wǔ_.**
(*lit.* he one metre seven five)
He is one metre seventy-five.

17.1.3 The particle **ne** can be added to the end of a question-word question usually to convey a slightly quizzical tone:

Shū zài nǎr?   Where is the book?
Shū zài nǎr _ne_?   Where can the book be?

Tā wèi shénme méi lái?   Why didn't he come?
Tā wèi shénme méi lái _ne_? Why didn't he come then?

17.2 _General questions_ in Chinese can be formed by adding the particle **ma** to the end of the sentence. There is no change in word order. The answer to such questions is likely to be 'yes' or 'no'; this is usually expressed by repeating the verb or adjective used in the question, in the case of 'no' with the negative (**bù** or **méi**). If the question has a modal verb, the response uses the modal verb:

Q: **Nín shì Zhāng Yún ma?**
Are you Zhang Yun?

A: **Shì. (Wǒ shì Zhāng Yún.)**
Yes. (I'm Zhang Yun.)

Q: **Zhè shì zhōngdiǎn zhàn ma?**
Is this the terminus?

A: **Bù shì.**
No.

Q: **Nǐ tóngyì ma?**
Do you agree?

A: **Tóngyì.**
Yes. (*lit.* agree)

Q: **Tā yǒu yī gè dìdi ma?**
Has s/he got a younger brother?

A: **Méi yǒu. (Tā méi yǒu dìdi.)**
No. (S/he doesn't have a younger brother.)

Q: **Nǐ jiějie chōuyān ma?**
Does your elder sister smoke?

A: **Chōu.**
Yes. (*lit.* smoke)

Q: **Qìchē jiāle yóu ma?**
Have you filled the car with petrol?

A: **Jiāle.**
Yes. (*lit.* filled)

Q: **Nǐ dāngguo bīng ma?**
Have you ever been a soldier?

A: **Méiyǒu. (Méi dāngguo.)**
No. (I have never been (one).)

Q: **Nǐ huì shuō Zhōngwén ma?**
Can you speak Chinese?

A: **Bù huì.**
No. (*lit.* cannot)

Q: **Nǐ yào hē bēi chá ma?**
Would you like a cup of tea?

A: **Yào.**
Yes. (*lit.* like)

Q: **Nèi gè jiémù yǒuqù ma?**
   Was that programme interesting?

A: *Hěn* **yǒuqù.**
   Yes, very interesting.

Q: **Nǐ zuìjìn máng ma?**
   Are you busy recently?

A: **Bù** *tài* **máng.**
   Not very. (*lit.* not too busy)

Q: **Nàr lěng ma?**
   Was it cold there?

A: **Lěng** *jí le.*
   Extremely cold.

Note: As in last three examples, a degree adverb or complement of some kind normally precedes or follows the adjectival predicate in the responses. We have seen earlier (6.2.1 and 13.6) that adjectival predicates do not usually occur without some form of marker.

When the question is enquiring about a state of affairs rather than an action, the initial response is usually **shì** (**de**) 'yes' or **bù** (**shì**) 'no':

Q: **Nǐ gǎnmào le ma?**
   (*lit.* you get-cold asp p)
   Have you got a cold?

A: **Shì (de). Wǒ gǎnmào le.**
   (*lit.* be [p]. I get-cold p)
   Yes. I've got a cold.

Q: **Nǐ huí lái de hěn zǎo ma?**

   (*lit.* you back-come p very
      early p)
   Did you come back early?

A: **Bù (shì). Wǒ huí lái de hěn**
   wǎn.
   (*lit.* not [be] I back-come p
      very late)
   No, I came back quite late.

Q: **Tā jiéle hūn le ma?**
   (*lit.* s/he get asp married p p)

   Is s/he married?

A: **Bù, tā hái méi (yǒu) jiéhūn.**
   (*lit.* no, s/he still not have
      marry)
   No, s/he is not married yet.

It should be noted that in Chinese the response to a question posed in the negative is to affirm or deny the negative, whereas in English the convention is to link the 'yes' or 'no' with the response:

Q: **Nǐ bù gāoxìng ma?**
   (*lit.* you not happy p)
   Aren't you pleased?

A: **Bù, wǒ hěn gāoxìng.**
   (*lit.* no, I very happy)
   Yes, I am.

or, **Shì (de), wǒ bù gāoxìng.**
   (*lit.* yes, I not happy)
   No, I'm not.

Q: **Nǐ míngtiān bù lái ma?**
   (*lit.* you tomorrow not come p)
   Aren't you coming tomorrow?

A: **Bù, wǒ lái.**
   (*lit.* no, I come)
   Yes, I am.

or, **Shì (de), wǒ bù lái.**
   (*lit.* yes, I not come)
   No, I'm not.

Q: **Nǐ méi jiànguo tāmen ma?**
    (*lit.* you not see asp them p)
    Haven't you met them before?

A: **Bù, jiànguo.**
    (*lit.* no, see asp)
    Yes, I have.
or, **Shì (de), méi jiànguo.**
    (*lit.* yes, not see asp)
    No, I haven't.

Note: These questions can be made more *rhetorical* by introducing *nándào* 'do you mean to say', 'is it really the case' before or after the subject:

Nǐ nándào *bù* **xiǎng jiā** *ma*?
Don't you really miss your family?

Nándào nǐ *bù* **zhǐdao zhèi huí shì** *ma*?
Didn't you really know this?

17.3 To ask a general question, where the answer is expected or assumed, **ba** is used in place of **ma**. Such questions are similar to English tag questions with phrases like 'is(n't) it', 'are(n't) they', etc., at the end. We will call these questions *surmise questions*:

Nǐ huì qí mótuōchē ba?
(*lit.* you can ride motorcycle p)
You can ride a motorbike, can't you?

Nǐ bù chī shé ba?
(*lit.* you not eat snake p)
You don't eat snake, do you?

The answers to surmise questions (**ba** questions) follow the same lines as those to **ma** questions. If the enquiry is about a state of affairs, **shì (de)** 'yes' or **bù (shì)** 'no' can be used:

Q: **Nǐ huì liūbīng ba?**
    (*lit.* you can slide-ice p)
    You can skate, can't you?

A: **Bù. Wǒ bù huì.**
    (*lit.* no I not can)
    No, I can't.

Q: **Tā dǒng Guǎngzhōuhuà ba?**
    (*lit.* s/he understand Cantonese p)
    S/he knows Cantonese, doesn't
    s/he?

A: **Shì (de). Tā dǒng.**
    (*lit.* be [p]. s/he understand)
    Yes, s/he does.

Where the question is posed in the negative, the response affirms or denies that negative, as with negative **ma** questions (see 17.2):

Q: **Nǐ bù shì Zhāng xiānsheng ba?**
    (*lit.* you not be Zhang mister p)
    You aren't Mr Zhang, are you?

A: **Shì (de), wǒ bù shì.**
    (*lit.* yes, I not be)
    No, I am not.

<blockquote>

or, **Bù, wǒ shì Zhāng xiānsheng.**
(*lit.* no, I be Zhang mister)
Yes, I am Mr Zhang.

</blockquote>

是不是

17.4 Another common way to make a general enquiry is to use *affirmative-negative questions.* These take the form of an affirmative verb or adjective immediately followed by its negative, i.e. 'verb/adjective + **bù** verb/adjective'. In the case of **yǒu**, the negative is, of course, **méi**.

Q: **Nǐ *shì bù shì* Zhāng xiǎojie?**
Are you Miss Zhang (or not)?

A: **Shì./Bù shì.**
Yes./No.

Q: **Nǐ shēn shàng *yǒu méi yǒu* qián?**
Have you got any money on you?

A: **Yǒu./Méi yǒu.**
Yes./No.

Q: **Tā míngtiān *lái bù lái*?**
Is s/he coming tomorrow?

A: **Lái./Bù lái.**
Yes./No.

Q: **Nǐ *xiǎng bù xiǎng* hē píjiǔ?**
Would you like some beer?

A: **Xiǎng./Bù xiǎng.**
Yes./No.

Q: **Bēizi *gòu bù gòu*?**
Are there enough cups/glasses?

A: **Gòu./Bù gòu.**
Yes./No.

Q: **Yínháng *yuǎn bù yuǎn*?**
Is the bank far [from here]?

A: **Hěn yuǎn./Bù hěn yuǎn.**
Yes./No.

If the verb or adjective is disyllabic, the second syllable may be dropped from the first verb or adjective:

Q: **Nàr *ān(jìng) bù ānjìng*?**
Is it quiet there?

A: **Ānjìng./Bù ānjìng.**
Yes./No.

Q: **Tā *yuàn(yi) bù yuànyi*?**
Is s/he willing?

A: **Yuànyi./Bù yuànyi.**
Yes./No.

This also happens with 'verb + object' expressions :

Q: **Nǐ *qǐ bù qǐchuáng*?**
Are you getting up?

A: **Qǐchuáng./Bù qǐchuáng.**
Yes./No.

Q: **Nǐ *xǐ bù xǐzǎo*?**
Are you going to take a bath?

A: **Xǐ./Bù xǐ.**
Yes./No.

If the verb is preceded by a modal verb or **lái/qù**, then only the modal verb or **lái/qù** is made affirmative-negative:

Q: **Nǐ *huì bù huì* lā xiǎotíqín?**
Can you play the violin?

A: **Huì./Bù huì.**
Yes./No.

Q: **Míngtiān** *huì bù huì* **xià yǔ?**   A: **Huì./Bù huì.**
Will it rain tomorrow?   Yes./No.

Q: **Nǐ xiàwǔ** *qù bù qù* **yóuyǒng?**   A: **Qù./Bù qù.**
Are you going swimming this   Yes./No.
   afternoon?

Where the verb indicates a completed action or past experience, the affirmative-negative pattern can be created either by putting **méiyǒu** at the
end of the question or by placing **yǒu méiyǒu** before the verb:

Q: **Nǐ** *xué guo* **Zhōngwén** *méiyǒu?*   A: **Xuéguo./Méiyǒu** or **Méi**
  or, **Nǐ** *yǒu méiyǒu xuéguo*   **xuéguo.**
  Zhōngwén?
Have you ever learned Chinese?   Yes./No.

Q: **Nǐ** *chīle* **yào** *méiyǒu?*   A: **Chīle./Méiyǒu** or **Méi(yǒu)**
  or, **Nǐ** *yǒu méiyǒu chī* **yào?**   **chī.**
Did you take your medicine?   Yes./No.

Q: **Nǐ** *shōu dào le* **huíxìn** *méiyǒu?*   A: **Shōu dào le./Méiyǒu** or
  or, **Nǐ** *yǒu méiyǒu shōu dào*   **Méi(yǒu) shōu dào.**
  huíxìn?
Have you got a reply to your letter?   Yes./No.

Note: As seen in 8.3.1, the aspect marker **le** is not used in a negative statement with **méi(yǒu)**.
It would therefore be incorrect to say: *Nǐ yǒu méiyǒu chīle yào?

17.5 *Alternative questions* are posed by using **háishì** 'or' as a pivot
between two balanced verbal clauses to suggest alternative possibilities:

Nǐ jīntiān zǒu *háishì* **míngtiān zǒu?**
Are you leaving today or tomorrow?

Nǐ zuò qìchē qù *háishì* **zuò huǒchē qù?**
Are you going by coach or by train?

Tāmen xiǎng tiàowǔ *háishì* **xiǎng kànxì?**
Do they want to go to a dance or to see a play?

Nǐ lái *háishì* **tā lái?**
Are you coming or is s/he coming?

Note 1: **Háishì** is used to mean 'or' only in questions. In other sentences the word for 'or'
is **huòzhě** (see 24.2.1(2)).

Note 2: The adverbs **jiūjìng** and **dàodǐ**, meaning 'after all', are often used for emphasis with
alternative questions, affirmative-negative and with some question-word questions. They are
always placed before the first verb:

Tā *jiūjìng* xiǎng xué Hànyǔ háishì xiǎng xué Rìyǔ?	What does s/he really want to learn – Chinese or Japanese?
Nǐ *dàodǐ* yǒu méi yǒu kòng?	Are you free after all?
Tāmen *jiūjìng* shénme shíhou dào?	When exactly do they arrive?
Nǐ *jiūjìng* yào qù nǎr ne?	Where do you really want to go?

17.6 *Suggestions* in the form of questions can be made by adding a tag expression such as **hǎo bù hǎo**, **hǎo ma** or **zěnmeyàng** at the end of the sentence:

Zánmen qù pá shān, *hǎo bù hǎo*?
Shall we go climbing?

Qǐng guān shàng chuānghu, *hǎo ma*?
Could you please close the window?

Qǐng shuō de màn diǎnr, *hǎo ma*?
Would you please speak a little slower?

Zánmen hē yī bēi, *zěnmeyàng*?
How about (having) a drink?

Qǐng nǐ bāng wǒ xiū yī xiū, *hǎo ma*?
Can you please (help) fix [it] for me?

Positive answer to all these questions will usually be **hǎo** 'fine'/'OK'/'good'. A negative response will obviously involve explanation but will often begin with **duìbuqǐ** 'sorry'.

17.7 *Confirmation* can often be sought by adding the tag expression **shì ma** or **shì bù shì** at the end of a statement:

Q: **Tā bìng le, *shì ma*?**
   S/he is ill, isn't s/he?

A: **Shì de. Tā bìng le.**
   Yes. S/he's ill.

Q: **Nǐ xià gè xīngqī kǎoshì, *shì bù shì*?**
   You'll have exams next week, won't you?

A: **Bù shì. Shì zhèi gè xīngqī.**
   No. It's this week.

Note: For discussion of **shì** as an intensifier, see Chapter 22.

18 SUBJECT AND PREDICATE; TOPIC AND COMMENT

18.1 Chinese sentences may be divided into two broad categories: *subject-predicate* and *topic-comment*. These two categories are markedly distinct both in terms of definite and indefinite reference and in their use of different types of verb with or without aspect markers. The transformation of a subject-predicate structure into a topic-comment one, with modal verbs or the sentence particle **le**, is a key feature of Chinese sentence construction.

This dual patterning of syntax enables flexible and succinct expression, with less dependence on formal grammatical features and sharper focus on meaning in relation to the real world. For instance,

> **Dōngxi dōu fàng zài guìzi lǐ le.**
> (*lit.* things all put at cupboard-in p)
> Everything has been put in the cupboard.

This sentence does not need to be couched in the passive voice, though its English equivalent does. By relying on real-world knowledge, the Chinese speaker can be confident that no misunderstanding will arise, since the listener cannot possibly assume that the 'things' in the sentence are the subject and responsible for the action of putting. (Compare 18.4.1.)

18.2 A *subject-predicate* sentence usually relates an event and is therefore used for narrative purposes. It has the following features:

(1) The subject is often a noun or pronoun representing the initiator or recipient of the action (or non-action) expressed by the verb:

> **Dàjiā dōu dàile yǔsǎn.**   Everybody carried an umbrella with
>   them.
> **Tāmén shōu dào le bù shǎo**   They received quite a lot of presents.
> **lǐwù.**
> **Dìdi bù chī yú.**   My younger brother doesn't eat fish.
> **Tā méi(yǒu) qùguo Yìndù.**   S/he has never been to India.

(2) The subject must be of *definite reference*:

> **Tā zài xǐ wǎn.**   S/he is washing the dishes.
> **Lǎoshī zǒu jìn le jiàoshì.**   The teacher came into the classroom.
> **Háizimen zài mǎlù shàng tī qiú.** The children are playing football on
>   the road.
> **Māma diū diào le tāde**   Mother has lost her purse.
> **qiánbāo.**

A noun at the beginning of such a sentence, even if unqualified by a demonstrative (this, that), will have definite reference (e.g. **lǎoshī** in the above 'the teacher'). A personal pronoun is naturally of definite reference, and a pronoun like **dàjiā** refers to 'everybody of a definite group'. A noun of indefinite reference cannot normally be the subject of a subject-predicate construction, and it would therefore be unusual to say:

*Yī gè xuésheng **zhànle qǐlái.**   (*lit.* *A student stood up.)

However, it is possible to begin the sentence with the verb **yǒu** so that the noun of indefinite reference comes after a verb:

Yǒu yī gè xuésheng **zhànle qǐlái.**   A student stood up.

This accounts for the fact that many narrative sentences begin with a time or location expression followed by **yǒu**:

Zhèi shíhou yǒu **(yī) liàng chē kāile guòlái.**
(*lit.* this time there-was (one) mw car drive asp across-come)
At this moment a car approached.

Jīntiān wǎnshang yǒu **(yī) gè péngyou lái wǒ jiā zuò.**
(*lit.* today evening there-will-be (one) mw friend come my home sit)
A friend is coming round to my place this evening.

Wàimiàn yǒu **rén zhǎo nǐ.**
(*lit.* outside there-is person look-for you)
There is someone outside looking for you.

(3) The predicate verb is an action verb. Aspect markers are therefore almost always present in subject-predicate sentences (see Chapter 8).

Wǒ *hēle* **yī bēi niúnǎi.**	I drank/had a glass of milk.
Tā *kànguo* **zájì.**	S/he has seen acrobatics.
Tāmen *zhèngzài tánpàn.*	They are negotiating right now.
Tā *dàizhe* **yī dǐng bái màozi.**	S/he is wearing a white hat.

Note: Some action verbs can be followed by **zhe** to indicate a persistent state that results from the action of the verb. See the last example above and 8.3.4.

(4) It may be a sentence with a passive marker (e.g. **bèi, ràng, jiào,** etc.) or with **bǎ** (implying intentional manipulation or unintentional intervention). (See also Chapter 20):

Xìnfēng *bèi* **nòng de hěn zāng.**
(*lit.* envelope by handle p very dirty)
The envelope has been made very dirty.

Tāmen *bǎ* **qìchē tíng zài lù biān.**
(*lit.* they grasp car stop at road-side)
S/he parked their car by the side of the road.

(5) The predicate verb may be causative or dative (see 8.5 and 21.5).

Tā *qǐng* wǒ chī fàn.   S/he invited me to a meal. (*causative*)
Wǒ *sòng* tā yī gè lǐwù.   I gave him a present. (*dative*)

18.3 A *topic-comment* sentence, while usually following a subject-predicate structure with a noun phrase followed by a verb phrase provides a description or offers an opinion, rather than narrating an action or event. It is therefore a construction designed for descriptive, explanatory or argumentative purposes. The following features differentiate it from the subject-predicate sentence:

(1) The topic may be of any word class or any structure (e.g. a phrase or even a clause):

Zìdiǎn hěn yǒuyòng.   (*noun*: 'dictionaries')
(*lit*. dictionary very useful)
Dictionaries are useful.

Lǎnduò shì bù duì de.   (*adjective*: 'lazy')
(*lit*. lazy is not right p)
Being lazy is wrong.

Zuò shì yīnggāi rènzhēn.   (*verbal phrase*: 'doing anything')
(*lit*. do things should conscientious)
One should be conscientious when doing anything.

Tā bù lái bù yàojǐn.   (*clause*: 's/he does not come')
(*lit*. s/he not come not urgent)
It does not matter if s/he does not turn up.

(2) The topic may be of definite or indefinite reference:

Gōngjù yīnggāi fàng zài zhèr.
(*lit*. tool should put at here)
The tools should be placed here.

Yī gè rén bù néng bù jiǎng lǐ.
(*lit*. one mw person not able not talk reason)
A person must be reasonable.

(3) The comment can be an adjectival predicate, or it can contain the verbs **shì** or **yǒu**:

Zhèi gè háizi *hěn cōngmíng*.   This child is (very) intelligent.
Jīntiān *shì* wǒde shēngrì.   Today is my birthday.
**Měi gè rén dōu *yǒu* yī gè   Every person has a name.
  míngzi.**

18.3.1 In addition, topic-comments can be created in the following circumstances:

(1) When a *modal verb* is present, since a modal verb naturally signals a comment:

Tā *huì* shuō Zhōngwén.   He can speak Chinese.
Shéi dōu *yīnggāi* zūnshǒu jìlù.   Everybody should observe discipline.
Xuésheng yě *kěyǐ* cānjiā.   Students may also take part.

(2) By the addition of the *sentence particle* le. This can convert most subject-predicates into topic-comments since by definition it expresses a comment on the action, updating, indicating change, etc. (see 16.1):

Dìdi chī yú *le.*
(*lit.* younger-brother eat fish p)
My younger brother eats fish now.

Bìngrén xǐng guòlái *le.*
(*lit.* patient wake across-come p)
The patient has regained consciousness.

Biérén dōu líkāi *le.*
(*lit.* others all depart p)
The others have all left.

18.4 A posed topic may be followed by a subject-predicate structure. There are therefore a large number of sentences where both a topic and a subject are present. These '*topic | subject-predicate*' structures are often used for explanatory purposes:

Nèi běn zhēntàn xiǎoshuō | wǒmen mài wán le.
(*lit.* that mw detective novel | we sell finish p)
We have sold out of that detective/crime novel..

Xìn | tā jì chūqù le.
(*lit.* letter | s/he post out-go p)
S/he has posted the letter.

Nǐde kùzi | wǒ tàng hǎo le.
(*lit.* your trousers | I iron good p)
I've ironed your trousers.

18.4.1 The subject in these 'topic + subject-predicate' structures may be omitted if its sense is understood from the context. Sentences of this type superficially become 'topic + predicate' structures and can be seen as *notional passive* sentences in which the topic is notionally the object of the verb. The three examples in 18.4 may be re-formulated without the subject as:

Nèi běn zhēntàn xiǎoshuō | mài wán le.
(*lit.* that mw detective novel | sell finish p)
That detective novel is sold out.

Xìn | jì chūqù le.
(*lit.* letter | post out-go p)
The letter has been sent/posted.

Nǐde kùzi | tàng hǎo le.
(*lit.* your trousers | iron good p)
Your trousers have been ironed.

Other examples are:

Zhèi gè xì | yǎnle liǎng gè yuè le.
(*lit.* this mw play | perform asp two mw month p)
This play has been on for two months.

Bāoguǒ | shōu dào le.
(*lit.* parcel | receive arrive p)
The parcel has been received.

Dàibiǎotuán de fǎngwèn rìchéng | ānpái hǎo le.
(*lit.* delegation p visit itinerary | arrange good p)
The itinerary for the delegation's visit has been arranged.

Nǐ yào de dōngxi | mǎi huílái le.
(*lit.* you want p things | buy back-come p)
The things you want have been bought.

18.5 Conversely, a subject may be followed by a topic-comment structure to create a '*subject | topic-comment*' sentence. At first sight these sentences seem to have two subjects, but in fact what looks like a second subject is a topic (relating to the subject) on which a comment is expressed:

Tā | *shēntǐ* **bù hǎo.**
(*lit.* s/he | body not good)
His/her health is not good.

Wǒ | *gōngzuò* **hěn máng.**
(*lit.* I | work very busy)
I am busy with my work.

Dǒngshìzhǎng | *xīnshuǐ* **shífēn gāo.**
(*lit.* board-director | salary extremely high)
The director of the board has an extremely high salary.

Guǎngdōngshěng | *jīngjì fāzhǎn* **fēicháng kuài.**
(*lit.* Guangdong province | economic development extremely fast)
The economy of Guangdong developed/is developing very fast.

It is also possible for the possessive **de** to be used after the subject, thereby changing the subject-topic sequence into a simple topic and leaving the sentence in the topic-comment form:

Wǒ*de* gōngzuò | hěn máng.
(*lit.* my work | very busy)
I am busy with my work.

Guǎngdōngshěng *de* jīngjì fāzhǎn | fēicháng kuài.
(*lit.* Guangdong province p economic development | extremely fast)
The economy of Guangdong developed/is developing very fast.

19 PREPOSITIONS AND COVERBS

19.1 We have seen in 11.4 how the preposition **zài** 'in', 'at' followed by a location noun, pronoun or postpositional phrase can be placed before the verb as a location phrase:

Māma *zài chúfáng lǐ* zuò fàn.
(*lit.* mother at kitchen in make rice-meal)
Mother is preparing the meal/doing the cooking in the kitchen.

There are a number of prepositions that grammatically function like **zài**; because, like **zài**, they can be used as full verbs they may be called *coverbs*, i.e. verbs that occur in sequence with other verbs in a sentence. The coverb with its object can be referred to as a *coverbal phrase*. In the above example, **zài** is the coverb, and the location phrase **zài chúfáng lǐ**, in syntactic terms, is a coverbal phrase.

Note: We have observed in 11.3 that **zài** can be a full verb as in **Tāmen xiànzài *zài* Měiguó** 'They are in America now'.

The coverbal phrase normally comes after the subject and before the main verb; it provides background information about the place, time, methods, service, reference, reason, etc., associated with the main verb. Generally modal verbs (e.g. **néng**, **yào**) and the negators **bù** and **méi(yǒu)** come before the coverbal phrase, though occasionally, when they relate only to the main verb, they come after it (e.g. in the case of **lí** 'away from'). The main types of coverb are listed below.

19.1.1 Coverbs of place and time:

(1) **zài** 'in, at'

Tā *zài (fēi)jīchǎng* dāng fānyì.
(*lit.* s/he at airport act interpreter
S/he serves as an interpreter at the airport.

Wǒ *zài dàshǐguǎn* bàn qiānzhèng.
(*lit.* I at embassy deal visa)
I was applying for a visa at the embassy.

Wǒ kěyǐ *zài zhèr* chōuyān/xīyān ma?
(*lit.* I can at here inhale-smoke p)
May I smoke here?

(2) **dào** 'to'

Tāmen míngtiān *dào Éguó* qù.
(*lit.* they tomorrow to Russia go)
They are going to Russia tomorrow.

Tā méi *dào yīyuàn* lái kàn wǒ.
(*lit.* s/he not to hospital come see me)
S/he did not come to the hospital to see me.

Wǒmen bù *dào fànguǎn* qù chīfàn.
(*lit.* we not to restaurant go eat-rice)
We are not dining out at a restaurant.

As can be seen from the last example, a **dào** coverbal phrase with **lái** 'come' or **qù** 'go' may often be followed by another verb to indicate purpose.

(3) **wàng, xiàng, cháo** 'towards'

Qìchē *wàng nán* kāi qù.
(*lit.* car towards south drive go)
The car is heading south.

Tā *cháo wǒ* diǎn le diǎn tóu.
(*lit.* s/he towards me nod asp nod head)
S/he nodded to me.

Tā *xiàng jùlèbù* zǒu lái.
(*lit.* s/he towards club walk come)
S/he came towards the club.

(4) **cóng** 'from'

Fēng *cóng xībian* chuī lái.
(*lit.* wind from west-side blow come)
The wind blew from the West.

Nǐ *cóng zhèr* xiàng běi zǒu.
(*lit.* you from here towards north walk)
You go north from here.

Note: In this last example, there are two coverbal phrases: **cóng zhèr** and **xiàng běi**.

(5) **lí** '(distance) from (in terms of place or time)'

Wǒ jiā *lí dàxué* hěn yuǎn.
(*lit.* my home from university very far)
My home is very far from the university.

Wǒde bàngōngshì *lí shì zhōngxīn* hěn jìn.
(*lit.* my office from city centre very near)
My office is very close to the town centre.

Note 1: **Lí** 'from' simply indicates *distance* between two fixed objects, while **cóng** 'from' is always associated with *movement* from one place to another.

Note 2: The negator **bù** comes before the main predicate verb or adjective and not before **lí**: **Wǒ jiā lí dàxué *bù* yuǎn** 'My home is not far from the university'. NOT ****Wǒ jiā bù lí dàxué yuǎn**.

Wǒ jiā *lí Shànghǎi* yǒu èrshí gōnglǐ.
(*lit.* my home from Shanghai have twenty kilometres)
My home is twenty kilometres from Shanghai.

Xiànzài *lí Shèngdànjié* hái yǒu liǎng gè yuè.
(*lit.* now from Christmas still have two mw month)
There are still two months from now to Christmas.

Note: When the actual distance or time is specified, the verb **yǒu** is normally required.

(6) **Yánzhe** 'along'

Wǒmen *yánzhe nèi tiáo jiē* zǒu qù.
(*lit.* we along that mw street walk go)
We went along that street.

Chuán *yánzhe yùnhé* kāi lái.
(*lit.* boat along canal sail come)
The boat came along the canal.

Note: **Yán** on its own is only found in such expressions as **yán lù** 'all along the road', **yán hǎi** 'all along the coast', etc., which are generally used to indicate existence rather than movement:

Yán lù dǒu shì màitián.   There are wheatfields all along the road.

19.1.2 Coverbs of methods and means:

(1) **Yòng** 'with, using'

Tā *yòng máobǐ* huà huàr.
(*lit.* s/he use Chinese-brush paint picture)
S/he paints with a Chinese brush.

(2) **Zuò** '(travelling) on/by' (*lit.* sit)

Wǒ chángcháng *zuò dìtiě* shàngbān.
(*lit.* I often sit underground-rail go-to-work)
I often go to work by underground.

Wǒmen hěn xiǎng *zuò huǒchē/gōnggòng qìchē/fēijī/chuán* qù.
(*lit.* we very want sit train/bus/plane/boat go)
We'd very much like to go by train/bus/plane/boat.

Note: An alternative coverb for travel is **chéng**:

Wǒ chángcháng *chéng chūzū qìchē* shàngbān.
(*lit.* I often take hire-car go-to-work)
I often go to work by taxi.

19.1.3 Coverbs of human exchange and service:

(1) **duì** '(speaking) to'; '(behaving) towards'

Tā *duì wǒ* shuō ...
(*lit.* s/he to me said ...)
S/he said to me ...

Tāmen *duì wǒ* hěn hǎo.
(*lit.* they towards me very good)
They are very kind to me.

Note: **Duì** is also commonly used to mean 'with regard to':

Wǒ *duì měishù/yīnyuè* méi(yǒu) xìngqù.
(*lit.* I regarding fine-art/music not-have interest)
I have no interest in fine art/music.

(2) **gěi** 'to'; 'for'

Wǒ jīntiān wǎnshang *gěi nǐ* dǎ diànhuà.
(*lit.* I today evening to you make telephone-call)
I will give you a telephone call tonight.

Wǒ měi zhōu dōu *gěi bàba* xiě xìn.
(*lit.* I every week all to father write letter)
I write to my father every week.

Qǐng nǐ *gěi wǒ* kāi (yī) zhāng shōujù.
(*lit.* please you to me write (one) mw receipt)
Please write a receipt for me.

(3) **wèi/tì** 'for'; 'on behalf of'

Jiějie *tì wǒ* lǐ fà.
(*lit.* elder-sister for me cut hair)
My elder sister cut my hair for me.

Ménfáng *wèi wǒ* **jiào le yī liàng díshì/chūzū qìchē.**
(*lit.* porter for me call asp one mw taxi)
The porter called a taxi for me.

(4) **Gēn/hé/tóng ... yīqǐ** '(together) with'

Wǒ *gēn fùmǔ yīqǐ* **qù dùjià.**
(*lit.* I with father-mother together go spend-holiday)
I spent my holiday with my parents.

Note: **gēn** may also be used colloquially like **duì** above:

   Tā *gēn* **wǒ shuō** ...   S/he said to me...

19.1.4   Coverbs indicating reference:

(1) **àn/zhào/ànzhào** 'according to'

Qǐng nǐ *àn/zhào/ànzhào* **guīdìng qù bàn zhèi jiàn shì.**
(*lit.* please you according-to regulation go manage this mw matter)
Please do this according to the regulations.

(2) **Jiù** 'with reference to'

Wǒmen *jiù* **zhèi gè wèntí tǎolùn yī xià.**
(*lit.* we with-reference-to this mw question discuss a-moment)
Let's have a discussion of/discuss this question.

19.1.5   **Bǐ** and **gēn** in comparison expressions (as discussed in 7.2 and 7.2.3) are in fact coverbs.

Tā *bǐ* **wǒ dà.**   S/he is older than I.
Zhèi gè *gēn* **nèi gè yīyàng guì.**   This one is as expensive as that one.

Bǎ in manipulation constructions and **bèi** for passive voice (analysed in Chapter 20) are also coverbs.

19.2   There are a number of disyllabic *prepositions* which, though similar to coverb prepositions, are not strictly in that category, since they may be followed not only by nominal expressions but also in most cases by verbal phrases. These prepositional constructions usually come at the beginning of the sentence:

(1) **gēnjù/jù** 'on the basis of'

Gēnjù lùpái wǒmen zhǎo dào le tāde jiā.
(*lit.* basing-on road-sign we look-for-and-find asp his/her home)
We found his/her home with the help of road signs.

Jù tā suǒ shuō, **tāmen yǐjing zǒu le.**
(*lit.* basing-on s/he p say, they already leave p)
According to him/her, they have already left.

(2) **guānyú** 'as for, as regards'

Guānyú zhèi yī diǎn, **wǒ yǐjing tíchūguo wǒde yìjian.**
(*lit.* as-for this one point, I already raise-out asp my opinion)
As regards this point, I have already put forward my opinion.

(3) **yóuyú** 'because of'

Yóuyú dà xuě, **qiúsài zàntíng.**
(*lit.* because-of heavy snow, ball-contest temporary-stop)
The ball game was temporarily suspended because of the heavy
  snow.

Note: **Yóuyú** may also be regarded as a conjunction when it is followed by a clause.
(See Chapter 24.)

(4) **wèile** 'for the sake of'

Wèile zhèi jiàn shì, **wǒ qù le sān tàng.**
(*lit.* for this mw matter, I go asp three trip)
I made three trips there for this business.

Wèile kànwàng lǎo zǔmǔ, **tā měi xīngqī dōu huí jiā.**
(*lit.* in-order-to visit old grandma, s/he every week all return home)
S/he goes home every week in order to see her/his old grandma.

Note: We have consciously used the term 'preposition' for this group of words in order to
illustrate the uniformity of their function.

20 BǍ AND BÈI CONSTRUCTIONS

20.1   The **bǎ** *construction* is a grammatical feature unique to the Chinese
language. In this construction, the coverb **bǎ**, which as a verb has the
meaning 'to grasp', has the function of shifting the object of the verb to
a pre-verbal position in the pattern of 'subject + **bǎ** + object + verb' Three
interrelated features of the construction can be identified:

(1) As seen in 1.3.2, an unqualified object after the verb will generally
    be of indefinite reference. Employment of the coverb **bǎ**, which moves
    the object in front of the verb, automatically converts the noun to
    definite reference:

Wǒ qù mǎi shū.
(*lit.* I go buy book)
I am going to buy a book/some books.

Wǒ qù *bǎ* shū mǎi huílái.
(*lit.* I go grasp book buy back-come)
I am going to buy *the* book/books (and come back with it/them).

(2) In the discussion of complements in 13.4.3, it was apparent that with complements adjustments have to be made when the verb is followed by an object:

Zhèi gè rén *shuō* huà *shuō* de hěn kuài.
(*lit.* this mw person say words say p very fast)
This person speaks very fast.

In this example, the repetition of the verb **shuō** enables it to deal with the object and the complement one at a time. The coverb **bǎ** is used to similar effect, moving the object before the verb and leaving the post-verbal position clear for the complement.

Tā bǎ *shū* fàng *hǎo* le.
(*lit.* s/he grasp book put good p)
S/he placed the books in good order.

Tā bǎ *tā* gē *zài shūjià shàng*.
(*lit.* s/he grasp it leave at book-shelf on)
S/he placed it on the bookshelf.

Note: **Tā** 'it' cannot be omitted after **bǎ**

(3) **Bǎ**, which as noted derives from a verb meaning 'to grasp', also implies *intentional* (or sometimes unintentional) *manipulation* of the object on the part of the subject.

Tā *bǎ* yīfu xǐ nòng gānjìng *zāng*le.
(*lit.* s/he grasp clothes wash/handle clean/dirty p)
S/he has washed/dirtied her/his clothes.

The subject of a **bǎ** construction deliberately (or unwittingly) handles or deals with the object in such a way that some kind of consequence is registered in the complement that follows the verb.

The **bǎ** construction, therefore, cannot be used if any of the above conditions are not met. In other words, a **bǎ** construction must have an object of definite reference (shifted now to a pre-verbal position directly after **bǎ**); a complement of some kind after the verb to indicate the result achieved by the action of the verb; and, generally, an intention (or non-intention) on the part of the subject. The following sentences are therefore unacceptable:

(a) ***Wǒ bǎ wǔ tiào le yī cì.**
(*lit.* *I danced once)

(The noun **wǔ** 'dance' is not of definite reference in this context.)

(b) *Wǒ bǎ shū fàng.
   (*lit.* *I put the books.)

   (There is no complement and therefore no indication of any result achieved by the action of the verb **fàng** 'put'.)

(c) *Wǒ bǎ diànyǐng kàn le liǎng gè zhōngtóu.
   (*lit.* *I took two hours to watch the film.)

   (It is clearly beyond the power of the subject to decide how long the film will be. There are of course occasions when the subject can control the duration of something – see 20.1.1 below.)

(d) *Wǒ bǎ zhèi běn shū xǐhuan de hěn.
   (*lit.* *I like this book very much.)

   (The verb **xǐhuan** 'like' expresses the inclination of the subject and the complement **de hěn** 'very much' indicates the degree or extent of the liking; these cannot be regarded as a manipulative action and an achieved result.)

20.1.1 Complements in a **bǎ** construction may take various forms:

Wǒ bǎ lājī dào *diào* le.   (*result – verb*)
(*lit.* I grasp litter pour off p)
I have dumped the rubbish.

Tā bǎ xìn fēng *hǎo* le.   (*result – adjective*)
(*lit.* s/he grasp letter seal good p)
S/he has sealed the letter.

Tā bǎ huà guà *qǐlái* le.   (*direction*)
(*lit.* s/he grasp picture hang up-come p)
S/he hung the picture.

Dìdi bǎ kèwén fùxí le *liǎng biàn*.   (*frequency*)
(*lit.* younger-brother grasp text revise asp two times)
My younger brother revised the text twice.

Jǐngchá bǎ xiǎotōu guān le *liǎng gè yuè*.   (*duration*)
(*lit.* police grasp thief imprison asp two mw month)
The police kept the thief in prison for two months.

Jiějie bǎ fángjiān shōushí le *yī xià*.   (*brief duration*)
(*lit.* elder-sister grasp room tidy asp one stroke)
My elder sister tidied up the room.

Tā bǎ yǐzi lā *dào zhuōzi pángbiān*.   (*destination*)
(*lit.* s/he grasp chair pull to table side)
S/he pulled the chair to the side of the table.

Wǒ bǎ dàyī guà *zài yījià shàng*.   (*location*)
(*lit*. I grasp overcoat hang at clothes-hanger on)
I hung my overcoat on the clothes-hanger.

Wǒmen bǎ lǐwù sòng *gěi tā*.   (*dative*)
(*lit*. we grasp gift present give him/her)
We presented the gift to him/her.

Tāmen bǎ wūzi dǎsǎo *de gāngānjìngjìng de*. (*manner*)
(*lit*. they grasp room sweep p clean-clean p)
They swept the room clean.

Note: Reduplicated adjectival complements are usually followed by **de**.

Tā bǎ wǒ qì *de huà dōu shuō bù chūlái le*.   (*consequential state*)
(*lit*. s/he grasp me anger p words all speak not out-come p)
S/he made me so angry that I could not speak a word.

20.1.2 The aspect markers **le** and **zhe** may also be used as complements in **bǎ** sentences.

(1) **le** (indicating completed action with verbs which have an inherent meaning of result):

Tā bǎ chá hē*le*.   **Shéi bǎ mén suǒ*le*?**
(*lit*. s/he grasp tea drink asp)   (*lit*. who grasp door lock asp)
S/he drank up/finished the tea.   Who has locked the door?

(2) **zhe** (indicating persistence in an *imperative* sentence):

Qǐng bǎ dēng ná*zhe*.   **Bǎ cài liú*zhe*.**
(*lit*. please grasp lamp hold asp) (*lit*. grasp dishes keep asp)
Please hold the lamp.   Keep the food.
                                   (i.e. don't throw it away or eat it)

20.1.3 One type of complement regularly used with **bǎ** is the resultative complement beginning with **chéng**, **zuò** or **wéi** all meaning 'become', 'act as':

Zuòjiā bǎ zìjǐ xiě de gùshì fānyì *chéng* Fǎwén.
(*lit*. writer grasp self write p story translate become French)
The writer translated his/her own story into French.

Tā *bǎ* wǒ dàng *zuò* zuì hǎo de péngyou.
(*lit*. s/he grasp me regard become most good p friend)
S/he regarded me as her/his best friend.

20.1.4 **Nòng** and **gǎo** are two versatile colloquial verbs meaning loosely 'to handle' which feature regularly in **bǎ** sentences:

Wǒ bǎ hézi *nòng* pò le.
(*lit.* I grasp box handle break p)
I broke the box.

Bié bǎ jīqì *gǎo* huài le.
(*lit.* don't grasp machine handle bad p)
Don't damage the machine.

20.1.5 In negative **bǎ** sentences, the negator must precede **bǎ**:

Yīnyuèjiā hái *méi(yǒu) bǎ* tāde gēqǔ guàn chéng chàngpiàn.
(*lit.* musician still not-have grasp his/her song record become record)
The musician has not yet recorded his/her song.

***Bié bǎ* huāpíng pèng dǎo.**
(*lit.* don't grasp vase bump fall-over)
Don't knock the vase over.

Tā cóng *bù bǎ* bèizi dié hǎo.
(*lit.* s/he always not grasp quilt fold-good)
S/he never folds up [her/his] quilt properly.

Note: **Bù** with **bǎ** is comparatively rare, occurring normally with verbs indicating habitual action or sometimes intention. It also occurs in composite sentences (see 24.3).

20.1.6 Modal verbs may come before **bǎ**:

Wǒ *néng bǎ* chuāng dǎ kāi ma?
(*lit.* I can grasp window hit open p)
May I open the windows?

Nǐ *kěyǐ bǎ* gōngjù shōu qǐlái le.
(*lit.* you can grasp tool collect up-come p)
You can put the tools away [now].

The negator **bù** generally precedes the modal verb in a **bǎ** construction, though it may occasionally come after it if required by meaning:

Tā *bù kěn bǎ* cídiǎn jiè gěi tā.
(*lit.* s/he not willing grasp dictionary lend give her/him)
S/he was not willing to lend her/his dictionary to her/him.

Nǐ *néng bù bǎ* lājī dào zài zhèr ma?
(*lit.* you can not grasp litter dump at here p)
Can you not tip [your] litter here?

20.2 The **bèi** *construction* in Chinese is similar to the *passive voice* in English, though it is not as commonly used. The coverb **bèi** 'by' marks the agent and with it forms a coverbal phrase, which like other coverbal phrases comes after the subject and before the verb. The agent may be either definite or indefinite reference.

The **bèi** construction has features in common with the **bǎ** construction: the verb is usually one of 'manipulation', involving action, handling, changing, etc., and is normally complex, that is followed by some form of complement. Additionally, the **bèi** construction often conveys the sense that something has gone wrong:

Tā bèi jīnglǐ pīpíngle yī dùn.
(*lit.* s/he by manager criticise asp one mw)
He was criticised by the manager.

Tā bèi rén dǎle yī quán.
(*lit.* s/he by someone hit asp one fist)
S/he was struck by someone.

Tā bèi lǎobǎn jiěgù le.
(*lit.* s/he by boss dismiss p)
S/he was dismissed by [her/his] boss.

20.2.1 In colloquial speech, **ràng** or **jiào** may be used instead of **bèi**:

Xiāngjiāo *ràng* háizi chī diào le.
(*lit.* banana by child eat off p)
The banana was eaten by the child.

Wǒde yǔsǎn *jiào* rén jiè zǒu le.
(*lit.* my umbrella by someone borrow away p)
My umbrella was borrowed by someone.

In addition, **gěi** may be added before the verb:

Zúqiúmí *jiào* liúmáng *gěi* dǎ shāng le.
(*lit.* football-fan by hooligan by hit hurt p)
The football fan was beaten up by hooligans.

20.2.2 It is possible for the construction to be used without an agent. In these cases, **bèi** (or **gěi**), but not **ràng** or **jiào**, is placed before the verb:

Tāmen *bèi* guān zài wàitou le.
(*lit.* they by shut at outside p)
They were shut outside.

Tā *gěi* tīle yī jiǎo.
(*lit.* s/he by kick asp one mw)
S/he was kicked.

20.2.3 As with the **bǎ** structure, the negator and modal verbs precede **bèi**:

Tāmende zhǔzhāng *méi(yǒu)* **bèi jiēshòu.**
(*lit.* their proposal not-have by accept)
Their proposal was not accepted.

Bié ràng **tā** *gěi* **piàn le.**
(*lit.* don't by him/her by cheat p)
Don't be fooled by him/her.

Jìsuànjī *huì bèi* **rén tōu zǒu ma?**
(*lit.* computer likely by someone steal away p)
Is the computer likely to be stolen by someone?

Note: **bù** is not normally used in **bèi** sentences.

20.3 While the **bèi** construction, usually describing an event, parallels the passive voice, sentence forms of the topic-comment variety (see 18.3) may be defined as *notional passives*. In these sentences, the topic is often inanimate (or non-human), and therefore no ambiguity arises as to the relationship between the topic and the verb. For example, in the first sentence below, the *letter* cannot possibly be taken as initiating the action of *writing* itself.

Xìn *xiě* **wán le.**
(*lit.* letter write finish p)
The letter has been written.

Bēizi *dǎ* **pò le.**
(*lit.* cup/mug hit broken p)
The cup/mug was broken.

Chuānghu dōu *qī* **chéng lǜsè le.**
(*lit.* window all paint become green p)
All the windows have been painted green.

Chuángdān hé bèitào dōu *xǐ* **gānjìng,** *zhédié* **hǎo le.**
(*lit.* bedsheets and blanket-cover all wash clean, fold good p)
All the bedsheets and blanket covers have been washed [and] neatly folded up.

21 SERIAL CONSTRUCTIONS

21.1 Chinese, unlike English, does not have the grammatical means to construct participles or infinitives, nor sets of prepositions capable of diversified meanings. Instead, it makes use of sequences of verbal phrases in what we will call serial constructions.

A *serial construction* normally consists of two (or more) verbal predicates or comments which share the same subject or topic and follow one another without any conjunction(s). A serial construction may have adjectival as well as verbal predicates.

21.2   The semantic relations between serial predicates or comments may belong to any of the following categories:

(1) *Sequence*: The action of the first verb takes place before that of the second. The first verb often carries the aspect marker **le**:

Tā *xià le kè huí jiā qù* **le.**
(*lit.* s/he finish asp class return home go p)
S/he finished class and went home..

Tā *chī le yào qù shuìjiào* **le.**
(*lit.* s/he eat asp medicine go sleep p)
S/he took his/her medicine and went to bed.

Note: As discussed in 8.3.1, if an unqualified noun follows a verb carrying the aspect marker **le**, the sentence needs to be completed with another clause or verbal phrase.

(2) *Purpose*: The action described by the second verb is the purpose of the first verb (often **lái** 'to come' or **qù** 'to go'):

Tāmen *lái Lúndūn tànwàng wǒmen.*
(*lit.* they come London visit us)
They came to London to visit us.

Wǒ *qù shāngdiàn mǎi dōngxi.*
(*lit.* I go shop buy things)
I am going to the shops to do some shopping.

Zánmen *yuē (yī) gè shíjiān tán (yī) tán* **ba.**
(*lit.* we appoint (one) mw time talk (one) talk p)
Let's make an appointment to have a talk.

Wǒ *dàibiǎo dàjiā xiàng nín zhùhè.*
(*lit.* I represent everybody to polite:you congratulate)
On behalf of everybody I congratulate you.

Note: Coverbal phrases indicating 'service' may often be used after **lái** 'come' or **qù** 'go' in a purpose serial construction:

Tā lái tì wǒ yùn yīfu.
(*lit.* s/he come for me iron clothes)
S/he came to iron my clothes for me.

Wǒ qù gěi tā lǐfà.
(*lit.* I go for him/her arrange-hair)
I'll go and cut his/her hair.

Sometimes **lái** may lose its motion meaning and simply indicate an intention:

Wǒ *lái* tántán.
(*lit.* I come talk-talk)
I'll say a few words.

Wǒ *lái* gěi nǐmen jièshào yī xià.
(*lit.* I come for you introduce one time)
Let me introduce you.

To enhance the meaning of purpose (or lack of purpose), words such
as **yǐbiàn** 'so as to' and **yǐmiǎn** 'so as not to' are used before the
second verbal expression.

Tā xuéxí Zhōngwén, *yǐbiàn* dào Zhōngguó qù lǚyóu/lǚxíng.
(*lit.* s/he studies Chinese, so-that to China go travel)
S/he is studying Chinese so that s/he can go and travel in China.

Wǒ méi(yǒu) bǎ zhèi jiàn shì gàosu tā, *yǐmiǎn* shǐ tā nánguò.
(*lit.* I not grasp this mw matter tell him/her, so-as-not-to make him/her
  sad)
I did not tell him/her about this matter so as not to make him/her sad.

(3) In constructions we have met which are essentially serial constructions, for example:

    (a) Using coverbs ~~yòng, zuò,~~ etc.:

        Wǒmen *zuò diàntī* shàng sān lóu.
        (*lit.* we sit lift go-up three floor)
        We went up to the second floor by lift.

        Nǐ néng *yòng Zhōngwén* shuō ma?
        (*lit.* you can use Chinese say p)
        Can you say [it] in Chinese?

    (b) Using the aspect marker **zhe**:

        Tā *wòzhe wǒde shǒu* shuō: 'Xièxie nǐ'.
        (*lit.* s/he grasp asp my hand say: thank-thank you)
        Shaking my hand, s/he said: 'Thank you'.

    (c) **bǎ**, **bèi**, **bǐ** constructions (see Chapters 7 and 20).

(4) Where the main verbal phrase is followed by a second verbal phrase
which conveys no new information but reiterates the same idea from
a different perspective by means of a *negative, antonymous expression*:

Tā zhuā zhù wǒ *bù fàng*.
(*lit.* s/he catch hold me not let-go)
S/he held me firmly and didn't let me go.

Wǒ yǎole yī kǒu miànbāo *méi(yǒu) tūn xiàqù.*
(*lit.* I bite asp one mw bread not-have swallow down-go)
I took a bite from the bread but did not swallow it.

(5) Where the verb **yǒu**, indicating possession or existence, is followed
by its object and then by another verb (sometimes preceded by a
modal verb) expressing *intentional action* directed back to the object:

Wǒ *méiyǒu* **qián** *yòng.*
(*lit.* I not-have money use)
I haven't got any money to spend.

Wǒ *yǒu* **yī fēng xìn** *yào xiě.*
(*lit.* I have one mw letter want write)
I have got a letter to write.

Nǐ *yǒu* **shénme yīfu** *yào yùn* **ma?**
(*lit.* you have what clothes want ironing p)
What clothes have you got [for me] to iron?

Nǎr *yǒu* **(xiāng)yān** *mài?*
(*lit.* where there-are cigarette sell)
Where do they sell cigarettes?

If the object of **yǒu** is an abstract noun, the following verb phrase may
be of any length, expressing the need (or lack of need) for further action:

Wǒ *méiyǒu* **zérèn** *gàosu* **tā.**
(*lit.* I not-have responsibility tell him/her)
I don't have the responsibility of letting him/her know.

Nǐ *yǒu* **lǐyóu** *bù* **tóngyì.**
(*lit.* you have reason not agree)
You have reasons to disagree.

Nǐ *méiyǒu* **quánlì** *měi* **tiān dào zhèr lái húshuō bādào.**
(*lit.* you not-have right every day to here come talk-nonsense)
You don't have the right to come here and talk nonsense every day.

21.3 Adjectives or state verbs may be placed at any position in a serial
construction to introduce a descriptive element into the narrative:

Xiǎo māo tiào shàng tiào xià, *kě'ài jí* **le.**   (*adjective*)
(*lit.* little kitten jump up jump down, lovable to-the-extreme p)
The kitten was extremely lovable as it jumped up and down.

Dàjiā *jìng* **le xiàlái, zuòzhe bù dòng.**   (*state verb*)
(*lit.* everybody quieten asp down, sit asp not move)
Everybody quietened down and remained motionless in their seats.

21.4 *Dative* verbal expressions regularly feature in serial constructions. A verb taking a *direct object* is followed by the verb **gěi** with an *indirect object*:

Bàba mǎi le yī liàng qìchē *gěi* wǒ.
(*lit.* father buy asp one mw car give me)
Father bought a car for me.

Wǒ jì le yī zhāng míngxìnpiàn *gěi* tóngshì.
(*lit.* I post asp one mw postcard give colleague)
I sent a postcard to my colleague.

This extended dative construction with **gěi** generally does not apply in the case of verbs expressing speech activity:

Wǒ gàosu nǐ yī gè mìmì.
(*lit.* I tell you one mw secret)
I'll tell you a secret.

not ***Wǒ gàosu yī gè mìmì gěi nǐ.**
(*lit.* *I tell one mw secret give you)

Note: See 8.5 for a fuller discussion of direct and indirect objects.

21.5 A common form of serial is the *causative construction*, in which the object of the first verb becomes the subject of the second verb/adjective:

Wǒ *qǐng* tā *chī* fàn.	I invited him to dinner.
Wǒmen *xuǎn* tā *dāng* zhǔxí.	We elected him president.
Zhè *shǐ* wǒ hěn *gāoxìng*.	This made me very happy.
Tāmen *yào* wǒ *bié qù*.	They wanted me not to go.

Note 1: Verbs which produce a causative construction include those in the following semantic categories:

(i)   Request or command: **qǐng** ask, **jiào** make, **pài** send, **mìnglìng** order.

Tā *jiào* wǒ bǎ hùzhào *ná* chūlái.
S/he asked me to take out my passport.

(ii)   Wish: **yào** want.

Tā *yào* wǒ dào fēijīchǎng *qù* jiē tā.
S/he wanted me to go and meet him/her at the airport.

(iii) Persuasion or requirement: **quàn** persuade, urge, **cuī** press, **yāoqiú** require.

Wǒ *quàn* tā *xué* dǎ quán.
I urged him/her to learn shadow-boxing.

Lǎoshī *yāoqiú* xuésheng *zhùyì* ānquán.
The teacher required the students to pay attention to safety.

(iv) Permission: **ràng** let, **yǔnxǔ** allow, **zhǔn** permit.

Bàba *yǔnxǔ* **wǒ** *qù* **tiàowǔ.**
Father allowed me to go dancing.

(v) Coercion: **bī** force, **qiángpò** compel.

Qiángdào *bī* **wǒ bǎ qián ná chūlái gěi tā.**
The robber forced me to get out my money and hand it over to him.

(vi) Prevention: **jìnzhǐ** forbid, ban, **zǔzhǐ** prevent.

Zhèi tiáo lù *jìnzhǐ* **huòchē** *tōngguò*.
(*lit.* this mw road forbid lorry go through)
Lorries are not allowed to use this road.

(vii) Others: **děng** wait, **tīng** listen to.

Wǒ *děng* **nǐ** *lái*.
I'll wait till you come.

Tīng **wǒ** *shuō*.
Listen to me.

Note 2: Causative verbs do not take aspect markers:

*Wō *bīle* tā qù kàn yīshēng.
(*lit.* *I force asp him/her go see doctor)
*I forced him/her to go and see the doctor.

21.5.1 Polite requests are often a serial construction using the causative
verb **qǐng** 'to ask politely' (cf. 8.6.1).

(1) With an object:

Qǐng nǐ bǎ zhèngjiàn ná chūlái.
(*lit.* ask you grasp document take out-come)
Please take out your documents.

Qǐng *dàjiā* **ānjìng yī diǎnr.**
(*lit.* ask everybody quiet a little)
Please be quiet, everyone./Would everyone please be quiet.

(2) Without an object:

Qǐng zài shuō yī biàn.
(*lit.* ask again say one time)
Please say it again.

Qǐng shuō de màn yī diǎnr.
(*lit.* ask say p slow a little)
Please speak more slowly.

Qǐng bié yòng shǒu mō zhǎnpǐn.
(*lit.* ask don't use hand touch exhibits)
Please don't touch the exhibits with your hands.

21.5.2 In an extended causative construction, the second verb (i.e. next but one) after the causative verb may refer to either the object or the subject of the causative verb:

(1) Referring to the subject:
Wǒ yuē tā zài túshūguǎn děng wǒ, *yǒu* yī fēng xìn yào jiāo gěi tā.
(*lit.* I make-appointment him/her at library wait-for me, have one
  mw letter want hand-over give him/her)
I asked him/her to wait for me at the library, [as] I had a letter to
pass on to him/her.

(2) Referring to the object:

Wǒ qǐng tā bāngzhù wǒ, *jiāo* wǒ zěnme dú nà/nèi liǎng gè (hàn)zì.
(*lit.* I asked him/her help me, teach me how read those two mw
  Chinese-characters)
I asked him/her to help me and teach me how to read those two
Chinese characters.

21.6 All the predicate (or comment) types mentioned above may, of
course, combine in longer serial constructions:

**Wǒ xǐle zǎo, huànle yīfu, dàizhe dìdi kāi chē dào Xiǎo Lǐ jiā, qǐng tā
gēn wǒmen yīqǐ qù kàn diànyǐng.**
(*lit.* I wash asp bath, change asp clothes, bring asp younger-brother
drive car to Xiao Li home, ask him with us together go see film)
Having taken a bath and changed my clothes, I drove with my
younger brother to Xiao Li's place and asked him to go with us to
see a film.

22 EMPHASIS AND THE INTENSIFIER SHÌ

22.1 Emphasis in language can be conveyed in various ways. The most
common is to focus on a particular word or phrase through sentence stress,
word order or other intensifying devices. Sentence stress is the concern
of phonology, and we shall not dwell on it here. In our discussion of
subject-predicate and topic-comment constructions, we have seen how
change in word order can bring about different emphases. What concerns
us here is the use of the verb **shì** as an *intensifier* to highlight specific
elements in a sentence. We will distinguish between its use in sentences
referring to the past (i.e. with **de**) and in those referring to the continuous

present or future (i.e. generally without **de**). (In the literal translation of the examples in this chapter, **shì** appears as int[ensifier].)

22.2 Where an event or action took place in the past, **shì** may be used in conjunction with **de** to highlight the adverbials or modifying elements in a sentence, e.g. time expressions; coverbal phrases indicating location, method or instrument; adverbial phrases of manner; or 'purpose' constructions beginning with **lái** or **qù**. It is as if a statement with the **shì . . . de** *construction* represents an answer to a question about when, where, how, to what purpose, at the hands of whom, etc., an action took place. **Shì** is placed immediately before the adverbial expression or verb followed by purpose expression/complement, and **de** generally comes at the end of the sentence.

(1) Time expression:

> **Wǒ** *shì zuótiān* **lái** *de*.
> (*lit*. I int yesterday come p)
> I came *yesterday*./It was yesterday that I came.

> **Nǐ** *shì qùnián* **háishi** *jīnnián* **dào** *de*?
> (*lit*. you int last-year or this-year arrive p)
> Did you arrive here last year or this year?

(2) Coverbal phrases indicating location, method, instrument, etc.:

> **Tā** *shì zài Xīnjiāpō* **shēng/chūshì** *de*.
> (*lit*. s/he int at Singapore be-born p)
> S/he was born in *Singapore*.

> **Wǒmen** *shì cóng Cháoxiān* **lái** *de*.
> (*lit*. we int from Korea come p)
> We come from Korea.

> **Nǐ** *shì zuò chē* **háishi** *zǒulù* **lái** *de*?
> (*lit*. you int sit car or walk-road come p)
> Did you come by car or on foot?

> **Wǒ** *shì yòng máobǐ* **xiě** zhèi **fēng** xìn *de*.
> (*lit*. I int use pen-brush write this mw letter p)
> I wrote this letter with a writing brush.

(3) 'Purpose' constructions beginning with **lái** or **qù**:

> **Wǒ** *shì lái* **kàn** bìng *de*.
> (*lit*. I int come see illness p)
> I've come to see the doctor.

Tā *shì qù* zhǎo nǐ *de*.
(*lit.* s/he int go find you p)
S/he went to look for you.

(4) **Bèi** or similar phrase introducing an agent:

Xǐyījī *shì bèi tā* nòng huài *de*.
(*lit.* washing-machine int by him/her mess-with bad p)
The washing-machine was damaged by him/her.

Qìché *shì ràng sījī gěi* xiū hǎo *de*.
(*lit.* car int by driver by repair good p)
The car was repaired by the driver.

(5) Adverbial phrase of manner:

Tā *shì lǎolǎo shíshí de* gàosu wǒ *de*.
(*lit.* s/he int honest p tell me p)
S/he told me honestly.

Chuán *shì mànmàn de* chén dào hǎi dǐ qù *de*.
(*lit.* boat int slow p sink to the bottom go p)
The boat slowly sank to the bottom of the sea.

(6) Complement of manner:

Wǒmen *shì* tán *de* hěn tóujī *de*.
(*lit.* we int talk p very congenial p)
We had a very congenial conversation.

Tāmen *shì* wánr *de* fēicháng gāoxìng *de*.
(*lit.* they int play p extremely high-spirited p)
They had a happy time.

Note: In colloquial speech, **shì** may often be omitted from the **shì ... de** structure:

Tā zuótiān lái *de*.	S/he came *yesterday*.
Tāmen zuò fēijī qù *de* ma?	Did they go by plane?

22.2.1 The **shì ... de** construction may also be used to emphasise either the subject or the object of the verb.

(1) If the emphasis is on the subject, **shì** is placed directly before the subject:

Shì wǒ dǎ pò zhèi gè bēizi *de*.
(*lit.* int I hit break this mw cup/mug)
I was the one who broke this cup/mug.

Shì jǐngchá zhuā zhù xiǎotōu *de*.
(*lit.* int policeman/woman catch hold thief p)
It was the policeman/woman who caught the thief.

Zhèi běn xiǎoshuō *shì shéi/shuí* xiě *de?*
(*lit.* this mw novel int who write p)
Who wrote this novel?/Who was this novel written by?

Nèi bēi kāfēi *shì wǒ* dào gěi nǐ *de.*
(*lit.* that mw coffee int I pour give you p)
(It was) I (who) poured that cup of coffee for you.

Note: The last two sentences above are *topic | subject-predicate* constructions (see 18.4). The subject embedded in this structure can be emphasised, but the topic is emphatic by definition and cannot be intensified by a **shì ... de** construction. Therefore, the sequence 'shì topic | subject-predicate de' is impossible:

*****Shì xìn wǒ jì de.**
(*lit.* int letter I post p)

(2) If the emphasis is on the object of a verb, **shì** is placed before the verb, while **de** comes before the object instead of at the end of the sentence:

Wǒ *shì* **mǎi** *de* **féizào.**
(*lit.* I int buy p soap)
I bought some *soap*.

Tā *shì* **hē** *de* **júzishuǐ.**
(*lit.* s/he int drink p orange-juice)
S/he drank *orange juice*.

22.2.2 The **shì ... de** construction, though it refers to past events, may only be negated by **bù** (not by **méiyǒu**). **Bù** comes before **shì**:

Wǒ *bù shì* **lái jiè qián** *de.*
(*lit.* I not int come borrow money p)
I've not come to borrow money.

Bù shì **wǒ gàosu tā zhèi jiàn shì** *de.*
(*lit.* not int I tell him/her this mw matter p)
I wasn't the one who told him/her about this.

Wǒmen nèi tiān *bù shì* **chī de** *yú.*
(*lit.* we that day not int eat p fish)
We didn't eat *fish* that day.

22.3 When **shì** is used for emphasis in relation to present continuous or projected events or actions, it generally occurs alone without **de**.

22.3.1 **Shì** can be employed in the contexts listed under 22.2 (1), (2) and (3) for the **shì ... de** structure (i.e. with time expressions, coverbal phrases and 'purpose' constructions), and to emphasise either subject or object:

Wǒ *shì míngtiān* **lái.**
(*lit.* I int tomorrow come)
I'll be coming *tomorrow*.

Tāmen *shì dào hǎibiān* **qù dùjià.**
(*lit.* they int go seaside spend-holiday)
They are going to the *seaside* for [their] holidays.

Wǒmen *bù shì zuò diànchē* **qù.**
(*lit.* we not int travel-by tram go)
We won't be going by tram.

If the emphasis is on the subject, **shì** is placed immediately before the subject:

Shì nǐ **qù ma?**
(*lit.* int you go p)
Will *you* be going?

Shì tā **yīnggāi xiàng dàjiā dàoqiàn.**
(*lit.* int s/he must towards everybody say-sorry)
S/he's the one who should apologise to everybody.

If the emphasis is on the object, **shì** is placed immediately before the predicate verb, but the object will naturally be stressed in speech:

Wǒ *shì* **qù kàn** *tā.*
(*lit.* I int go see him/her)
I am going to see *him/her*.

Tāmen *shì* **xiǎng chī** *bīngjilíng/bīngqílín.*
(*lit.* they int want eat ice-cream)
It is ice-cream that they want to eat.

22.3.2 **Shì** is also used alone to emphasise a comparison construction. It is placed immediately before **bǐ** in affirmative and **méi(yǒu)** in negative comparisons:

Nǐde fángzi *shì* **bǐ wǒde dà.**
(*lit.* your house int compare mine big)
Your house *is* bigger than mine.

Wǒ shuō Zhōngwén *shì* **méi(yǒu) nǐ shuō de hǎo.**
(*lit.* I speak Chinese int not-have you speak p good)
I *don't* speak Chinese as well as you do.

22.3.3 The negative of **shì** sentences, like that of **shì ... de** sentences, is formed by placing **bù** before **shì**:

Wǒmen *bù shì* **zuò diànchē qù.**　　**Wǒ** *bù shì* **qù chǎojià.**
(*lit.* we not int travel-by tram go)　　(*lit.* I not int go quarrel)
We are not going by tram.　　　　　　I am not going (in order) to have a
　　　　　　　　　　　　　　　　　　row.

22.4 The above discussion has focused on **shì** as an intensifier of elements in the predicate that modify the verb (adverbials, 'purpose' constructions, etc.) or subjects/objects of the verb. In addition, **shì** as an intensifier may occur alone in topic-comment sentences with gradable adjectives or state verbs.

(1) Gradable adjectives:

Tā *shì* **hěn ǎi.**　　　　　**Tāmen** *shì* **bù gāoxìng.**
(*lit.* s/he int very short)　　(*lit.* they int not happy)
S/he *is* short.　　　　　　　　They *are* unhappy.

(2) State verbs:

Wǒ *shì* **bìng le.**　　　　　**Wǒmen** *shì* **cuò le.**
(*lit.* I ill p)　　　　　　　　　(*lit.* we int wrong p)
I *am* ill.　　　　　　　　　　　We *are* wrong./It's *our* fault.

It can also be introduced in a subject-predicate sentence where the emphasis is on the whole predicate. Its presence in effect makes the sentence topic-comment:

Wǒmen *shì* **qùle sān cì.**　　**Wǒ** *shì* **chīguo wōniú.**
(*lit.* we int go asp three-times)　(*lit.* I int eat snail)
We (really) *did* go three times.　I *have* eaten snails.

Tāmen *shì* **bù zhīdao.**　　　**Zhèi gè wèntí** *shì* **kěyǐ tí chūlái.**
(*lit.* they int not know)　　　　(*lit.* this mw question int can raise
　　　　　　　　　　　　　　　　out-come)
They *really* don't know.　　　　This question *can* be raised.

22.4.1 The sentences in 22.4, in fact, all have an undertone of reservation or contradiction. It is often the case that the implicit reservation in such sentences is immediately made explicit by a contradictory statement:

Tā *shì* **cōngmíng,** *bùguò* **tài jiāo'ào le.**
(*lit.* s/he int clever, but too proud p)
S/he *is* clever, *but* s/he's too conceited.

Zhèi gè gōngzuò wǒ *shì* **xǐhuan,** *kěshì* **xīnshui tài shǎo.**
(*lit.* this mw job I int like, but salary too little)
I *do* like this job, *but* the salary is too little.

22.4.2 The pattern of this last structure (in 22.4.1) in colloquial speech can take the form of 'verb-**shì**-verb' or 'adjective-**shì**-adjective':

Zhèi gè gōngzuò wǒ *xǐhuan shì xǐhuan*, dànshì ...
(*lit.* this mw job/work I like int like, but ...)
I *do* like this job, but ...

Nèi běn shū *hǎo shì hǎo*, bùguò tài guì le.
(*lit.* that mw book good int good, nevertheless too expensive p)
(It is true) that book *is* good, but it is too expensive.

22.5 Apart from the use of the intensifier **shì**, emphasis in Chinese may also be expressed through repetition. This occurs particularly when agreement, disagreement, thanks or welcome are expressed:

A: **Zhèi yàng xíng ma?**   B: **Xíng, xíng, xíng.**
    (*lit.* this type OK p)   (*lit.* OK, OK, OK)
    Will this do?   It is perfectly all right.

A: **Wǒ lái bāng nǐ máng.**   B: **Bù, bù, bù. Wǒ zìjǐ lái.**
    (*lit.* I come help you busy)   (*lit.* no, no, no. I self come)
    I'll come and help you.   No, no, no. I'll manage myself.

A: **Nǐ Yīngwén shuō de zhēn hǎo.** B: **Bù, bù, bù.**
    (*lit.* you English speak p really   (*lit.* no, no, no)
        good)
    You speak really good English.   Not at all. (Being modest)

Note: When praised, an English speaker is likely to say 'thank you', while a Chinese person will probably make a modest denial such as **bù, bù, bù**.

Huānyíng, huānyíng.   Welcome.
Qǐng jìn, qǐng jìn.   Please come in.
Nǎli, nǎli.   It was nothing. (polite response to thanks)

23 ABBREVIATION AND OMISSION

23.1 Like most languages, Chinese has a considerable number of *conventional* phrases or constructions which habitual usage has made acceptable despite apparent grammatical incompleteness. Similarly, Chinese makes use of abbreviated expressions when allowed or demanded by the *context* (i.e. the actual situation in which the utterance takes place). There is also a tendency, already observed, for Chinese to omit words from a sentence that are not strictly necessary for the meaning. This is possible because the sentence is formulated within a *cotext* (i.e. the spoken or written text that precedes and/or follows). For example, the subject and/or object may be omitted in response to a question (see Chapter 17.2). There is, of course, likely to be some overlap between context and cotext.

23.2 *Conventional abbreviations* normally take the form of *subjectless sentences* and occur in the following types of expression:

(1) Thanks, good wishes, apologies, etc.:

Xièxie, or **Xièxie nǐ.**
(*lit.* thank-thank, or thank-thank you)
Thanks, or Thank you.

Bù xiè, or **Bù kèqi.**
(*lit.* not thank, or not polite)
You're welcome. (in response to **xièxie**)

Bié kèqi, or **Bù yào kèqi.**
(*lit.* don't polite)
Don't stand on ceremony, *or* Make yourself at home.

Duìbuqǐ.
(*lit.* face not rise)
Sorry.

Hěn/zhēn bàoqiàn.
(*lit.* very/really be-apologetic)
[I] must apologise.

Gōngxǐ, gōngxǐ.
(*lit.* respectfully-[wish]-happy, respectfully-[wish]-happy)
Congratulations!

Others include **màn zǒu** take care (*lit.* slow walk) (said when seeing off a guest), **xīnkǔ le** you must be tired (after such a long journey)/sorry to have put you to so much trouble (*lit.* tiring p), **yī lù píng'ān** have a safe/pleasant journey (*lit.* all way peace-safe), **zhù nǐ shēntǐ jiànkāng** wish you good health (*lit.* wish you body healthy), **jìng nǐ yī bēi** your health! (*lit.* respectfully-[offer] you one cup/glass), **zàijiàn** good-bye (*lit.* again-see), **gān bēi** bottoms up; cheers (*lit.* dry glass).

(2) Approval, commendation, etc.:

Duì!
(*lit.* correct)
(You're) right!

Hǎo.
(*lit.* good)
That's good/All right.

Bù yàojǐn.
(*lit.* not important)
It doesn't matter.

Others include: **méi guānxì** never mind/it doesn't matter (*lit.* no concern), **méi wèntí** no problem, **zhēn qiǎo a** what a coincidence (*lit.* really coincidental p), **hǎo xiāng a** how sweet (of smell)/how tasty (*lit.* very fragrant/savoury p).

(3) Requests, warnings, etc:

Qǐngbiàn.
(*lit.* please convenient)
Please yourself, *or* Do as you please.

Qǐng zhǐzhèng.
(*lit.* please point-correct)
Please make comments/corrections.

(usually when presenting a piece of writing, etc. and politely seeking opinion).

Xiǎoxīn.
(*lit.* small concern)
Be careful, *or* Take care.

Jìde guān mén.
(*lit.* remember close door)
Remember to close the door.

Others include: **kàn hǎo** look out/watch out (*lit.* look well), **kāihuì le** let's start (the meeting) (*lit.* start/hold meeting p), **jiùmìng a** help! (*lit.* save life p).

(4) Standard prohibitions, often found as public notices:

Qǐng wù xīyān!
(*lit.* please no inhale-smoke)
No smoking!

Qǐng wù suídì diū lājī!
(*lit.* please no over-all-floor throw rubbish)
No litter!

Bù zhǔn tíng chē.
(*lit.* not allow stop car)
No parking (on these premises).

Jìnzhǐ rù nèi.
(*lit.* forbid enter inside)
No entry.

(5) Proverbial sayings:

Huó dào lǎo, xué dào lǎo.
(*lit.* live till old, learn till old)
It's never too old to learn.

Jǐ suǒ bù yù, wù shī yú rén.
(*lit.* self that-which not want, do-not impose on people)
Do unto others as you would be done by.

(6) Sentence starters, characteristic of oral or written narrative:

Xiǎngbùdào **huì zài zhèr jiàn dào nǐ.**
(*lit.* think-not-reach can at here bump into you)
[I] never thought/expected [I] would see you here.

Bù zhīdao **tā míngtiān lái bù lái.**
(*lit.* not know s/he tomorrow come not come)
[I] don't know whether s/he is coming tomorrow or not.

Kǒngpà **wǒ gǎnmào le.**
(*lit.* afraid I catch-cold p)
[I] am afraid I have caught a cold.

Others include **jìde** ... [I] remember ... (*lit.* remember), **bù liào** ... unexpectedly ... (*lit.* not expect), **tīng shuō** ... [I] have heard that ... (*lit.* hear say).

(7) Statements about the weather (often including a change in the weather, or a realisation about the state of the weather on the part of the speaker – see discussion on sentence **le** in Chapter 16):

Xià **yǔ le.**   下雨了
(*lit.* fall rain p)
It's raining.

Chū **tàiyáng le.**   出太阳了
(*lit.* out sun p)
The sun is out.

Others include **guā fēng le** it's windy, **qǐ wù le** it's getting foggy, **dǎ shuāng le** it's frosty/there's a frost, **dǎ léi le** it's thundering, **shǎn diàn le** it's lightning.

23.3 *Contextual abbreviation* usually takes the form of a one-word (or two-word) expression.

(1) Calling out to somebody:

Wèi!   Hello! Hey! (or on the telephone Hello).
Lǎo Lǐ!   Old Li!
Fúwùyuán!   Waiter!

(2) Calling attention to something:

Huǒ!	Fire!
Xìn.	A letter (for you).
Piào.	Tickets. (said perhaps by a bus conductor)

(3) Enquiring about the 'whereabouts' of something or the 'condition' of somebody:

Xié ne?	Where are the shoes?
Qián ne?	Where is the money?
Nǐ ne?	How about you?
Tāmen ne?	How about them?

(4) Written instructions:

nán(cè)	gentlemen	(*lit.* man-lavatory)
nǚ(cè)	ladies	(*lit.* female-lavatory)
wú rén	vacant (of lavatory)	(*lit.* no people)
yǒu rén	engaged (of lavatory)	(*lit.* have people)
tuī	push	
lā	pull	

23.4 *Cotextual omissions* take a number of forms. As observed earlier, numbers/demonstratives with measures and attributives with **de** do not need to be followed by a noun once that noun has been identified:

zhèi gè	this one
dì sān gé	the third one
wǒde	mine
Wáng xiānsheng de	Mr Wang's
huáng sè de	yellow one(s)
zuótiān mǎi de	the one(s) bought yesterday

23.4.1 Where a noun is made up of a defining element and a headword, once the noun is identified, subsequent reference may be to the headword alone. Thus when it is already clear that references are to respectively **gōngòng qìchē** 'bus', **zhíshēng fēijī** 'helicopter', and **jīngshénbìng yuàn** 'mental hospital', the following sentences can occur:

Wǒmen zài nǎr děng *chē*?	Where do we wait for the bus?
Wǒmen jǐdiǎn (zhōng) dēng *jī*?	When do we board the helicopter?
Tā yǐjing rù *yuàn* le.	S/he is already been admitted to the mental hospital.

23.4.2   As seen in 17.2, positive or negative answers to a question are regularly expressed by repeating the verb in the question. With cotextual abbreviations, usually the verb is retained as the core element, and repetition of other parts of the sentence, especially pronouns, becomes unnecesary:

Q: **Nǐ xǐhuan zhèi jiàn máoyī ma?**   A: **Xǐhuan.**   (*lit.* like)
  (*lit.* you like this mw sweater p)   Yes.
  Do you like this sweater?

                                            Bù xǐhuan.(*lit.* not like)
                                            No.

Q: **Nǐ rènshi tā ma?**   A: **Rènshi.**   (*lit.* know)
  (*lit.* you know him/her p)   Yes.
  Do you know him/her?

                                            Bù rènshi. (*lit.* not know)
                                            No.

23.4.1   In written or spoken passages, omissions of previous references are similarly possible, because the reader or listener is able to make sense of the material on the basis of contextual/cotextual evidence:

Wǒ yòng Zhōngwén xiěle yī piān wénzhāng gěi wǒ laǒshī kàn, shuō kàn hòu, qǐng zhǐzhèng, jīnhòu kěyǐ chóngxiě.
(*lit.* I use Chinese write asp one mw essay give my teacher look, say look after, please correct, afterwards can re-write)
I wrote an essay in Chinese and gave [it] to my teacher to look at, saying that after [s/he] had seen [it] could [s/he] please correct [it], (so that) afterwards [I] could re-write [it].

The seven bracketed pronouns in the translation are not present in the Chinese original. Such omissions are possible because the speaker/writer is confident that the passage is intelligible on the basis of contextual/ cotextual evidence.

24 COMPOSITE SENTENCES: CONJUNCTIONS AND CONJUNCTIVES

24.1   In Chapter 21, we looked at serial constructions, in which a subject (or topic) is followed by more than one verb (or adjective) without any linking device(s). Here we deal with *composite sentences*. We use this term to describe sentences which have either (1) more than one clause in a coordinated or subordinated relationship, or (2) more than one predicate or comment pertaining to the same subject or topic. The common feature of these two types of composite sentence is that their parts are usually linked by *conjunctions* and/or *conjunctives*.

It is possible, however, for the first type of construction to have no conjunctions or conjunctives; the clauses are then bound together in rhythmic or lexical balance or contrast (see 24.3 below). When the second type of construction has no conjunctions or conjunctives, it becomes a serial construction. We deal here first with sentences marked by conjunctions or conjunctives.

Note: We have discussed conjunctions that link words and expressions e.g. **hé**, **gēn**, etc. (see Chapter 1), but not those that link clauses.

24.2 *Conjunctions* in Chinese occur independently (e.g. **dànshì**, **kěshì**, **bùguò** 'but'; **fǒuzé/bùrán** 'otherwise'; **suǒyǐ/yīncǐ** 'therefore', etc.) or in related pairs (e.g. **suīrán** ..., **dànshì** ... 'although ..., (however) ...'; **yīnwèi** ..., **suǒyǐ** ... 'because ..., (therefore) ..., etc.):

Wǒmen tuìrànglè, *kěshì* **tāmen hái bù tóngyì.**
(*lit.* we give-way asp, but they still not agree)
We gave way *but* they still would not agree.

Yīnwèi **māma bìng le,** *suǒyǐ* **wǒ dāi zài jiā lǐ kānhù tā.**
(*lit.* because mother ill asp, therefore I stay at home in nurse her)
Because Mother was ill, (*therefore*) I stayed at home to nurse her.

Suīrán **nèi gè háizi hěn cōngmíng,** *dànshì* **xuéxí bù gòu nǔlì.**
(*lit.* though that mw child very intelligent, but study not sufficient hard)
Though that child is very clever, (*however*) s/he does not study hard
   enough.

From the second and third examples above, it can be seen that pairs of related conjunctions (e.g. **yīnwèi** and **suǒyǐ**, **suīrán** and **dànshì**) are split such that one is placed at the beginning of the first clause and the other at the beginning of the second. The conjunction in the first clause may alternatively come after the subject, generally when the two clauses share the same subject:

Nèi gè háizi *suīrán* **hěn cōngmíng,** *dànshì* **xuéxì bù gòu nǔlì.**
(*lit.* that mw child though very intelligent, but study not sufficient hard)
Though that child is very clever, (*however*) s/he does not study hard
   enough.

Conjunctives, on the other hand, are adverbs such as **jiù** 'then', **cái** 'only then', etc., which function as *referential adverbs* in simple sentences (see 14.3), but in compound sentences occur at the beginning of the second (main) clause after the subject to link that clause to the previous (subordinate) clause. The previous clause may include a conjunction such as **rúguǒ, yàoshì, jiǎrú** 'if', **chúfēi** 'unless', etc.). Conjunctives also occur as related pairs (e.g. **yī** ... **jiù** ... 'as soon as ...,, ...', **yòu** ... **yòu** ... 'both ... and ...', etc.).

> **Nǐ *rúguǒ* méi kòng, wǒmen *jiù* gǎitiān tán ba.**
> (*lit.* you if not free, we then change-day talk p)
> *If* you are busy, we'll talk [about it] another day.

Sometimes a second conjunction may be included with the conjunctive in the second clause:

> **Nǐ *rúguǒ* méi kòng, *nàme* wǒmen *jiù* gǎitiān tán ba.**
> (*lit.* you if not free, in-that-case we then change-day talk p)
> *If* you are busy, we'll talk [about it] another day.

24.2.1 Composite sentences have a wide range of meanings and functions. We will give examples in the following categories: contrast, choice, addition, cause and effect, inference, condition, 'non-condition', supposition, concession, preference, and time relations:

(1) *Contrast*:

> **Tā xiǎng shuì yī huìr, *kěshì* shuì bù zháo.**
> (*lit.* s/he want sleep one while, but sleep not attain)
> S/he wanted to have a sleep *but* could not go to sleep.
> (*conjunction*: **kěshì** 'but')

> **Kuài zǒu ba, *fǒuzé* nǐ huì chídào de.**
> (*lit.* quick go p, otherwise you probably late-arrive p)
> Be quick, *or* you'll be late.
> (*conjunction*: **fǒuzé** 'otherwise')

> **Wǒ méi yǒu qián, *bùrán* wǒ *jiù* mǎi wēibōlú le.**
> (*lit.* I not-have money, otherwise I then buy microwave-stove p)
> I don't have any money, *otherwise* I would have bought a microwave.
> (*conjunction*: **bùrán** 'otherwise', reinforced by *conjunctive*: **jiù** 'then')

> **Wǒmen de fángzi hěn xiǎo, *bùguò* yǒu (yī) gè hěn piàoliàng de huāyuán.**
> (*lit.* our house very small, but have (one) mw very beautiful garden)
> Our house is small, *but* we have a beautiful garden.
> (*conjunction*: **bùguò** 'however')

> **Tā *suīrán* hěn è, *dànshì* bù xiǎng chī fàn.**
> (*lit.* s/he though very hungry, but not want eat rice)
> *Though* s/he was very hungry, (*however*) s/he did not want to touch any food.
> (*paired conjunctions*: **suīrán** 'though' and **dànshì** 'but')

Tā *bùdàn* bù zébèi zìjǐ, *fǎn'ér* zéguài biérén.
(*lit.* s/he not-only not blame oneself, on-the-contrary blame others)
Not only did s/he not blame her/himself *but* s/he laid blame on others.
(*paired conjunctions*: **bùdàn** 'not only' and **fán'ér** 'on the contrary')

(2) *Choice*:

Nǐ kěyǐ fù xiànjīn *huòzhě* kāi zhīpiào.
(*lit.* you may pay cash or write cheque)
You may pay cash *or* by cheque.
(*conjunction*: **huòzhě** 'or')

Tā *bùshì* chōuyān *jiùshì* hējiǔ.
(*lit.* s/he not-be inhale-cigarette then-be drink-wine)
If s/he is not drinking, (*then*) s/he is smoking.
(*paired conjunctions*: **bùshì** 'if not' and **jiùshì** 'then')

Bùshì tāmen lái, *jiùshì* wǒmen qù.
(*lit.* not-be they come, then-be we go)
If they didn't come, (*then*) we would go.

(3) *Addition*:

Tā hěn cōngmíng, *érqiě* hěn yònggōng.
(*lit.* s/he very intelligent, moreover very hardworking)
S/he is very intelligent, *and also* extremely diligent.
(*conjunction*: **érqiě** 'moreover')

Tā *bùjǐn/bùdàn* mà rén *érqiě* dǎ rén.
(*lit.* s/he not-only scold people but-also hit people)
S/he *not only* used abusive language *but also* resorted to blows.
(*paired conjunctions:* **bùjǐn/bùdàn** 'not only' and **érqiě** 'but also')

(4) *Cause and effect*:

Tā bìng le, *yīncǐ* méi lái cānjiā yànhuì.
(*lit.* s/he ill p, therefore not come attend banquet)
S/he was ill *and so* did not come to the banquet.
(*conjunction*: **yīncǐ** 'therefore')

Yīnwèi tāmen méi dài dìtú, *suǒyǐ* mílù le.
(*lit.* because they not bring map, therefore lose-way p)
Because they did not have a map with them, they lost their way.
(*paired conjunctions*: **yīnwèi** 'because' and **suǒyǐ** 'therefore')

Yóuyú tiānqì bù hǎo, bǐsài zàntíng.
(*lit.* owing-to weather not good, contest suspend)
Owing to bad weather, the contest was postponed.
(*conjunction*: **yóuyú** 'owing to')

Note: **Yóuyú** may often be used in the first clause without any conjunction or conjunctive in the second clause.

In cause and effect sentences, the 'effect' may be expressed before the 'cause'. The first (main) clause is then unmarked, and the second (subordinate) clause begins with **yīnwèi** 'because'. Sometimes **yīnwèi** is preceded by **shì** 'to be':

Wǒ méi(yǒu) qù jiàn tāmen (shì) *yīnwèi* wǒ yǒu lìngwài yī gè yuēhuì.
(*lit.* I not go see them (be) because I have another one mw
   appointment)
I didn't go and see them *because* I had another appointment.

Tā tūrán yūndǎo le *yīnwèi* tā hē le tài duō de jiǔ.
(*lit.* s/he suddenly faint-fall p because s/he drink asp too much p
   wine/spirit)
S/he suddenly passed out, *because* s/he had had too much to drink.

(5) *Inference*:

Jìrán nǐ bù shūfu, *jiù* bié lái le.
(*lit.* since you not comfortable, then don't come p)
Since you aren't well, don't come (*then*).
(*conjunction*: **jìrán** 'since', linked with *conjunctive*: **jiù** 'then')

Jìrán tāmen shuō bù lái, wǒmen *jiù* bié děng tāmen le.
(*lit.* since they say not come, we then don't wait-for them p)
Since they said that they would not come, we had better not wait
   for them (*then*).

(6) *Condition*:

Zhǐyào nǐ xiǎoxīn, *jiù* bù huì chū shénme wèntí.
(*lit.* provided you small-concern, then not likely emerge any problem)
Provided you are careful, there won't be any problem.
(*conjunction*: **zhǐyào** 'provided', linked with *conjunctive*: **jiù** 'then')

Zhǐyǒu nǐ xué hǎo Zhōngwén, nǐ *cái* néng qù Zhōngguó gōngzuò.
(*lit.* only-if you study well Chinese, you only-then can go China work)
Only if you do well in your study of Chinese will you (*then*) be
   able to go and work in China.
(*conjunction*: **zhǐyǒu** 'only if', linked with *conjunctive*: **cái** 'only then')

Chúfēi nǐ qù shuōfú tāmen, tāmen *cái* huì tóngyì hézuò.
(*lit.* unless you go convince them, they only-then likely agree
   cooperate)

Only if you go and convince them will they (*then*) agree to cooperate.
(*conjunction*: **chúfēi** 'unless', linked with *conjunctive*: **cái** 'only then')

Note: **chúfēi** is also regularly paired with **fǒuzé/bùrán** 'otherwise':

Chúfēi nǐ qù shuōfú tāmen, *fǒuzé/bùrán* tāmen bù huì tóngyì hézuò.
(*lit.* unless you go convince them, otherwise they not likely agree cooperate)
You must go and convince them, *otherwise* they won't agree to cooperate.

(7) '*Non-condition*':

Bùguǎn tā lái bù lái, wǒmen yě ànzhào jìhuà chūfā.
(*lit.* no-matter s/he come not come, we also according-to plan set-out)
No matter whether s/he turns up or not, we'll *still* set out according
   to plan.
(*conjunction*: **bùguǎn** 'no matter', linked with *conjunctive*: **yě** 'also')

Wúlùn tiān qíng háishi xià yǔ, wǒ *dōu* zǒulù qù.
(*lit.* regardless sky fine or fall rain, I all walk-road go)
Whether it's fine or raining, I'm going on foot.
(*conjunction*: **wúlùn** 'regardless', linked with *conjunctive*: **dōu** 'all')

(8) *Supposition*:

Nǐ rúguǒ yuànyì, wǒ *jiù* tì nǐ xiě huíxìn.
(*lit.* you if willing, I then for you write reply-letter)
I'll reply to the letter for you *if* you want.
(*conjunction*: **rúguǒ** 'if', linked with *conjunctive*: **jiù** 'then')

Yàoshi tāmen jiā méi yǒu diànhuà, wǒ *jiù* qù diànhuàtíng dǎ.
(*lit.* if their home not-have telephone, I then go telephone-booth
   make-a-call)
I'll go and use the public telephone *if* there isn't one at their
   place.
(*conjunction*: **yàoshi** 'if', linked with *conjunctive*: **jiù** 'then')

Jiǎrú dōngtiān méi yǒu nuǎnqì, nǐ zěnme bàn?
(*lit.* suppose winter there-isn't heating, you how manage)
How do you manage *if* there isn't any heating in winter?
(*conjunction*: **jiǎrú** 'if'; since the second clause is a question, no
   linking conjunction or conjunctive is necessary)

Note: The phrase **... de huà** 'if' may be used at the end of the first clause, either alone
or with one of the conjunctions **rúguǒ, jiǎrú, yàoshi** earlier in the clause.

Míngtiān (*rúguǒ***) xià xuě *de huà*, wǒmen jiù qù huáxuě.**
(*lit.* tomorrow (if) fall snow that-is-the-case, we then go ski)
We'll go skiing *if* it snows tomorrow.

(9) *Concession*:

(a) referring to the past:

Jǐnguǎn tiānqì bù hǎo, bǐsài *háishi* zhàocháng jìnxíng.
(*lit.* though weather not good, contest still as-usual go-on)
Though the weather was not good, the match was held as planned.
(*conjunction*: **jǐnguǎn** 'although', linked with *conjunctive*: **háishi** 'still')

(b) referring to the future:

Jíshǐ/jiùsuàn hěn wēixiǎn, wǒ *yě* bù pà.
(*lit.* even-if very dangerous, I also not afraid)
Even if it is dangerous, I'm (*still*) not afraid.
(*conjunction*: **jíshǐ/jiùsuàn** 'even if/though', linked with *conjunctive*:
   yě 'also')

Nǎpà shìqíng zài duō, wǒ *yě* yào chōu shíjiān xué Zhōngwén.
(*lit.* even-though affairs more much, I also want find time study
   Chinese)
Even if things get even busier, I will *still* find time to study
   Chinese.
(*conjunction*: **nǎpà** 'even if/though', linked with *conjunctive*: **yě**
   'also')

(10) *Preference*:

Yǔqí zài jiā lǐ dāizhe, *bùrú* chū qù zǒuzǒu.
(*lit.* rather-than at home-in stay asp, better-to go-out walk-walk)
(I) would *rather* go out for a walk *than* stay at home.
(*paired conjunctions*: **yǔqí** 'rather than' and **bùrú** 'better to')

Wǒ *nìngké* è sǐ, *yě bù* chī gǒuròu.
(*lit.* I would-rather hungry die, also never eat dog-meat)
I would *rather* starve to death *than* eat dog-meat.
(*conjunction*: **nìngkě** 'would rather', linked with *conjunctive*: **yě bù**
   'and definitely not')

(11) *Time relations*:

(a) as soon as

Wǒ *yī* xǐ wán zǎo *jiù* shàng chuáng shuìjiào le.
(*lit.* I as-soon-as wash finish bath then up bed sleep p)
As soon as I had finished my bath, I (*then*) went to bed.
(*paired conjunctives*: **yī** 'once' and **jiù** 'then')

(b) not yet

Wǒ děng dào xiàwǔ liǎng diǎn (zhōng), tā *hái* méi(yǒu) lái.
(*lit.* I wait till afternoon two o'clock, s/he still not come)
I waited till two o'clock in the afternoon [but] s/he *still* had
  not turned up.
(*conjunctive*: **hái** 'still')

(c) only then

Wǒ zuò wán gōngkè *cái* xià lóu qù kàn diànshì.
(*lit.* I do finish coursework only-then down stairs go watch
  television)
I did *not* go downstairs to watch television *until* I finished my
  coursework.
(*conjunctive*: **cái** 'only then')

(d) then

Tā kū qǐlái, *yúshì* wǒ *jiù* zǒu guòqù.
(*lit.* s/he cry/weep start, so I then go across)
S/he started weeping, *so* (then) I went over (to her/him).
(*conjunction*: **yúshì** 'thereupon', reinforced by *conjunctive*: **jiù**
  'then')

Wǒmen hǎohāo de shuì le yī jiào, *ránhòu jiù* qù yóuyǒng.
(*lit.* we well-well p sleep asp one sleep, after-that then go swim)
We had a good sleep, and then we went swimming.
(*conjunction*: **ránhòu** 'after that', reinforced by *conjunctive*: **jiù**
  'then')

Note 1: **Yúshì** and **ránhòu** are often accompanied by the conjunctive **jiù**.

Note 2: The expressions **... de shíhou** 'when ...', **... yǐhòu** 'after ...' and **... yǐqián**
'before ...', (see 10.3) are also regularly linked with **jiù** 'then' in the main clause:

Xì yǎn wán *yǐqián* guānzhòng *jiù* hē dàocǎi le.
Before the performance (of the play) had ended, the audience booed.

Fǎguān jìn lái *de shíhou*, dàjiā *jiù* zhàn qǐlái le.
When the judge entered, everyone (*then*) stood up.

Nǐ dào le *yǐhòu* jiù gěi wǒ dǎ diànhuà.
After you've arrived, telephone me.

24.2.2   There are a few *conjunctives* which repeat to form related pairs.
In a sentence, these are placed immediately before two verbal predicates/
comments sharing the same subject/topic:

Tāmen *yībiān/yīmiàn* hē jiǔ *yībiān/yīmiàn* tán tiān.
(*lit.* they one-side drink wine one-side chat)
They drank as they chatted.

Note: Other commonly used conjunctives of this type are:

yòu … yòu …	**Wǒ yòu è yòu kě.**	I was *both* hungry *and* thirsty.
yuè … yuè …	**Tā yuè pǎo yuè kuài.**	S/he ran fas*ter* and fas*ter*.

Some conjunctions are used in a similar way:

Zánmen huòzhě qù huáxuě huòzhě qù yóuyǒng.
(*lit.* inclusive: we or go ski or go swim)
We either go skiing or go swimming.

24.3   Composite sentences can also be formed without using conjunctions or conjunctives, by placing clauses in parallel with each other. This is done in a number of ways:

(1) By repeating the same interrogative adverb or pronoun in the second clause:

Shéi shū, shéi qǐngkè.
(*lit.* who lose, who invite-guest)
Whoever loses will pay for the meal.

Nǎr piányi dào nǎr qù mǎi.
(*lit.* where cheap to where go buy)
We'll go and buy wherever is cheaper.

Zěnme hǎo zěnme zuò.
(*lit* how good how do)
We'll do it whichever way seems best.

(2) By posing a condition in the first clause and then answering or countering it in the second:

Dōngxi tài guì, wǒ bù mǎi.
(*lit.* thing too expensive, I not buy)
If things are too expensive, I won't buy (anything).

Tiānqì bù hǎo, wǒmen bù lái le.
(*lit.* weather not good, we not come p)
If the weather isn't good, we won't come.

Tāmen qù, wǒ bù qù.
(*lit.* they go, I not go)
If they are going, I won't go.

Bù bǎ wénzhāng xiě wán, wǒ bù shuìjiào.
(*lit.* not grasp essay/article write finish, I not sleep)
I won't go to bed before I finish the essay/article.

It would, of course, be acceptable to use one of the conditional conjunctions **rúguǒ**, **jiǎrú**, **yàoshi** (or … **de huà**) or the conjunctive **jiù**, or both a conjunction and the conjunctive in these sentences:

Rúguǒ dōngxi tài guì (*de huà*), wǒ *jiù* bù mǎi le.
If things are too expensive, I won't buy (anything).

(3) By binding the two clauses in a rhythmic and semantic balance:

Chī zhōngcān yòng kuàizi, chī xīcān yòng dāochā.
(*lit.* eat Chinese food use chopsticks, eat Western food use knife and fork)
(You) eat Chinese food with chopsticks (and) Western-style food with knives and forks.

Tā kànkàn wǒ, wǒ kànkàn tā.
(*lit.* s/he look-look me, I look-look him/her)
S/he looked at me (and) I looked at him/her.

24.4 Finally, there are a few verbs which take *object clauses* and form sentences that may be regarded as composite. We list some of these verbs in categories of meaning:

(1) Estimation, thought:

Wǒ *rènwéi* nǐ shì duì de.
(*lit.* I think you be right p)
I think you are right.

Wǒ *juéde* shíjiān bù zǎo le.
(*lit.* I feel time not early p)
I feel it's getting late.

In these examples, **nǐ shì duì de** and **shíjiān bù zǎo le** are the object clauses.

(2) Suggestion and promise:

Wǒ *shuō* nǐ yīnggāi zuò huǒchē qù.
(*lit.* I say you should travel-by train go)
I say (that) you should go by train.

Wǒ *jiànyì* dàjiā yīqǐ gàn.
(*lit.* I suggest everyone together work)
I suggest we should do it together.

Wǒ *dāying* míngtiān qù kàn tā.
(*lit.* I promise tomorrow go see him/her)
I promised to go and see him/her tomorrow.

Note: From this last example, it can be seen that if the object clause has the same subject as the main clause, the subject need not be repeated.

(3) Belief:

Wǒ *xiāngxìn* dìqiú shì yuán de.
(*lit.* I believe earth be round p)
I believe that the earth is round.

(4) Wish:

Wǒ *xīwàng* nǐ néng lái cānjiā wǒmen de wǎnhuì.
(*lit.* I hope you can come attend our evening-gathering)
I hope you will be able to come to our party.

(5) Worry:

Wǒ *dānxīn* míngtiān huì xià yǔ.
(*lit.* I worry tomorrow possible fall rain)
I am worried that it might rain tomorrow.

Object clauses also naturally take the form of direct speech:

Tā *shuō*: 'Bù yàojǐn!'
(*lit.* s/he say: not important)
S/he said: 'It doesn't matter'.

Háizi *wèn* bàba: 'Nǐ néng mǎi yī zhī wánjùxióng gěi wǒ ma?'
(*lit.* child ask father: you can buy one mw toy-bear give me p)
The child asked his father: 'Can you buy a teddy bear for me?'

25   EXCLAMATIONS AND INTERJECTIONS; APPOSITIONS; AND APOSTROPHES

25.1 *Exclamations* in Chinese, as in most languages, can be partial or full statements. Vehemence or emphasis is normally expressed by adding the particle **a** to the end of the exclamation. Degree adverbs such as **duō(me)** 'how'/'what' or **zhēn** 'really' regularly occur before adjectives to intensify emotions.

(1) Partial statements (i.e. only the comment is present):

Duō(me) měilì de jǐngsè a!	*Zhēn* bàng a!
(*lit.* how beautiful p scenery p)	(*lit.* really great p)
What a beautiful view!	Really great!

(2) Full statements:

Zhèi gè xiāngzi *zhēn* zhòng a!	Zhèr de kōngqì *duōme* xīnxiān a!
(*lit.* this mw box really heavy p)	(*lit.* here p air how fresh p)
This case is really heavy!	How fresh the air is here.

Note: The pronunciation of the particle **a** may be influenced by the vowel or consonant that precedes it:

(1) **a > wa** following **ao**, etc.

Duō hǎo *wa*!
(*lit.* how good p)
How good it is!

(2) **a > ya** after **i**, **ai**, etc.

Zhēn qíguài *ya*!
(*lit.* really strange p)
How strange!

(3) **a > na** after words ending
with **n**, etc.

Tiān *na*!
(*lit.* heaven p)
Good heavens!

(4) **le + a > la**:

Wán *la*! (originally: **wán le a!**)
(*lit.* finish p)
All over!

25.1.1 In another regular formulation, the adverb **tài** 'too' is placed
before an adjectival or verbal predicate followed by **le**:

Tài **hǎo** *le*!
(*lit.* too good p)
Terrific!

Tài **měi** *le*!
(*lit.* too beautiful p)
How beautiful!

Tài gǎnxiè nǐ le.
(*lit.* too thank you p)
I'm truly grateful!

25.1.2 Exclamations may also be shaped as question-word questions,
generally ending with **a**, **ya**, etc.

Nǐ zuótiān *wèi shénme* bù lái *ya*?
(*lit.* you yesterday for-what not come p)
Why didn't you come yesterday?!

Note: **Bù** is used here instead of **méi** because, although the action is in the past, the speaker
wants to emphasise not the *fact* but the *intention* of the listener, who didn't turn up the day
before.

Nǐ zěnme méi bāngmáng a?
(*lit.* you how not help p)
How come you didn't help?

Wǒ zěnme bàn na?
(*lit.* I how deal p)
What am I to do?

Nǐ zěnme shuō zhèyàng de huà *ya*?
(*lit.* you how say like-this p words p)
How could you say such a thing?!

25.2 Chinese has a wide range of *interjections* used at the beginning of
sentences to express various kinds of emotion or attitude:

Ā, yǔ tíng le.
(*lit.* oh, rain stop p)
Hey! It's stopped raining.

Pèi, zhēn bēibǐ!
(*lit.* bah really base)
Gosh! How mean!

Wèi, nǐ qù nǎr?
(*lit.* hello, you go where)
Hello there! Where are you going?

Hèi, xià xuě le.
(*lit.* hey, fall snow p)
Why, it's snowing.

Note: Other commonly used interjections include:

Āiyā	for impatience	**Āiyā! Bié fán wǒ!** Dammit! Don't bother me. (see 25.2.1 below)
Āi	for remorse or regret	**Āi, yòu nòng cuò le.** Oh dear, I've got it wrong again.
Hng	for dissatisfaction	**Hng, tā xiǎng piàn wǒ.** Huh, s/he wants to fool me.
Ǹg	for agreement	**Ng, xíng.** Mm. O.K.
Āiyō	for pain	**Āiyō! Huángfēng zhēle wǒ le.** Ouch, I've been stung by a wasp.

25.2.1 Tones are important for interjections in Chinese, and the same interjection with different tones can convey different feelings:

A 1st tone (pleasant surprise):

Ā, chū tàiyáng la!
(*lit.* interj come-out sun p)
Hey! The sun has come out.

A 2nd tone (pressing a point):

Á, nǐ dàodǐ qù bù qù?
(*lit.* interj you after-all go not go)
Well, are you going or not?

A 3rd tone (doubt or suspicion):

Ǎ, zhè shì zěnme (yī) huí shì a?
(*lit.* interj this be how (one) mw matter p)
What? What is this all about?

A 4th tone (sudden enlightenment):

À, wǒ míngbai le.
(*lit.* interj I understand p)
Oh, I think I understand it now.

An interjection may also, in different contexts, convey different feelings with no change of tone:

Āiyā, zhèi gè háizi zhǎng de zhème gāo la!
(*lit.* interj this mw child grow p so tall p)
Goodness, this child has grown so tall.

Āiyā, nǐ zěnme bǎ wǒ de yīfu nòng zāng le.
(*lit.* interj you how p grasp my clothes handle dirty p)
Oh dear, how could you have dirtied my clothes.

25.3 *Appositions* are another form of independent element in Chinese sentences. They function in a way similar to appositions in English, being placed immediately after the word or words they refer to:

Dàjiā dōu pèifú Xiǎo Lǐ, *yī gè chūsè de gōngchéngshī*.
(*lit.* everybody all admire little Li, one mw outstanding p engineer)
Everybody admires Xiao Li, *an outstanding engineer*.

Tā shì dúshēngnǚ, *tā māma de zhǎngshàng míngzhū*.
(*lit.* she be only-daughter, her mother's palm-on bright-pearl)
She is an only daughter, *the apple of her mother's eye*.

Pronouns or pronominal expressions such as **zìjǐ** 'self', **yī gè rén** (*lit.* one mw person 'alone'/'by myself'), **liǎ** 'both'/'the two', etc., are commonly used appositions:

Wǒ *zìjǐ* lái.
(*lit.* I self come)
I'll help myself. (i.e. to food, etc)

Tā *yī gè rén* zǒu le.
(*lit.* s/he one mw person go p)
S/he left by him/herself.

Tāmen *liǎ* chǎo qǐlái le.
(*lit.* they two quarrel start p)
The two of them started to quarrel.

25.4 *Apostrophe* is another independent element, which in Chinese normally comes at the beginning of a sentence rather than at the end:

Lǐ *xiānsheng*, nǐ zǎo!
(*lit.* Li Mr, you early)
Good morning, Mr Li!

Zhāng jiàoshòu, qǐng nín jiǎng huà.
(*lit.* Zhang professor, please polite:you say words)
Professor Zhang, please say a few words.

Xiǎo Chén, nǐ shàng nǎr qù?
(*lit.* little Chen, you to where go)
Little Chen, where are you going to?

Lǎo Wáng, jìnlái zěnyàng?
(*lit.* old Wang, recently what-like)
How are things with you lately, *Old Wang*?

GLOSSARY OF GRAMMATICAL TERMS

adjectives	Words used to describe, define or evaluate qualities or characteristics associated with nouns, such as 'big, green, good'. Gradable adjectives are adjectives that generally can be modified by a degree adverb. That is, they can be graded to varying degrees using a range of adverbs such as 'very, extremely', etc. Non-gradable adjectives are usually not modifiable by degree adverbs as they have more absolute meanings (e.g. 'male, female, square, black') and define rather than describe.
adverbial	In Chinese, a word or phrase placed directly before a verb to modify it, usually providing background information such as time, location, means, method, manner, etc. (e.g. 'yesterday, in London, by train, with chopsticks, slowly', etc.).
aspect markers	The functional words **le**, **guo**, **zhe** and **zài** which are closely associated with verbs. **Le**, **guo** and **zhe** are suffixed to the verb, and **zài** immediately precedes it; they indicate the aspectual notions of completion, immediate or past experience, simultaneousness, persistence, and continuation. Chinese aspect markers are NOT indicators of tense. Tense is specified by time expressions placed before the verb or at the beginning of the sentence.
attitudinal verb	In Chinese, a verb which reflects the speaker's attitude. It may be followed by verbal as well as nominal objects (e.g. 'I *like* tea, I *like* to drink tea).
attributive	In Chinese, a word, phrase or clause placed before a noun to qualify or identify it (e.g. '*nice* weather, a *very useful* book', or – a clause – 'a *nobody-will-ever-forget* experience').
causative verb	A verb which causes its object to produce an action or to change state (e.g. '*ask* him to come, *make* him happy', etc.).
clause	A term employed to describe a subject-predicate or topic-comment construction which relates to other

	similar constructions, with or without conjunctional devices, to constitute a *sentence* in Chinese.
comment	The part of a sentence in a topic-comment sentence which follows the *topic*. The topic establishes the theme or focus of interest in the sentence, while the comment describes, defines, explains or contends, etc. In contrast with a subject-predicate sentence which narrates an incident (e.g. somebody did something), a *topic-comment* sentence makes observations, provides descriptions, offers explanations, etc. The verb **shì** 'to be', adjectives, modal verbs and the particle **le** are all regular elements in a comment.
complement	A word, phrase or clause which comes directly after either a verb (i.e. a *verbal complement*) to indicate the duration, frequency, terminal location or destination, result, manner or consequential state of the action expressed by the verb, or after an adjective (i.e. an *adjectival complement*) to indicate its degree or extent.
composite sentence	A general term referring to a sentence which consists of more than one clause or predicate linked together by (a) conjunction(s) or conjunctive(s). A composite sentence may therefore be of a compound or complex nature, using coordinate or subordinate conjunctions.
conjunctions	Words used to join two words, phrases or clauses (e.g. 'and, otherwise, because', etc.). Conjunctions in Chinese often form related pairs (e.g. 'because ... therefore, though ... however', etc.).
conjunctives	*Referential adverbs* used to link two clauses or predicates/comments.
context	The extralinguistic situation or environment in which a verbal event takes place.
cotext	The verbal text (in speech or in writing) that goes before or after the verbal event under consideration.
coverb	In Chinese, a preposition-like verb which is not normally used on its own but is followed by another verb (or other verbs). A coverb with its object forms a *coverbal phrase*, which indicates location, method, instrument, reference, etc.
dative verb	A verb which requires two objects: a direct object and an indirect object (e.g. give him a present, in which 'him' is the indirect object and a 'present' is the direct object).

definite reference and indefinite reference	Terms used in connection with nominal or pronominal items. The difference between definite and indefinite reference may be illustrated by the use of the definite article 'the' and the indefinite article 'a(n)' in English.
degree adverb	See *adjective*
direction indicators	A set of *motion verbs* which follow other verbs as direction complements to indicate the spatial direction or, sometimes, the temporal orientation (i.e. beginning, continuing or ending) of the actions expressed by those verbs.
indefinite reference	See *definite reference*
intensifier	A word used to emphasise or highlight elements in a sentence.
intentional verb	A verb which expresses the speaker's intentions. It is generally followed by another verb indicating the action which the speaker intends to take (e.g. 'I plan to study Chinese').
location phrase	A location word or postpositional phrase preceded by the *coverb* **zài** '(be) in, at' .
measure words	Also known as *classifiers*, these are words which must be used between a numeral or demonstrative and the noun it qualifies. English equivalents are 'a *piece* of cake, a *glass* of beer', but in Chinese measure words are used with all nouns.
modal verbs	A set of verbs which are used directly before other verbs to indicate possibility, probability, necessity, obligation, permission, willingness, daring, etc. (e.g. 'can, must, should, may, dare', etc.).
notional passive	A term used to refer to a construction in which the object of the verb is brought forward to a subject position before the verb, while the verb is still encoded in its active form. Hence the passive voice is not realised in its actual form but can only be notional.
onomatopoeia	A word which is used to approximate to a natural sound in real life. There are a considerable number of conventionalised onomatopoeic words in Chinese, but they are also regularly created spontaneously.
particle	In Chinese, a monosyllabic item which has no independent meaning of its own but serves to deliver a structural or functional grammatical message. The sentence particle **ma**, for example, has no independent semantic significance, but its presence has the

	function of changing a statement into a general question.
phonaesthemes	Two-syllabled items which are suffixed to an adjective to add to its descriptive power by introducing some kind of sound connotation.
postposition	A word placed after a noun to indicate a part of the noun or a spatial/temporal relationship to the noun (e.g. 'on, in, outside, above', etc.), A noun followed by a postposition is called a *postpostional phrase*, which usually indicates location or time, and resembles a *prepositional phrase* in English (e.g. the prepositional phrase 'on the table' in English is rendered in the word order 'the table on' in Chinese).
predicate	The part of a sentence that follows the *subject*. The subject is usually the initiator or recipient of the action expressed by the verb or verb phrase in the predicate. In a Chinese *subject-predicate* sentence, the subject is generally of *definite reference*.
referential adverbs	A set of monosyllabic adverbs such as **jiù**, **cái**, **dōu**, **yě**, **yòu**, **zài**, **hái**, **dào**, **què**, etc., which in a sentence refer either backwards to elements before them or forwards to elements after them, echoing or reinforcing the meaning of those elements.
serial construction	A type of Chinese sentence in which more than one verb occurs in succession without any conjunctional devices.
state verb	In Chinese, a verb which is formed by placing the particle **le** after an adjective. A state verb indicates a state of affairs rather than an action or an event.
subject	See *predicate*
tense	See *aspect markers*
topic	See *comment*

GLOSSARY OF CHINESE CHARACTERS

Items are listed alphabetically according to syllable. Where a character is the first element in one or more compound words, the words are listed alphabetically under that character. Chapter numbers in bold indicate chapters in which items are discussed as grammatical forms.

Pinyin	Character	English/explanation	Chapter(s)
A			
ā	啊	exclamatory particle	**25**
āi	哎	interjection	25
āiyā	哎呀	interjection: oh dear, etc.	25
āiyō	哎哟	interjection: ouch	25
ǎi	矮	short (of stature), low	16, 22
ānjìng	安静	quiet	7, 17, 19, 21
ānpái	安排	to arrange	18
ānquán	安全	safe, secure	21
ànzhào	按照	according to	19, 24
àngsī	盎司	ounce	3
Àodàlìyà	澳大利亚	Australia	10
B			
bā	八	eight	2, 7, 10, 12, 16, 17
bǎ	把	(a) mw for knife, chair, etc. (b) coverb in **bǎ**-construction	**3**, 6, 16, 18 **20**, 21, 22, 23, 25
ba	吧	particle for imperatives, etc.	4, **8**, 14, **17**, 21, 24

Pinyin	Character	English/explanation	Chapter(s)
bàba	爸爸	father	4, 5, 7, 16, 19, 21, 24
bái	白	white	5, 6, 8, 18
báicài	白菜	cabbage	1
bǎi	百	hundred	2, 7, 15
bǎifēn zhī ...	百分之...	... per cent	2
bǎihuò shāngdiàn	百货商店	department store	5
bān	班	class; work-shift	12
bān	搬	to take away, move (house)	13
bàn	半	half	2, 10, 12
bàn	办	to deal with	19, 25
bànfǎ	办法	method	9
bàngōngshì	办公室	office	8, 19
bāng	帮	to help	22
bāngmáng	帮忙	to help	25
bāngzhù	帮助	to assist; assistance	4, 8, 10, 15, 21
bàng	镑	pound sterling	2, 3, 5, 8, 17
bāo	包	to wrap up	3, 9
bāoguǒ	包裹	parcel	5, 18
bǎozhòng	保重	to take care	14
bǎo	饱	full (after a meal)	13
bào	报	newspaper	11
bàoshuì	报税	to declare (at customs)	15
bàozhǐ	报纸	newspaper	5
bào	抱	to hug	16
bàoqiàn	抱歉	to feel apologetic	23

Pinyin	Character	English/explanation	Chapter(s)
bēi	杯	mw meaning cup, glass, mug	2, 3, 8, 11, 16, 17, 18, 22
bēizi	杯子	cup, glass, mug	17, 20, 22
běi	北	north	19
běibian/ běimian	北边	to the north (of)	11
Běijīng	北京	Beijing	1, 8, 9, 10, 11, 12, 14
bèi	被	coverb introducing agent in a passive; in words for quilt	18, **20**, 22
bèitào	被套	quilt	20
bèizi	被子	quilt	20
bēibǐ	卑鄙	contemptible	25
Bèiduōfēn	贝多芬	Beethoven	8
běn	本	mw for books, etc.	3, 6, 7, 17, 20, 22
bèn	笨	foolish, stupid	16
bī	逼	to force, compel	21
bǐ	笔	pen	1, 3
bǐjìběn	笔记本	notebook	1
bǐmíng	笔名	pseudonym, pen-name	1
bǐshì	笔试	written examination	1
bǐ	比	to compare; coverb 'compared with', in comparison expressions	**7**, 13, 15, 19, 22
bǐjiào	比较	comparatively, relatively	7, 13
bǐsài	比赛	contest, competition	11, 24
bì	闭	to close, shut	9
bìxū	必须	must	**15**
bìyè	毕业	to graduate	10

Pinyin	Character	English/explanation	Chapter(s)
biān	边	side	11, 18
biǎn	扁	flat	6
biàn	变	to change	16
biànhuà	变化	change	7
biàn	遍	number of times (from beginning to end)	20, 21
biǎo	表	wrist watch; list, table; in words for cousins	5
biǎodì	表弟	younger cousin (on mother's side)	12
biǎogē	表哥	older cousin (on mother's side)	15
biāoyǔ	标语	slogan	5
bié	别	don't; in words for other	15, 20, 21, 23, 24, 25
biéren	别人	other people	18, 24
bīng	兵	soldier	17
bìng	病	ill, sick; illness	10, 16, 17, 22, 24
bìngrén	病人	patient, invalid	8, 18
bīngqílín/ bīngjilíng	冰淇淋/冰激凌	ice-cream	22
bīngxiāng	冰箱	refrigerator	11
bówùguǎn	博物馆	museum	14, 18
bù	布	cloth	3, 6
bù	不	no, not	4, 5, 6, 7, 8, 9, 11, 13, 15, 16, 17, 18, 19, 20, 21, 22, 23, 24, 25
bùbì	不必	no need, unnecessary	**15**
bùdàn	不但	not only	24

Pinyin	Character	English/explanation	Chapter(s)
bùguǎn	不管	in spite of, despite	24
bùguò	不过	however	22, 24
bùjǐn	不仅	not only	24
bùrán	不然	otherwise	24
bùrú	不如	it would be better to	24
bùshì ... jiùshì ...	不是... 就是...	if not ..., then ...	17, 22, 24
bù tíng de	不停地	non-stop	14
bùxìng	不幸	unfortunately	14, 25
bùyòng	不用	not necessary, no need	**15**
bùzhī bùjué	不知不觉	without realising it	14

C

cāi	猜	to guess	13
cái	才	only then	**14**, 16, 24
cài	菜	food (to go with rice)	3, 6, 11, 16, 20
cǎisè	彩色	multi-coloured	5
cānguān	参观	to visit, go round (a place)	15
cānjiā	参加	to take part in	18, 24
cāngying	苍蝇	fly	3
cǎo	草	grass	3, 8, 11
cǎodì	草地	lawn	11
cèsuǒ	厕所	toilet	11
chā	插	to insert	16
chā	叉	fork	1, 21
chá	茶	tea	3, 11, 15, 17, 20
chà	差	to ... (in hours of the day); to lack	10

Pinyin	Character	English/explanation	Chapter(s)
chǎnpǐn	产品	product	21
cháng	长	long	4, 7
Chángchéng	长城	The Great Wall	1
chángfāngxíng	长方形	rectangle	6
chángtú qìchē	长途汽车	(long distance) coach	1
chǎng	场	mw for games, films, etc.	3, 16
chàng	唱	to sing	9, 12, 13
chànggē	唱歌	to sing (songs)	13, 24
chángcháng	常常	often	10, 16, 19
cháo	朝	towards	19
chǎo	吵	to quarrel	25
chǎojià	吵架	to quarrel	8
chē	车	car	2, 5, 15, 18, 22, 23
chēfáng	车房	garage	13
chēliàng	车辆	cars, vehicles	1
chēpiào	车票	ticket (for bus, coach, train, etc.)	4
chēzhàn	车站	(train) station, bus-stop	17
chén	沉	to sink	22
chènshān	衬衫	shirt	3, 6, 9
chéngjī	成绩	achievement	3
chéng	城	town, city	9, 10, 11, 20
chéngshì	城市	town, city	6
chéng	乘	to travel by	19
chī	吃	to eat	3, 4, 8, 10, 14, 15, 16, 17, 18, 19, 20, 21, 22, 24

Pinyin	Character	English/explanation	Chapter(s)
chídào	迟到	to be late for (class, work, etc.)	24
chóngxiě	重写	to re-write	23
chōu	抽	to pull	17, 24
chōuti	抽屉	drawer	7
chōuyān	抽烟	to smoke	8, 10, 16, 17, 19, 22, 24
chū	出	(a) mw word for plays, films, etc.	3
		(b) to exit; out (direction indicator)	**9**, 16, 23, 24, 25
chūfā	出发	to set out	10, 19, 24
chūlái	出来	to come out	9, 20, 21, 22, 23
chūqù	出去	to go out	9, 16, 25
chūshén de	出神地	absent-mindedly	14
chūshì	出世	to be born	8, 22
chūzū qìchē	出租汽车	taxi	19
chúfáng	厨房	kitchen	19
chúfēi	除非	unless	24
chuān	穿	to wear	8, 9
chuán	船	boat, ship	3, 19, 22
chuǎn	喘	to pant	16
chuǎnqì	喘气	to pant	13
chuāng	窗	window	11
chuānghu		window	9, 11, 17
chuáng	床	bed	5, 10, 24
chuángdān	床单	(bed)sheet	20
chuī	吹	to blow	14, 19
chūntiān	春天	spring	9, 10

Pinyin	*Character*	*English/explanation*	*Chapter(s)*
cí	瓷	porcelain	6
cì	次	number of times	10, **12**, 16, 20
cídiǎn	词典	dictionary	1, 3
cóng	从	from (coverb)	19
cóng(lái) bù	从(来)不	never	10
cōngming	聪明	clever, intelligent	6, 18, 22, 24
cùn	寸	inch	3
cuò	错	wrong, incorrect	22, 23, 25
cuòwù	错误	error, mistake	5, 6

D

dǎ	打	to hit, beat	3, 8, 12, 13, 15, 16, 19, 20, 21, 22, 23, 24
dǎban	打扮	to dress up	13
dǎ diànhuà	打电话	make a telephone call	24
dǎduàn	打断	to interrupt	13
dǎjià	打架	to fight	13
dǎ pò	打破	to break	13
dǎsǎo	打扫	to sweep	20
dǎsuàn	打算	to plan (to do something)	15
dǎzhēn	打针	to have an injection	15
dǎzì	打字	to type, typewrite	13
dāying	答应	to promise	24
dà	大	big	5, 6, 7, 10, 11, 15, 16, 19, 22
dàjiā	大家	everybody	4, 9, 12, 13, 14, 18, 21, 22, 24, 25
dàrén	大人	adult	2, 5

Pinyin	Character	English/explanation	Chapter(s)
dàshǐ	大使	ambassador	9
dàshǐguǎn	大使馆	embassy	19
dàtīng	大厅	hall	11
dàxué	大学	university	1, 8, 9, 11, 14, 19
dà xuě	大雪	heavy snow	19
dàyī	大衣	overcoat	3, 5, 8, 20
dàyuē	大约	approximately	2
dāi	待/呆	to stay	12, 15, 24
dài	戴	to wear (on the head or hands)	5
dàizhe	戴着	wearing (on the head or hands)	18
dài	带	to carry; take, bring	8, 15, 18, 21, 24
dàibiǎo	代表	delegate, representative; to represent	21
dàibiǎotuán	代表团	delegation	18
dàifu	大夫	medical doctor	6
dānchéng	单程	single (journey)	7
dàngāo	蛋糕	cake	3
dànshì	但是	but	22, 24
dānxīn	担心	to worry about	24
dāng	当	when; to act as, be	**10**, 19, 20, 21
dāngrán	当然	of course	14
dāo	刀	knife	1, 3, 21
dāochā	刀叉	knives and forks	24
dào	到	to arrive; to (coverb)	8, 10, 13, 14, 15, 16, 17, 19, 20, 21, 22, 23, 24

Pinyin	Character	English/explanation	Chapter(s)
dàodǐ	到底	after all, in the end	17, 25
dào	倒	on the other hand, on the contrary, however	13, 14, 20, 22
dàocǎi	倒彩	catcalls	24
dàoqiàn	道歉	to apologise	22
dǎoshī	导师	tutor, supervisor	14
dǎoyóu	导游	tourist guide	15
de	得	particle, to introduce a complement; in words for attain, achieve, etc.	7, **13**, 14, 16, 17, 20, 21, 22, 23, 25
dédào	得到	to get, obtain	8
de	的	particle, to mark an attributive	4, **5**, 6, 7, 8, 10, 11, 12, 13, 14, 15, 16, 17, 20, 22, 23, 24, 25
de huà	的话	if	20, **24**
de shíhou	的时候	when	**10**, 14, 17, 18, 24
de	地	particle, to indicate an adverbial	**22**
děi	得	must	14, **15**
dēng	灯	lamp, light	20
děng	等	to wait (for)	8, 12, 17, 21, 24
dī	滴	a drop (of water, blood, etc.)	3
dǐ	底	bottom	2
dì	递	to pass, hand over	8
dì	地	ground	3, 11, 12
dìfang	地方	place	5
dìqiú	地球	globe	24

Pinyin	Character	English/explanation	Chapter(s)
dìtǎn	地毯	carpet	5, 16
dìtiě	地铁	the underground, subway	19
dìtú	地图	map	4, 24
dìdi	弟弟	younger brother	7, 9, 17, 18, 20
díshì	的士	taxi	19
diǎn	点	hour, point; a little; to nod	2, 10, 16, 19
diǎnr	点儿	a little, a bit	3, 7, 14, 17, 21
diǎntóu	点头	to nod	14
diǎn(zhōng)	点(钟)	o'clock	10, 13, 17, 24
diàn	电	electricity, power	23
diànchē	电车	tram, trolley-bus	22
diànhuà	电话	telephone	5, 24
diànhuàtíng	电话亭	telephone box	24
diànnǎo	电脑	computer	13
diànshì	电视	television	5, 14, 24
diànshìjī	电视机	television set	3, 7, 14
diàntī	电梯	lift, elevator	21
diànyǐng	电影	film	3, 8, 12, 14, 17, 18, 20
diànyǐngyuàn	电影院	cinema	5
diào	掉	to drop	13, 18, 20
diàoyú	钓鱼	to go angling, fishing	14, 16
dié	叠	to fold	20
dǐng	顶	top, peak	3, 18
diū	丢	to lose	11, 18, 23
dǒng	懂	to understand	13, 17

Pinyin	*Character*	*English/explanation*	*Chapter(s)*
dòng	动	to move	13, 14, 15, 21
dòngrén	动人	moving, touching	17
dòngwùyuán	动物园	zoo	11
dōng	东	east	
dōngbian/ dōngmian	东边/东面	(to the) east (of)	11
Dōngjīng	东京	Tokyo	10
dōngxi	东西	thing	10, 15, 16, 18, 21, 24
dǒngshìzhǎng	董事长	director (of a board)	18
dōngtiān	冬天	winter	10, 14, 16, 24
dōu	都	all, both	10, 11, 12, 13, **14**, 15, 16, 18, 19, 20, 24, 25
dòuliú	逗留	to stay	10
dú	读	to read	21
dǔ	堵	mw for walls	5
dùjià	度假	to go on holiday	15, 19, 22
dúshēngnǚ	独生女	only daughter	25
duànliàn	锻练	to train, take physical exercise	10
duī	堆	heap, pile	11
duì	队	queue, line	11
duì	对	(a) yes, right, correct (b) to (coverb)	13 / 3, 13, 14, 19, 23, 24, 25
duì . . . láishuō	对... 来说	as far as . . . is concerned	14
duìbuqǐ	对不起	sorry	23
duìlián	对联	couplet	8
duìmiàn	对面	opposite	11

Pinyin	Character	English/explanation	Chapter(s)
dùn	顿	mw for meals	10, 20
duō	多	many; how	1, 2, 5, 7, 11, 12, 13, 14, 24, 25
dūo dà	多大	how big, large	17
duō gāo	多高	how tall, how high	17
duō jiǔ	多久	how long (in time)	17
duōme	多么	how (with adjective, e.g. how beautiful, how cold, etc.)	25
duōshao	多少	how many/much	17
duōxiè	多谢	many thanks	14
duō yuǎn	多远	how far	17
duǒ	朵	mw for flowers, etc.	3, 9
E
Éguó	俄国	Russia	19
ér	而	but	5
èr	二	two	2, 7, 10, 11
èryuè	二月	February	10
ěrhuán	耳环	earring	3, 4
F
fādǒu	发抖	to shiver, tremble	13
fǎguān	法官	judge (in a court)	24
fákuǎn	罚款	to pay a fine, be fined	5
fāshāo	发烧	to have a fever	14
Fǎwén	法文	French (language)	20
fāyán	发言	to speak, make a speech	13
fāzhǎn	发展	to develop	7, 18
fán	烦	to trouble	25

Pinyin	Character	English/explanation	Chapter(s)
fàn	饭	meal (of rice)	3, 8, 10, 18, 19, 21, 24
fànguǎn	法官	restaurant	19
fǎnduì	反对	to oppose, object to	15
fǎn'ér	反而	on the contrary	24
fánmáng	繁忙	busy (street, etc.)	6
fānyì	翻译	to translate, interpret	19, 20
fāng	方	square	6
fāngfǎ	方法	method	3
fáng	房	room	11
fángjiān	房间	room	5, 20
fángzi	房子	house	3, 5, 6, 8, 22, 24
fàng	放	to let go, release, put	8, 11, 18, 20, 21
fàngjià	放假	to have a vacation or holiday	14
fǎngwèn	访问	to visit (a person)	10, 15, 18
fēi	飞	fly	9, 14
fēijī	飞机	plane, aircraft	3, 12, 19, 22
(fēi)jīchǎng	(飞)机场	airport, airfield	19, 21
fēicháng	非常	extremely	6, 7, 15, 18
féizào	肥皂	soap	1, 3, 22
fēizhèngshì	非正式	informal	6
Fēizhōu	非洲	Africa	8
fēn	分	minute (of an hour), cent	2, 3, 15
fèn	份	portion	10, 15
fēng	封	mw for letters	3, 4, 8, 21, 22, 23

Pinyin	Character	English/explanation	Chapter(s)
fēng	风	wind	14, 15, 19, 23
Fójiào	佛教	Buddhism	8
fǒuzé	否则	or, otherwise, if not	24
fú	幅	mw for paintings	11
fù	副	mw for spectacles	3, 4, 8
fù	付	to pay	5, 24
fùjìn	附近	nearby, in the neighbourhood	11
fùmǔ	父母	parents	10, 19
fùqīn	父亲	father	6
fúwùyuán	服务员	service worker, waiter, etc.	17, 23
fùxí	复习	to revise	20
fúzhuāng	服装	articles of clothing	6
G			
gāi	该	must	**15**
gǎitiān	改天	some other time, another day	24
gǎizhèng	改正	to correct, rectify	23
gǎn	敢	dare	**15**
gānjìng	干净	clean	5, 3, 16
gāngānjìngjìng	干干净净	clean	20
gǎnmào	感冒	to catch a cold	14, 17, 23
gǎnxiè	感谢	to express thanks	25
gāng	钢	steel	6
gāngbǐ	钢笔	pen, fountain pen	8
gānggāng	刚刚	just now	10, 11
gāngqín	钢琴	piano	15
gāo	高	(a) tall, high	5, 6, 7, 13, 18, 22, 23, 25
		(b) surname	1

Pinyin	Character	English/explanation	Chapter(s)
gāoxìng	高兴	happy, glad	15, 17, 21, 22
gǎo	搞	to do, make, handle	20
gàosu	告诉	to tell	8, 14, 15, 21, 22
gē	割	to cut grass, etc.	11
gē	歌	song	3, 9, 12
gējù	歌剧	opera	12
gēyǒngduì	歌咏队	choir	13
gē	搁	to put	20
gè	个	common mw passim	
gèbié	个别	individual	5
gēge	哥哥	elder brother	4, 7
gémìng	革命	revolution	5
gěi	给	to give; for (coverb)	8, 19, 20, 21, 22, 23, 24
gēn	跟	with (coverb)	1, 7, 8, 13, 19, 21
gēn	根	root	3
gēnběn	根本	fundamental	5
gēnjù	根据	according to, based on	19
gèng	更	even more	7
gōng'ānjú	公安局	public security bureau	1
gōngchǎng	工厂	factory	15
gōngchéngshī	工程师	engineer	25
gōngdào	公道	fair, reasonable	17
gōngdiàn	宫殿	palace	3
gōnggòng qìchē	公共汽车	bus	19
gōngjīn	公斤	kilogram	3, 8, 16
gōngjù	工具	tool	18

Pinyin	Character	English/explanation	Chapter(s)
gōngkè	功课	homework	15, 24
gōnglǐ	公里	kilometre	19
gōngrén	工人	worker, workman	2
gōngsī	公司	company	9
gōngxǐ	恭喜	congratulations	22, 23
gōngyè	工业	industry	1
gōngyuán	公园	park	5, 7, 11, 13
gōngzuò	工作	to work; work	7, 12, 15, 22, 23, 24
gǒu	狗	dog	1, 3, 15, 17
gǒuròu	狗肉	dog-meat	24
gòu	够	enough	24
gūniang	姑娘	young girl	5
gùshi	故事	story	20
guā	刮	to blow	23
guāfēng	刮风	to be windy	15
guà	挂	to hang	11
guān	关	to close	9, 17, 20
guānyú	关于	regarding	19
guàn	罐	tin, can (of food)	3
guānzhòng	观众	audience, spectators	24
guǎngbō	广播	to broadcast	8, 16
Guǎngdōng	广东	Guangdong	1
Guǎngdōng shěng	广东省	Guangdong Province	18
Guǎngzhōu	广州	Guangzhou	15
Guǎngzhōuhuà	广州话	Cantonese (language)	17
guǐ	鬼	ghost	15
guì	贵	expensive	6, 16, 17, 19, 22, 24

Pinyin	Character	English/explanation	Chapter(s)
guīdìng	规定	regulation	19
guīgēn jiédǐ	归根结底	in the final analysis	25
guìzi	柜子	cabinet	7, 18
guo	过	asp for 'past experience'; over (direction indicator); to cross	**8, 9**, 12, 14, 16, 17, 18, 19 22
guòlái	过来	(come) over here	9, 14, 18
guòqù	过去	(go) over there	9, 16, 24
guójiā	国家	country, state	3
H			
hái	还	still	7, **14**, 17, 19, 20, 24
háishi	还是	or (in questions)	**17**, 22, 24
hǎibiān	海边	seaside	22
hǎitān	海滩	beach	11
hǎi'ōu	海鸥	gull	9
Hǎidé gōngyuán	海德公园	Hyde Park	11
háizi	孩子	child	1, 2, 5, 6, 8, 9, 11, 13, 14, 16, 18, 20, 23, 24, 25
Hànyǔ	汉语	the Chinese language	7, 14, 17
Hànzì	汉字	Chinese characters	21
hǎo	好	good	1, 4, 5, 6, 9, 13, 16, 18, 19, 20, 22, 24, 25
hǎochī	好吃	tasty, delicious	6
hǎohǎo	好好	well, nicely	14
hǎokàn	好看	good-looking	6
hǎo ma/ hǎo bù hǎo	好吗/好不好	How about . . .?	17

Pinyin	Character	English/explanation	Chapter(s)
hǎotīng	好听	pleasant to the ear	6
hǎowán	好玩	interesting; amusing	6
hào	号	number (of date, bus, room, telephone, etc.)	2, 10
hàomǎ	号码	number (of telephone, etc.)	5
hē	喝	to drink	8, 10, 13, 16, 17, 18, 20, 22, 24
hē jiǔ	喝酒	to drink wine/spirit/liquor	24
hé	河	river	3, 9
hé	盒	box	3, 8
hézi	盒子	box	20
hé	和	and	**1**, 4, 7, 15, 20
Héběi	河北	Hebei	1
hé bu lǒng	合不拢	to be unable to close (of mouth, etc.)	13
hèsè	褐色	brown	6
hésuàn	合算	cheap, worthwhile	7
hézuò	合作	to cooperate	24
hēi	嘿	interjection: hello there, hey	25
hēi	黑	black	5, 6
hēibǎn	黑板	blackboard	13
hěn	很	very	1, 4, **5**, 6, 7, 8, 11, 12, 13, 14, 15, 16, 17, 18, 19, 20, 21, 22, 23, 24
héng guò	横过	to cross (the road)	9
hóng	红	red	6

Pinyin	Character	English/explanation	Chapter(s)
hōngzhàjī	轰炸机	bomber	3
hòu	后	after, behind	10, 11, 23
hòubian/ hòumian/hòutou	后边/后面/后:	at the back, behind	11
hòulái	后来	later, afterwards	10
hòutiān	后天	day after tomorrow	14
Hú	胡	surname	1
hūhū de	呼呼地	noise made by the wind	14
hūshì	忽视	to overlook, neglect	9
húshuō bādào	胡说八道	to talk nonsense	21
hùxiāng	互相	mutual	4
hùzhào	护照	passport	21
huā	花	flower	3, 5, 6, 8, 11, 20
huācóng	花丛	groups of flowers	14
huāpíng	花瓶	vase	8, 16
huār	花儿	flower, blossom	1, 3, 5, 9, 16, 19
huāshēng	花生	peanut, groundnut	3
huāyuán	花园	garden	3, 11, 16, 24
huà	画	to draw, paint; picture	5, 11, 13, 19
huàjiā	画家	painter	1, 16
huàxué	化学	chemistry	24
huài	坏	bad	13, 20, 22
huán	还	to return, give back	8
huàn	还	to exchange	15, 21
huàn jù huà shuō	换句话说	in other words	25
huānyíng	欢迎	(to) welcome	22

Pinyin	Character	English/explanation	Chapter(s)
huáng	黄	(a) yellow	6
		(b) a surname	1
huángfēng	黄蜂	wasp	25
huí	回	(a) (number of) times	8, 9, **12**, 13, 19, 25
		(b) mw for matter, business	17
		(c) to return); (back – direction indicator)	
huídá	回答	to reply, answer	15
huí jiā	回家	to return home	10, 14, 16, 21
huílái	回来	to come back	9, 13, 14, 17, 20
huíqù	回去	to go back	9
huíxìn	回信	to reply (to a letter); letter of reply	10, 17, 24
huì	会	able to; likely to	5, 11, **15**, 17, 18, 20, 22, 23, 24
huìr	会儿	a short while	24
huìyì	会议	meeting	16
huīchén	灰尘	dust	16
huīsè	灰色	grey	5
húnshēn	浑身	all over the body	13
huó	活	alive	23
huǒ	火	fire	23
huǒchē	火车	train	1, 11, 16, 17, 19, 21, 24
huǒchēzhàn	火车站	railway station	17
huò	或	or	**1**, 4, 15
huòzhě	或者	or	24

Pinyin	Character	English/explanation	Chapter(s)
J			
jǐ	几	several, a few; how many (up to ten)	2, 12
jǐ diǎn (zhōng)	几点(钟)	what time is it	17
jǐ	己	self	23
jì	寄	to send by post, post	16, 21, 22
jìde	记得	to remember	15, 23
Jīdūjiào	基督教	Christianity	8
jìhuà	计划	plan	24
jīhuì	机会	opportunity, chance	15
jíle	极了	extremely	5, 13, 17, 21
jìlǜ	纪律	discipline	18
Jǐnán(shì)	济南(市)	(City of) Jinan	1
jīqì	机器	machine	3, 20
jìrán	既然	since, as	24
jíshǐ	即使	even if	24
jìsuànjī	计算机	calculator, computer	20
jìzhě	记者	journalist	1
jiā	家	home	7, 8, 9, 10, 11, 12, 13, 17, 18, 19, 21, 24
jiājù	家具	furniture	5
jiātíng	家庭	family	5
jiā	加	to add; plus	9, 17
jiǎ	假	false	6
jià	架	mw for plane	5
jiǎkè	甲克	jacket	5
jiàqián	价钱	price	17
jiàqī lǐ	假期里	during the vacation	10

Pinyin	Character	English/explanation	Chapter(s)
jiǎrú	假如	if, supposing	24
jiàshǐ	驾驶	to drive (cars), pilot (planes)	15
jiàshǐyuán	驾驶员	driver, pilot	1
jiàn	见	to see	12, 13, 14, 15, 17, 22, 23, 24
jiàndào	见到	to succeed in seeing	3
jiàn	件	mw for shirt, coat, etc.	3, 4, 5, 6, 7, 8, 9, 13, 14, 17, 19, 21, 22, 23
jiànjiànde	渐渐地	gradually	14
jiànyì	建议	suggestion	3, 24
jiǎng	讲	to talk, speak	12, 18
jiǎnghuà	讲话	to talk, speak	25
jiānglái	将来	future	10
jiǎnglǐ	讲理	to be reasonable	18
jiǎngxuéjīn	奖学金	scholarship	22
jiāo	交	to hand over	8, 21
jiāoxiǎng yuètuán	交响乐团	symphony orchestra	8
jiāo	教	to teach	8, 15, 21
jiàoliàn	教练	coach, trainer	12
jiàoshì	教室	classroom	18
jiàoshòu	教授	professor	25
jiǎo	脚	foot	7, 12, 13, 20
jiǎo	角	corner, angle	15
jiào	叫	to call	5, 13, 19, 20, 21
jiāo'ào	骄傲	proud	4, 22
jiē	接	to meet; receive	15, 21

Pinyin	Character	English/explanation	Chapter(s)
jiēshòu	接受	to accept	20
jiēzhe	接着	then, after that	10
jiē	街	street	6, 19
jiè	借	to borrow, lend	20, 22
jiěgù	解雇	to dismiss, fire, sack	20
jiéhūn	结婚	to marry, get married	10, 17
jiějie	姐姐	elder sister	1, 3, 8, 9, 11, 17, 19, 20
jiémù	节目	program	5, 17
jièshào	介绍	to introduce	12, 21
jiéshù	结束	to finish	16
jīn	金	gold	6
jīn	斤	catty	3, 17
jìn	进	to enter; in, into (direction indicator)	9, 10, 15, 18, 22
jìnbù	进步	progress	7
jìnlái	进来	to come in	9, 14, 15, 24
jìnqù	进去	to go in	9, 13
jìnxíng	进行	to go on, be in progress	11, 24
jìn	近	near, close to	4, 7, 11, 19
jìnlái	进来	recently, lately	10, 25
jǐnguǎn	尽管	despite, in spite of	24
jīnhòu	今后	from now on, afterwards	23
jīnnián	今年	this year	8, 10, 16, 17, 22
jīntiān	今天	today	7, 8, 13, 15, 17, 18, 19
jīn(tiān) wǎn(shang)	今天	this evening, tonight	11, 18
jìnzhǐ	禁止	to forbid	21, 23

Pinyin	Character	English/explanation	Chapter(s)
jìng	静	quiet	9, 21
jìngjìng	静静	quietly	14, 16
jǐngchá	警察	policeman	2, 13, 20
jīngjì	经济	economy	7, 18
jīngjù	京剧	Beijing opera	8
jīnglǐ	经理	manager	1, 9, 15, 20
jǐngsè	景色	scenery	25
jǐngtàilán	景泰蓝	cloisonné	8
jīngyàn	经验	experience	7, 22
jìngzi	镜子	mirror	11
jiǔ	酒	wine, spirit, liquor	3, 8, 24
jiǔ	九	nine	2
jiǔ	久	a long time	12
jiù	就	then	8, 10, **14**, 16, 19
jiù	旧	old	5
jiùhùchē	救护车	ambulance	9, 10, 11
jiùhuǒchē	救火车	fire engine	10
jiūjìng	究竟	after all	17
jiùmìng	救命	Help!	23
jiùshì	就是	even if	24, 25
jiùsuàn	就算	even if	24
jù	句	sentence	9
jù	据	according to	19
jùlèbù	俱乐部	club	19
jǔxíng	举行	to hold (meetings, contests, etc.)	11
júzi	橘子	(mandarin) orange	2
júzishuǐ	橘子水	orange juice	8, 22

Pinyin	Character	English/explanation	Chapter(s)
juéde	觉得	to feel	17, 24
juédìng	决定	to decide	5, 15
K			
kāfēi	咖啡	coffee	3, 15, 22
kāfēisè	咖啡色	brown	6
kāfēiguǎn	咖啡馆	cafe	17
kāi	开	(a) to bloom (of flowers)	11
		(b) to open, start	8, 9, 13, 16, 8, 19, 21, 23, 24
kāichē	开车	to drive a car	15
kāihuì	开会	to hold a meeting	10
kāishǐ	开始	start, begin	5, 14, 16
kàn	看	to look, read	5, 8, 10, 12, 14, 19, 20, 21, 22, 24, 25
kàncuò	看错	to misread	13
kànhǎo	看好	to watch one's step	23
kànhù	看护	to look after	24
kànjiàn	看见	to see	13
kànwàng	看望	to visit	19
kàn xì	看戏	to see a play, film, etc.	17
kǎo	考	to take an examination	9, 13
kǎolǜ	考虑	to consider	14
kǎoshì	考试	to take an examination	17
kào	靠	against	5
kǎoyā	烤鸭	roast duck	8
kē	棵	mw for trees	3
kē	颗	mw for pearls, stars, etc.	3

Pinyin	Character	English/explanation	Chapter(s)
kè	刻	a quarter of an hour	10
kè	课	lesson	8, 12, 17, 21
kèběn	课本	textbook	3
kèwén	课文	text	20
kěài	可爱	lovely	4, 21
kěkào	可靠	reliable	6
Kělè	可乐	Coke	17
kēmù	科目	subject, discipline	11
kěnéng	可能	possible	14
kèqi	客气	polite	23
kèren	客人	guest	2, 9, 11, 22
kěshì	可是	but	4, 22, 24
kètīng	客厅	lounge	8, 11
kěxī	可惜	unfortunately	25
kěyǐ	可以	can, may	**15**, 18, 19, 22, 23, 24
kěn	肯	be willing	**15**
kěndìng	肯定	definite	14
kǒngpà	恐怕	to be afraid	23
kōngqì	空气	air	25
kōngtiáo	空调	air-conditioning	15
kǒu	口	mouth	3, 14, 21
kū	哭	to cry, weep	9, 16, 24
kùzi	裤子	trousers	3, 18
kuài	块	piece	3
kuài	快	quick, fast	13, 14, 16, 18, 20, 24
kuàizi	筷子	chopsticks	3, 10, 24
kuānchàng	宽敞	spacious	6
kùn	困	tired, sleepy	13

Pinyin	Character	English/explanation	Chapter(s)
L			
lā	拉	to pull	17, 20, 23
lā kāi	拉开	to pull apart	13
la	啦	exclamatory particle	25
lājī	垃圾	litter, rubbish	20, 23
lái	来	(a) to come	2, 8, 5, **9**, 10, 11, 12, 14, 15, 16, 17, 18, 19, 21, 22, 23, 24, 25
		(b) for the last (time expression)	12
láibīn	来宾	visitor	2
láihuí piào	来回票	return ticket	7, 8
lán	蓝	blue	6, 9
lǎnchē	缆车	cable car	15
lǎnduò	懒惰	lazy	18
lánqiú	篮球	basket ball	8
lǎnyāngyāng	懒洋洋	idly, lazily	14
láng	狼	wolf	3
lǎo	老	old	7, 19, 23
lǎobǎn	老板	boss	20
lǎolǎoshishí	老老实实	sincerely, honestly	22
Lǎo Lǐ	老李	Old Li	8
lǎoshī	老师	teacher	1, 2, 5, 8, 10, 11, 18, 21
le	了	(a) asp marker	**8**
		(b) sentence particle	4, 8, 9, 10, 11, 12, 13, 14, **16**, 17, 18, 19, 20, 21, 22, 23, 24, 25

Pinyin	Character	English/explanation	Chapter(s)
léi	雷	thunder	23
lèi	累	tired	7
lěng	冷	cold	7, 13, 17
lí	离	away from	17, 19
líkāi	离开	to go away (from), leave	10, 18
lí	梨	pear	2
lǐ	里	in	5, 11, 12, 13, 15, 16, 18, 19, 22, 24
lǐbian/ lǐmian/lǐtou	里边/里面/里头	inside	11
lǐ	理	to bother about	4, 18
lǐfà	理发	to cut hair, have one's hair cut	19, 21
Lǐ	李	surname	1, 17, 25
lì	粒	mw for (rice, etc.)	3
lǐbài	礼拜	week	15
lìjí	立即	immediately	10
lìkè	立刻	at once	10
lǐmào	礼貌	polite	7
lǐtáng	礼堂	auditorium	6, 13, 16
lǐwù	礼物	present, gift	5, 18, 20
lǐyóu	理由	reason	21
liǎ	俩	two (people)	25
lián	连	even	13, **14**
liǎng	两	two	1, 2, 3, 4, 5, 7, 8, 10, 11, 12, 14, 15, 16, 17, 18, 19, 20, 24
liáng	凉	cool	16

Pinyin	Character	English/explanation	Chapter(s)
liángkuài	凉快	cool	6, 7
liàng	晾	to hang (clothes) out to dry	11, 16
liàng	辆	mw for vehicles	3, 7, 11, 13, 18, 19, 21
liáotiān	聊天	to chat	8
línjū	邻居	neighbour	17
líng	零	zero	2
lǐngdài	领带	tie (an article of clothing)	5
lìngwài	另外	other	24
liú	留	to stay behind	20
liù	六	six	2, 12, 13, 16
liūbīng	溜冰	to go skating	17
liúlì	流利	fluent	13
liúmáng	流氓	hooligan	20
liúxué	留学	to go abroad to study	15
lóu	楼	storey, floor	2, 9, 11, 21
lóufáng	楼房	(storeyed) building	7
lù	路	road, route	4, 5, 7, 15, 17, 18, 19, 21
lùpái	路牌	road sign	19
lùyīnjī	录音机	(tape) recorder	5
Lúndūn	伦敦	London	9, 21
luóbo	萝卜	turnip, carrot	1
lǚkè	旅客	tourist	10, 15
lǜ shī	律师	lawyer	11
lǚ xíng	旅行	to travel	5, 10, 15
lǚ xíngshè	旅行社	travel agent	5
lǚ yóu	旅游	to tour	21

Pinyin	Character	English/explanation	Chapter(s)
M			
ma	吗	sentence particle	7, 11, 13, 15, **17**, 19, 20, 21, 22, 23, 24
mǎ	马	horse	1, 3, 8, 13
mǎlù	马路	road, highway	9, 11, 18
mǎ	码	yard	3
mà	骂	to scold, abuse	15, 24
māma	妈妈	mother	4, 7, 9, 11, 13, 18, 19, 25
mǎshàng	马上	immediately	10, 11
mǎi	买	to buy	4, 5, 8, 9, 10, 15, 20, 21, 22, 24
mǎi bu qǐ	买不起	to be unable to afford	13
mài	卖	to sell	5
màitián	麦田	wheat-field	19
mǎn	满	full	16
màn	慢	slow	14, 17, 21
mànmàn	慢慢	slowly	16, 22
máng	忙	busy	17, 18, 22
māo	猫	cat	4, 5, 16, 21
máobǐ	毛笔	writing brush	1, 19, 22
máojīn	毛巾	towel	1
Máotái	茅台	Maotai (a Chinese spirit, i.e. liquor)	8
máoyī	毛衣	sweater	9, 23
màozi	帽子	hat, cap	3, 18
méi	没	not (with **yǒu** 有)	7, 12, 13, 14, 17, 18, 19, 24, 25

Pinyin	Character	English/explanation	Chapter(s)
méi(yǒu)	没(有)	did not, have not (negative of completed action, etc.)	**8**, 13, 14, 16, 18, 21, 22, 24
méi yǒu	没有	haven't got (negative of possession, existence)	**7**, 16, 17, 19, 20, 21, 22, 24
měi	每	every	10, 19
měinián	每年	every year	14
měitiān	每天	every day	8, 10, 21
měi	美	beautiful	25
Měiguó	美国	America, United States	19
měilì	美丽	beautiful	7, 25
méiguìhuā	玫瑰花	rose	16
mèimei	妹妹	younger sister	1, 7, 8, 17
méiqì	煤气	gas	1
měishù	美术	fine art	19
men	们	plural suffix	**1**, 4, 18
mén	门	door	5, 8, 9, 11, 15, 20, 23
ménfáng	门房	porter	19
mǐ	米	metre	3, 7, 16, 17
mìfēng	蜜蜂	bee	3, 14
mílù	迷路	to go astray, lose one's way	24
mìshū	秘书	secretary	5, 20
mìtáng	蜜糖	honey	7
miànbāo	面包	bread	3, 16, 21
miànfěn	面粉	flour	3
míng	名	name	7
míngzi	名字	name	18
míngbai	明白	to understand, be clear about	25

Pinyin	Character	English/explanation	Chapter(s)
míngnián	明年	next year	10
míngtiān	明天	tomorrow	7, 10, 14, 15, 17, 19, 22, 24
míngxìnpiàn	明信片	postcard	2
mō	摸	to touch	21
mòmòde	默默地	silently, quietly	14
mótuōchē	摩托车	motor-cycle, motor-bike	13, 17
mù	木	wood	6
mùqián	目前	at present	16
N			
ná	拿	to take	9, 21
nǎ/něi	哪	which	4, **17**, 21, 25
nǎli	哪里	it's nothing	22
nǎpà	哪怕	even if	24
nǎr	哪儿	where	1, 11, **17**, 21, 24, 25
nà/nèi	那	that	**4**, 5, 8, 11, 13, 14, 15, 16, 17, 19, 22, 24
nàme	那么	then	7, 13, 24
nàr	那儿	there	11, 17, 24
nán	南	south	19
nánbian/ nánmian	南边/南面	(to the) south (of)	11
nán	男	male	2, 16, 23
nán	难	difficult	6, 7
nánchī	难吃	unpleasant to the taste	6
nándào	难道	could it be true that ..., do you mean to say that ...	17

Pinyin	Character	English/explanation	Chapter(s)
nán dǒng	难懂	difficult to understand	6
nánguò	难过	sad	6, 21
nánkàn	难看	ugly	6
nántīng	难听	unpleasant to the ear	6
ne	呢	sentence particle	8, **17**
nèi	内	within	23
néng	能	can	**15**, 18, 24
nénggòu	能够	can	13, 15
nénglì	能力	ability	1, 3
ǹg	唔	interjection	25
nǐ	你	you	4, 5, 8, 10, 11, 13, 15, 17, 18, 19, 21, 22, 23, 24, 25
nǐde	你的	your, yours	4, 5, 7, 15, 18, 22, 23
nǐmen	你们	you (plural)	3, 21
nǐmende	你们的	your, yours (plural)	4
nílóng	尼龙	nylon	6
nián	年	year	8, 10, 12, 16
niánjí	年级	year (of study)	2
niánqīng	年轻	young	5, 7
niàn	念	to read (aloud), study	8, 12
niǎor	鸟儿	bird	1, 3
nín	您	you (polite)	4, 15, 17, 21, 25
nínde	您的	your, yours (polite)	4
nìngkěn	宁肯	would rather	24
niú	牛	ox	3
niúnǎi	牛奶	milk	3, 18

Pinyin	Character	English/explanation	Chapter(s)
niúzǎikù	牛仔裤	jeans	13
nòng	弄	to handle, play with	18, 20, 22, 25
nòng huài	弄坏	to damage, ruin	13
nóngyè	农业	agriculture	1
nǔlì	努力	to work hard	24
nuǎnhuo	暖和	warm	7, 9, 14
nuǎnqì	暖气	central heating	24
nǚ	女	female	2, 4, 5, 6, 9, 23
nǚshìmen	女士们	ladies (addressing an audience)	1

O

Ōuzhōu	欧洲	Europe	8

P

pá	爬	to climb	9
pá shān	爬山	to climb hills	10, 17
pà	怕	to fear, be afraid	15, 24
pái	排	row, line	11
páiduì	排队	to queue (up)	10
páizi	牌子	brand, trademark	7
pán	盘	plate	3
pàng	胖	fat	8
pángbiān	旁边	side	11, 20
pǎo	跑	to run, leave	9, 13, 14, 15
pǎobù	跑步	to run, go jogging	13
pēi	呸	interjection	25
pèifú	佩服	admire	25
pén	盆	basin	11

Pinyin	Character	English/explanation	Chapter(s)
pēnqìjī	喷气机	jet-plane	3
péngyou	朋友	friend	2, 5, 11, 13, 14, 18, 20, 23
pī	批	batch	3
pí	皮	leather	5, 6
pǐ	匹	mw for horses	3, 13
píjiǔ	啤酒	beer	2, 3, 16, 17
pīpíng	批评	to criticise	20
piān	篇	mw for compositions	8
piàn	片	mw: slice	3, 16
piàn	骗	to cheat	20, 25
piányi	便宜	cheap	7, 24
piāo	飘	to float (in the air)	9, 16
piào	票	ticket	3, 7, 23
piàoliang	漂亮	pretty	5, 24
píng	瓶	mw: bottle	8
píngzi	瓶子	bottle	1
píngguǒ	苹果	apple	2, 3
pīngpāngqiú	乒乓球	ping-pong, table tennis	8
dǎ**pīngpāngqiú**	打乒乓球	to play ping-pong, table tennis	8
pò	破	broken	13, 20, 22

Q

qī	七	seven	2, 16, 17
qī	漆	to paint, decorate	20
qí	骑	to ride	17
qí mǎ	骑马	to ride (a horse)	8
qǐ	起	up (direction indicator)	**9**, 10, 13, 23

Pinyin	Character	English/explanation	Chapter(s)
qǐchuáng	起床	to get up, get out of bed	10, 17
qǐfēi	起飞	to take off	16
qǐlái	起来	to get up	8, 9, 14, 16, 18, 20, 24, 25
qì	气	air	14, 16, 20
qìqiú	气球	balloon	16
qìchē	汽车	car	3, 9, 10, 13, 17, 19, 21, 22
qíguài	奇怪	strange, odd	6, 25
qiān	千	thousand	2
qián	前	before	10, 11, 14
qiánbian/ qiánmian/qiántou	前边/前面/前头	ahead, in front (of)	11, 17
qiánnián	前年	the year before last	10
qiántiān	前天	the day before yesterday	23
qián	钱	(a) money	4, 5, 7, 8, 14, 17, 21, 22, 24
		(b) a surname	1
qiánbāo	钱包	purse, wallet	13, 18
qiānbǐ	铅笔	pencil	1, 4
qiānzhèng	签证	visa	19
qiáng	墙	wall	5, 11
qiáo	桥	bridge	9
qiáo	瞧	to look	14
qiāoqiāo	悄悄	quietly	14
qīng	轻	light (in weight)	7
qīngyīnyuè	轻音乐	light music	5
qíng	晴	fine (of weather)	4, 24
qǐng	请	please; to invite	8, 9, 15, 17, 18, 19, 20, 21, 23, 25

Pinyin	Character	English/explanation	Chapter(s)
qǐngbiàn	请便	please yourself	23
qǐng jìn	请进	please come in	22
qǐngkè	请客	to invite (a guest to a meal)	8, 24
qíngbùzìjìn	情不自禁	can't help but	14
qīngchu	清楚	clear	13
qíngkuàng	情况	situation	7
qiú	球	ball	18
qiúsài	球赛	ball game, match	19
qiūtiān	秋天	autumn	10
qù	去	to go	5, 8, **9**, 10, 12, 13, 14, 15, 16, 17, 18, 19, 20, 21, 22, 24, 25
qùnián	去年	last year	10, 11, 14, 16, 22
quán	拳	fist; boxing	12, 20, 21
quán	全	entirely	11
quàn	劝	to urge	21
quánlì	权利	rights	21
què	却	on the other hand, on the contrary, however	**14**
qún	群	crowd, throng	3
qúnzi	裙子	skirt	5, 6, 8, 13
R			
ránhòu	然后	then, after that	16, 24
ràng	让	to let, allow	12, 20, 22
rè	热	hot	13
rén	人	person, people	2, 3, 4, 5, 6, 7, 11, 13, 14, 15, 16, 18, 20, 23, 24, 25

Pinyin	Character	English/explanation	Chapter(s)
rénjiā	人家	others	4
rénkǒu	人口	population	1
rénmín	人民	the people	13
rènshi	认识	to recognise, know	4, 14, 15, 22, 23
rènwéi	认为	to regard, consider	24
rènzhēn	认真	conscientious	18
rènrènzhēnzhēn	认认真真	conscientiously	14
rì	日	day	10
rìchéng	日程	agenda	18
Rìyǔ	日语	Japanese	7, 17
róngyì	容易	easy	6, 7
ròu	肉	meat	14, 15, 22
rù	入	to enter	23
rùkǒuchù	入口处	entrance	11
rúguǒ	如果	if	24
rúhé	如何	how	25
rǔlào	乳酪	cheese	8
ruǎn	软	soft	13
ruǎnmiānmiān	软绵绵	soft	5
S			
sài	赛	contest, match	3
sān	三	three	2, 3, 5, 8, 9, 10, 11, 12, 16, 19, 21
sānyuè	三月	March	10, 12
sǎo	扫	to sweep	12
shā	沙	sand	3
shāfā	沙发	sofa	11

Pinyin	Character	English/explanation	Chapter(s)
shài tàiyáng	晒太阳	to sunbathe	11
shān	山	hill, mountain	3
Shāndōng (shěng)	山东(省)	Shandong (Province)	1
shǎn	闪	to flash	23
shàn	扇	fan	5
shàng	上	to go up; on, above; up (direction indicator)	5, **9**, 10, 11, 12, 13, 16, 17, 18, 20, 21, 24, 25
shàngbān	上班	to go to work	15, 19
shàngbian/ shàngmian/ shàngtou	上边/上面/上头	above	11
shàng (gè) xīngqī	上(个)星期	last week	10
shàng (gè) yuè	上(个)月	last month	10
Shànghǎi	上海	Shanghai	1, 14, 18, 19
shàngkè	上课	to go to class	10
shànglái	上来	to come up	9
shàngqù	上去	to go up	9
shàngxià	上下	approximately	2
shāngdiàn	商店	shop	5, 9, 21
shāngrén	商人	businessman	7
shǎo	少	little, few	5, 7, 11
shé	蛇	snake	3, 17
shéi/shuí	谁	who	4, 8, 14, 15, 18, 20, 22, 24
shéide/shuíde	谁的	whose	4, 17
shēn	身	body	14, 17

Pinyin	Character	English/explanation	Chapter(s)
shēntǐ	身体	body	10, 18
shénme	什么	what; any	4, 11, 15, **17**, 21, 24
shēnqǐng	申请	to apply for	15, 22
shènzhì	甚至	even	14
shēng	生	to be born	22
shēngcí	生词	new words	2
shēngháo	生蚝	live oyster	15
shēnghuó	生活	to live; life	7, 13
shēngrì	生日	birthday	18
shēngyì	生意	business	11
shēng	升	to rise	16
shěng	省	province	1
Shèngdàn lǐwù	圣诞礼物	Christmas present	5
Shèngdànjié	圣诞节	Christmas	1, 12, 19
shī	诗	poem, poetry	16
shī	施	to impose on	23
shí	十	ten	2, 5, 15, 16
shí èr	十二	twelve	2
shífēn	十分	extremely	5, 14, 18
shí yī	十一	eleven	2
shí	时	time; when	**10**
shíjiān	时间	period of time	3, 4, 5, 21, 24
shǐ	使	to make, cause	21
shì	市	city, town	1, 19
shìchǎng	市场	market-place	11
shìzhǎng	市长	mayor	6
shìzhèngtīng	市政厅	town hall	11

Pinyin	*Character*	*English/explanation*	*Chapter(s)*
shì	事	matter, affair, thing	3, 4, 5, 6, 8, 9, 13, 14, 17, 19, 21, 22, 25
shìqing	事情	matter, affair, thing	24
shì	是	to be	4, 5, 6, 11, 14, 16, 17, 18, 19, 22, 23, 24, 25
shì(de)	是的	yes	17, 23
shì . . . de	是...的	framework for emphasis	**6, 22**
shīfàn dàxué	师范大学	normal university	1
shìjiè	世界	the world	11
shípǐn	食品	food	15
shìwēi yóuxíng	示威游行	demonstration	11
shíyànshì	实验室	laboratory	12
shōu	收	to receive	1, 23
shōu dào	收到	to receive	8, 17, 18
shōujù	收据	receipt	19
shōurù	收入	income	7
shǒu	首	mw for poem, song, etc.	3
shǒu	手	hand	12, 21
shǒubiǎo	手表	wrist-watch	3, 5, 15
shǒutào	手套	gloves	3
shōushi	收拾	to tidy up	8, 20
shǒuxiàng	首相	prime minister	14
shū	输	to lose (a match, a war)	24
shū	书	book	1, 3, 4, 5, 6, 11, 13, 17, 20, 22
shūfáng	书房	study	11
shūjià	书架	bookshelf	11, 20

Pinyin	Character	English/explanation	Chapter(s)
shǔ	属	to belong to	6
shù	树	tree	11
shùyè	树叶	leaf	3
shùyīn	树荫	shade (of a tree)	11
shù	束	bouquet	8
shūcài	蔬菜	vegetables	14
shūfu	舒服	comfortable	6, 24
shuāng	霜	frost	23
shuāng	双	pair, couple	3
shuāngrén chuáng	双人床	double-bed	5
shuǐ	水	water	1, 3, 11, 15, 22, 23
shuǐguǒ	水果	fruit	11
shuǐpíng	水平	level, standard	7, 13
shuì	睡	to sleep	12, 14, 16
shuìjiào	睡觉	to sleep	15, 21, 24
shuì zháo	睡着	to fall asleep	14, 16
Shùndé	顺德	name of county	1
shuō	说	speak (a language), say	7, 8, 9, 10, 13, 15, 17, 18, 19, 20, 21, 22, 23, 24, 25
shuōfú	说服	convince	24
shuōhuà	说话	speak, say something	15, 20
sǐ	死	dead; to die	24
sì	四	four	2, 3, 12, 16
sījī	司机	driver (of a car)	22
sīrén	私人	private	5
sīxiǎng	思想	thought, ideas	3

Pinyin	Character	English/explanation	Chapter(s)
sìzhōu	四周	all around	11
sòng	送	to give (as a present), to see someone off	8, 18, 20
sǒng jiān	竦肩	to shrug one's shoulders	14
sōngshù	松树	pine tree	11
sùliào	塑料	plastic	1, 6
suàn	算	to calculate	9
suì	岁	years old, years of age	2, 7, 17
suídì	随地	everywhere, all over	23
suīrán	虽然	although	24
Sūn	孙	surname	1
suǒ	锁	lock; to lock	15, 20
suǒ	所	(a) mw for houses, etc. (b) that which	3, 5, 6 23
suǒyǐ	所以	therefore	24
T			
tā	他 (她, 它)	he (him), she (her), it	1, 4, 6, 7, 8, 9, 10, 11, 12, 13, 14, 15, 16, 17, 18, 19, 20, 21, 22, 23, 24, 25
tāde	他(她,它)的	his, her, hers, its	4, 5, 7, 13, 18, 19, 20
tāmen	他(她,它)们	they	4, 5, 7, 8, 9, 12, 13, 14, 15, 16, 17, 18, 19, 21, 22, 23, 24, 25
tāmende	他们的	their, theirs	4
tái	台	mw for machines, etc.	3
tài	太	too	15, 17, 22, 24, 25

Pinyin	Character	English/explanation	Chapter(s)
tàijíquán	太极拳	shadow-boxing	15
tàiyáng	太阳	the sun	11, 16, 23, 25
tán	弹	to play (the piano)	15
tán	谈	to talk, talk about	12, 14, 15, 21, 24
tántiān	谈天	to chat	24
tánpàn	谈判	to negotiate	16, 18
tàn	叹	to sigh	14
tànwàng	探望	to visit, look (somebody up)	21
táng	糖	sugar, sweets	8
tǎng	躺	to lie, lie down	11, 14
tàng	烫	to iron (clothes)	18
tàng	趟	number of times	12, 19
tào	套	a suit, a set	3
tǎolùn	讨论	to discuss	19
tǎoyàn	讨厌	to hate, loathe	15
tī	踢	to kick, play (football)	10, 12, 18, 20
tí	提	to lift	9, 15, 22
tíchū	提出	to raise, put forward	19
tígāo	提高	to raise, improve	7, 13
tíyì	提议	proposal	15
tì	替	for, on behalf of (coverb)	19, 21, 24
tǐcāo	体操	gymnastics	11
tǐyùguǎn	体育馆	gymnasium	11
tiān	天	sky, heaven, day	4, 5, 8, 10, 11, 15, 16, 22, 24, 25
tiānkōng	天空	sky	9, 16

Pinyin	Character	English/explanation	Chapter(s)
tiānqì	天气	weather	4, 7, 9, 14, 16, 19, 24
tiāntiān	天天	every day	8, 16
tiánxiě	填写	to fill in (a form)	15
Tiānzhǔjiào	天主教	Catholicism	8
tiáo	条	mw for trousers, etc.	3, 5, 6, 7, 8, 9, 13, 19, 21
tiào	跳	to jump, leap	9, 12, 13, 15, 21, 22
tiàowǔ	跳舞	to dance	13, 17, 20, 21, 24
tiē	贴	to stick on	8, 9
tiě	铁	iron	5, 6
tīng	听	to listen to	8, 13, 14, 16
tīngcuò	听错	to mishear	13
tīngjiàn	听见	to hear	13
tíng	停	to stop, park	9, 11, 13, 15, 18, 23, 25
tóng	同	with, together with	1
tóngshì	同事	colleague	21
tóngxué	同学	coursemate, schoolmate	5, 17
tóngyì	同意	to agree	10, 14, 15, 17, 21, 24
tōngguò	通过	to go through; through	21
tōu	偷	to steal	14, 20, 22
tōutōude	偷偷地	furtively	14
tóu	头	head; a noun suffix	3, 11, 16, 19
tóujī	投机	congenial	22
tūrán	突然	suddenly	24
túshūguǎn	图书馆	library	11, 13

Pinyin	Character	English/explanation	Chapter(s)
tùzi	兔子	rabbit, hare	11
tuī	推	to push	23
tuìràng	退让	to back out	24
tuìxiū	退休	to retire	15
tūn	吞	to swallow	21
tuō	脱	to take off (clothes)	9
W			
wa	哇	particle	25
wàzi	袜子	socks, stockings	5
wài	外	outside	11
wàibian/ wàimian/ wàitou	外边/外面/外头	outside	11
wàitào	外套	jacket	17
wán	完	to finish	13, 20, 24, 25
wǎn	碗	bowl	3, 8, 18
wǎn	晚	late; evening, night	14, 16, 17
wǎnhuì	晚会	evening party	24
wǎnshang	晚上	in the evening	7, 18, 19
wàn	万	ten thousand	2
wánjùxióng	玩具熊	teddy bear	24
wánr	玩	to enjoy oneself	22
Wáng	王	surname	1
wǎng	往	to, towards (coverb)	19
wàng	忘	to forget	15
wǎngqiú	网球	tennis	16
wèi	为	for (coverb)	19
wèi	喂	hello, hey	23

Pinyin	Character	English/explanation	Chapter(s)
wèi	位	(polite) mw for people	4
wēibōlú	微波炉	micro-wave (oven)	24
wéijīn	围巾	scarf	7
wèishénme	为什么	why	17, 25
wēixiǎn	危险	dangerous	24
wěn	稳	steady, firm	13
wèn	问	to ask	24
wèntí	问题	question	6, 15, 19, 22, 24
wénxué	文学	literature	17
wénzhāng	文章	essay	23
wēngwēngde	嗡嗡地	(humming noise)	14
wǒ	我	I, me	1, 4, 5, 6, 7, 8, 9, 10, 11, 12, 13, 14, 15, 16, 17, 18, 19, 20, 21, 22, 23, 24, 25
wǒde	我的	my, mine	4, 5, 7, 12, 13, 15, 18, 19, 20, 21, 22, 25
wǒmen	我们	we, us	4, 8, 9, 10, 11, 12, 13, 14, 15, 16, 19, 20, 21, 22, 24
wǒmende	我们的	our, ours	4
wò	握	to grasp, shake	21
wōniú	蜗牛	snail	22
wòshì	卧室	bedroom	3, 11
Wú	吴	surname	1
wǔ	五	five	2, 3, 7, 8, 10, 11, 12, 15, 17

Pinyin	Character	English/explanation	Chapter(s)
wù	雾	mist, fog	23
wǔfàn	午饭	lunch	14
wúkěnàihé	无可奈何	helplessly, with no alternative	14
wúlùn	无论	no matter	24, 25
wú rén	无人	vacant (of lavatory)	23
wǔtái	舞台	stage, platform	11
wūzi	屋子	room	3, 5, 9, 11, 20
X			
xī	西		west 19
Xī'ān	西安	Xi'an (city)	14
xībian/ xīmian	下边/下面/下	(to the) west (of)	11
xīfāngrén	西方人	Westerner	15
xī	锡	tin (a metal)	6
xǐ	洗	to wash	5, 8, 12, 13, 16, 17, 18, 21, 24
xǐyīdiàn	洗衣店	laundry	11
xǐyījī	洗衣机	washing machine	22
xǐzǎo	洗澡	to take a bath	10, 16
xì	戏	play	18, 24
xìyuàn	戏院	theatre	11
xǐhuan	喜欢	to like	1, 4, 11, 14, 15, 17, 20, 22, 23
xīwàng	希望	to hope	15, 23, 24
xīyān	吸烟	to smoke (cigarette)	15, 23
xià	下	to descend; down (direction indicator)	5, 8, **9**, 10, 11, 13, 14, 16, 17, 19, 20, 21, 23, 25

Pinyin	Character	English/explanation	Chapter(s)
xiàbian/ xiàmian/ xiàtou	下边/下面/下	below, beneath	11
xià gè yuè	下个月	next month	10
xiàkè	下课	after class	10
xiàlái	下来	to come down	9, 21
xiàlóu	下楼	to come downstairs	24
xiàqù	下去	to go down	9, 21
xiàwǔ	下午	afternoon	17, 24
xiàxuě	下雪	to snow	15, 24
xiàyǔ	下雨	to rain	15, 24
xiàtiān	夏天	summer	10
xiān	先	first	10
xiānsheng	先生	Mr	1, 17, 25
xiānshengmen	先生们	gentlemen (addressing an audience)	1
xiàn	县	county	1
xiànjīn	现金	cash	24
xiànzài	现在	now	7, 8, 10, 15, 19, 23
xiǎng	想	to think, think of; want (to do something)	9, 15, 17, 19, 22, 24, 25
xiǎng bù dào	想不到	did not expect, unexpected	23
xiǎng bù qǐ	想不起	to be unable to remember, recall	13
xiàng	向	towards (coverb)	14, 19, 21, 22
xiāngcháng	香肠	sausage	3
xiāngdāng	相当	fairly	6
Xiānggǎng	香港	Hong Kong	11, 14

Pinyin	Character	English/explanation	Chapter(s)
xiāngjiāo	香蕉	banana	3, 20
xiàngliàn	项链	necklace	5
xiāngxìn	相信	to believe, trust	24
(xiāng)yān	(香)烟	cigarette	3, 21
xiāngzi	箱子	box, trunk, suitcase	3, 4, 8, 25
xiǎo	小	small	5, 21, 24
xiǎofèi	小费	tips	5
xiǎohuǒzi	小伙子	young man	16
xiǎojie	小姐	miss, young girl	1, 17
Xiǎo Lǐ	小李	Little Li	21, 23, 25
xiǎoshí	小时	hour	12, 15, 17
xiǎoshuō	小说	novel	4, 7, 8, 17, 20, 22
xiǎotíqín	小提琴	violin	17
xiǎotōu	小偷	thief	13, 14, 20, 22
xiǎoxīn	小心	to take care	15, 23, 24
xiào	笑	to smile, laugh	8, 13, 14, 15
xiàomīmī	笑眯眯	smilingly	14
xiàoróng	笑容	smile	3
xiāoxi	消息	news	3
xiàozhǎng	校长	headmaster	1, 15
xiē	些	some, a few	3, 4, 6, 7, 14
xié	鞋	shoes	3, 5
xiě	写	to write	8, 14, 16, 19, 20, 21, 22, 23, 24
xiě/xuè	血	blood	3
xiè	谢	to thank	23
xièxie	谢谢	thanks	8, 21, 23

Pinyin	Character	English/explanation	Chapter(s)
xīn	新	new	5, 9, 10, 15
xìn	信	letter	3, 4, 8, 16, 18, 19, 20, 21, 23
xìnfēng	信封	envelope	1, 18
xìnjiàn	信件	correspondence, letters	1
Xīnjiāpō	新加坡	Singapore	22
xīnshì	新式	fashionable, new-style	5, 6
xīnshui	薪水	salary	18
xīnxiān	新鲜	fresh	25
xīng	星	star	3
xīngqī	星期	week	17, 19
xíng	行	all right, OK; to walk	4, 22, 25
xíngli	行李	luggage	7
xíngrén	行人	pedestrian	9
xǐng	醒	to wake	13, 18
xǐnglái	醒来	to wake up	10
xìngchōngchōng	兴冲冲	in high spirits	14
xìngqù	兴趣	interest	19
xióng	雄	male (of animals)	16
xióngmāo	熊猫	panda	11
xiū	修	to repair	13, 17, 22
xiūxi	休息	to rest, take a rest	10, 12
Xú	徐	surname	1
xuǎn	选	to choose, select	15, 21
xué	学	to learn, study	6, 12, 14, 15, 16, 17, 21, 23, 24
xuésheng	学生	student	1, 2, 18, 21
xuéwèn	学问	learning	6

Pinyin	Character	English/explanation	Chapter(s)
xuéxí	学习	to learn, study	11, 13, 21, 24
xuéxiào	学校	school	3, 5, 6, 11
xuézhě	学者	scholar	1
xuě	雪	snow	14, 16, 25
xùnsù	迅速	speedy	14
Y			
ya	呀	particle (for exclamations)	**25**
yágāo	牙膏	toothpaste	1
yáshuā	牙刷	toothbrush	1, 3
yān	烟	cigarettes	9
yán	沿	along (coverb)	5, 19
yǎn	演	to perform, act	18, 24
yǎnyuán	演员	actor, actress	7, 11
yǎnzòu	演奏	to perform (music)	8
yǎn	眼	eye	12, 14
yǎnjing	眼睛	eye	3, 5, 9, 13
yǎnjìng	眼镜	spectacles, glasses	13
yànhuì	宴会	banquet	24
yáng	羊	sheep	3
yǎng	养	to keep, rear	15
yǎnglǎojīn	养老金	old-age pension	5
yàng	样	kind, type	22
yǎo	咬	to bite	21
yào	药	medicine	8
yàofáng	药房	chemist's shop, pharmacy	21
yào	要	want	4, 5, 13, 14, **15**, 16, 17, 21, 23, 24

Pinyin	Character	English/explanation	Chapter(s)
yàojǐn	要紧	urgent; to matter	18, 23, 24
yàome ... **yàome ...**	要么... 要么...	either ... or ...	24
yāoqiú	要求	to require; requirement	21
yàoshi	要是	if	24
yàoshi	钥匙	key	11, 15
yě	也	also	4, 13, **14**, 18, 24, 25
yěxǔ	也许	perhaps, probably	14
yī	一	one	passim
yībiān/yīmiàn	一边/一面	as, while, at the same time	14, 24
yī bù yī bù de	一步一步地	step by step	14
yī cì	一次	one time, once	12
yīdìng	一定	definitely	14
yī fēn qián	一分钱	one cent	14
yī gè zì yī **gè zì de**	一个字 一个字地	one character by another	14
yī huìr	一会儿	(for) a while	12
yīqí	一齐	at the same time	24
yīqǐ	一起	together with	19
yīqiè	一切	all, everything	5
yīyàng	一样	the same	7, 13, 19
yīzhí	一直	all along	10
yì	亿	hundred million	2
yǐbiàn	以便	so as to	21
yīfu	衣服	clothes	4, 5, 11, 16, 20, 21, 25
yǐhòu	以后	after, afterwards	8, 14, 24
yījià	衣架	coat hanger, clothes stand	20

Pinyin	Character	English/explanation	Chapter(s)
yìjian	意见	idea, proposal	1, 15, 19
yǐjing	已经	already	10, 13, 18, 19
yǐlái	以来	since, for the last . . .	12
yǐmiǎn	以免	to avoid, so as not to	21
yǐqián	以前	before	8, 24
yīshēng	医生	doctor	8, 9, 22
Yīsīlánjiào	伊斯兰教	Islam	8
yī wǒ kàn	依我看	in my view	14
yīyuàn	医院	hospital	19
yǐzi	椅子	chair	6, 20
yín	银	silver	6
yínháng	银行	bank	11, 17
yīncǐ	因此	therefore	24
Yìndù	印度	India	18
yǐnliào	饮料	drink, beverage	15
yīnwèi	因为	because	24
yìnxiàng	印象	impression	1, 3
yīnyuè	音乐	music	11
yīnyuèhuì	音乐会	concert	10
yīnggāi	应该	must	15, 18, 22, 24
Yīngguó	英国	Britain	7, 10, 12
Yīnglǐ	英里	mile	2, 5, 7, 15, 17
Yīngwén	英文	English (language)	6, 7, 8, 20
Yīngyǔ	英语	English (language)	8
yòng	用	using (coverb)	10, 17, 19, 21, 22, 23, 24
yònggōng	用功	hard-working, diligent	24
yóu	油	oil, petrol	17

Pinyin	Character	English/explanation	Chapter(s)
yǒu	有	to have, there is/are	1, 4, 5, **7**, 10, 11, 14, 15, 16, 17, 18, 21, 24
yǒu kòng	有空	to be free, have spare time	7, 17, 24
yǒuqù	有趣	interesting	17
yǒu rén	有人	engaged (of lavatory)	23
yǒu yìsi	有意思	interesting	7
yǒuyòng	有用	useful	6, 18
yòu	又	again	**14**, 25
yòubian/ yòumian	右边/右面	on the right(hand side)	11
yóudìyuan	邮递员	postman	9
yǒuhǎo	友好	friendly	17
yóupiào	邮票	stamp	1, 9
yóutǒng	邮筒	pillar-box	11, 18
yóuyǒng	游泳	swim	24
yóuyǒngchí	游泳池	swimming-pool	10
yóuyú	由于	because (of)	19, 24
yú	于	at	23
yú	鱼	fish	9, 18, 22
yǔ	雨	rain	14, 16, 17, 23, 25
yǔsǎn		umbrella	18, 20
yǔ	与	and	**1**, 10
yù	欲	to want	23
yǔfǎ	语法	grammar	5, 6
yǔmáoqiú	羽毛球	badminton	10, 12
yǔqí	与其	instead of	24
yuán	元	basic unit of Chinese currency	15

Pinyin	Character	English/explanation	Chapter(s)
yuán	圆	round	6, 24
yuánzhūbǐ	圆珠笔	biro	1
yuǎn	远	far	7, 17, 19
yuànyi	愿意	willing	**15**, 24
yuánzé	原则	principle	5
yuē	约	(a) to make an appointment	21
		(b) approximately, about	2, 21
yuēhuì	约会	appointment	7, 24
yuè	月	month; moon	2, 3, 10, 12, 14, 16, 17, 18, 19, 20
yuèqǔ	乐曲	musical composition	8
yuètuán	乐团	orchestra	8
yùn	熨	to iron (clothes)	20, 21
yūndǎo	晕倒	to faint	24
yùndòngchǎng	运动场	sportsfield	5
yùndòngyuán	运动员	athlete	1, 9, 22
yùnhé	运河	canal	19
yǔnxǔ	允许	to allow, permit	21
Z			
zájì	杂技	acrobatics	18
zázhì	杂志	magazine	3, 5
zài	再	again	**14**, 15, 21, 24
zài	在	be at, at; asp for	1, **8**, 10, **11**, 12,
		continuous action	13, 14, 15, 16, 17, 18, 19, 20, 22, 23, 24, 25
zánmen	咱们	we, us (including the listener[s])	4, 8, 12, 17, 21, 24

Pinyin	Character	English/explanation	Chapter(s)
zánmende	咱们的	our	4
zàntíng	暂停	temporarily suspended	19, 24
zāng	脏	dirty	13, 18, 20, 25
zǎo	早	early	4, 13, 14, 17, 24
zǎoshang	早上	in the morning	10
zǎo	澡	bath	8, 21, 24
zébèi	责备	to blame	24
zéguài	责怪	to blame	24
zérèn	责任	responsibility	21
zěnme	怎么	how	**17**, 21, 24, 25
zěnmeyàng	怎么样	how about; what is (something) like	**17**
zěnyàng	怎样	what is (something) like	25
zēngjiā	增加	to increase	7
zhāi	摘	to pick, pluck	9
zhàn	站	to stand	8, 9, 13, 14, 16, 17, 18, 24
zhǎnlǎnguǎn	展览馆	exhibition	11
zhǎnpǐn	展品	exhibits	14
zhànshìmen	战士们	(the) soldiers	13
zhāng	张	(a) mw for paper, etc. (b) (with initial capital), surname	4, 6, 8, 9, 19 3, 15, 17, 21, 25
zhǎng	长	to grow	23, 25
zhànghù	帐户	account (in a bank)	11
zhǎngshàng míngzhū	掌上明珠	the apple of one's eye	25
zhǎo	找	to look for	4, 10, 14, 18, 19, 22, 24

Pinyin	Character	English/explanation	Chapter(s)
zhǎo dào	找到	to find	13, 19
Zhào	赵	surname	1
zhàocháng	照常	as usual	24
zhàoxiàngjī	照相机	camera	13
zhè/zhèi	这	this	5, 6, 7, 8, 9, 10, 11, 12, 13, 14, 15, 16, 17, 18, 19, 20, 21, 23, 25
zhème	这么	like this, thus	25
zhèr/zhèlǐ	这儿/这里	here	1, 7, 9, 10, 11, 14, 15, 17, 18, 19, 21, 23, 25
zhèyàng	这样	like this	25
zhe	着	asp for continuous or persistent state	**8**, 11, 14, 16, 20, 21
zhē	蜇	to sting	25
zhēn	真	real, really	5, 6, 7, 8, 16, 23, 25
zhēn bàng	真棒	Great!	25
zhēnzhū	珍珠	pearl	3
zhèng	正	just, exactly	13
zhèngzài	正在	in the process of	8, 11, 13, 15, 16, 18
zhèngjiàn	证件	document	21
zhěngqí	整齐	tidy, in good order	5
zhèngshì	正式	formal	6
zhī	之	particle in Classical Chinese indicating possession	2
zhījiān	之间	between	10
zhī	支	mw for pen, etc.	3, 4

Pinyin	Character	English/explanation	Chapter(s)
zhīchí	支持	to support	15
zhīpiào	支票	cheque	1, 5, 24
zhī	枝	mw for rifle, etc.	1
zhī	只	mw for animal, bird, insect	3, 4, 7, 8, 9, 11, 14, 15, 16, 24
zhǐyào	只要	only if	24
zhǐyǒu	只有	only when	24
zhí	直	straight	13
zhǐ	纸	paper	1, 3
zhǐ	指	to point at	23
zhǐzhèng	指正	to correct, point out to	23
zhīdào	知道	to know	4, 14, 17, 23
zhìliáo	治疗	treatment; to treat, cure	8
zhízhào	执照	(driving) licence	15
zhīzhū	蜘蛛	spider	7
zhōng	中	middle; Chinese	11, 14
zhōngcān	中餐	Chinese food	24
Zhōngguó	中国	China	1, 5, 10, 11, 15, 16, 17, 21, 22, 23, 24
Zhōngguórén	中国人	Chinese	10
zhōngjiān	中间	middle	11
zhōngniánrén	中年人	middle-aged person	16
Zhōngwén	中文	the Chinese language	1, 5, 6, 7, 12, 13, 16, 17, 18, 21, 22, 23, 24
Zhōngwénxì	中文系	the Chinese department	1, 14
zhōngxīn	中心	centre	19
zhǒng	种	category, kind	3, 16

Pinyin	Character	English/explanation	Chapter(s)
zhòng	重	heavy	5, 8, 25
zhōngdiǎn	终点	terminal, terminus	17
zhōngtóu	钟头	hour	12
zhòngyào	重要	important	6
Zhōu	周	surname	1, 19
zhū	猪	pig	7
zhù	住	to live	11, 12, 13, 21, 22
zhūbǎo	珠宝	jewellery	16
zhùhè	祝贺	to congratulate	21
zhǔrén	主人	host	9
zhǔxí	主席	chair person	21
zhǔyào	主要	primary	5
zhǔyi	主意	idea	3
zhùyì	注意	to pay attention to	21
zhǔzhāng	主张	proposal	3, 20
zhuā	抓	to grasp	21, 22
zhuā zhù	抓住	to grasp firmly	13
zhuǎn	转	to pass on (to)	14
zhuāntou	砖头	brick	1
zhuāng	装	to pack	15
zhuàng	幢	mw for houses	7
zhǔn	准	precise; to allow	23
zhǔnbèi	准备	to prepare	12, 15, 17
zhuōzi	桌子	table	5, 6, 11, 20
zǐ	紫	purple	6
zì	字	Chinese character	3, 4, 11, 13, 21, 23
zìdiǎn	字典	dictionary	18

Pinyin	Character	English/explanation	Chapter(s)
zǐdàn	子弹	bullet	3
zìjǐ	自己	oneself	20, 22, 24, 25
zìxíngchē	自行车	bicycle	7
zǒng'éryánzhī	总而言之	all in all	25
zōngjiào	宗教	religion	15
zǒnglǐ	总理	premier, prime minister	1
zǒng(shì)	总(是)	always	10
zǒngsuàn	总算	after all	14
zǒu	走	to leave, walk, go	4, 9, 11, 13, 14, 15, 17, 18, 19, 20, 23, 24, 25
zǒulù	走路	to walk, go on foot	22, 24
zūjīn	租金	rent	6
zǔmǔ	祖母	grandmother	19
zúqiú	足球	football, soccer	1, 3, 10
zúqiú mǐ	足球迷	football fan	20
zuǐ	嘴	mouth	13
zuì	醉	drunk, intoxicated	13, 16
zuì	最	most	7, 11, 13, 17, 20
zuìhòu	最后	finally, in the end	10
zuìjìn	租金	recently, lately	10, 17
zūnshǒu	遵守	to obey (discipline), follow (regulations)	18
zuò	坐	to sit; travel by	9, 11, 12, 13, 15, 16, 17, 18, 19, 21, 22, 24
zuò	作	to make	20
zuò	座	mw for mountains, houses, etc.	3

Pinyin	Character	English/explanation	Chapter(s)
zuòwèi	座位	seat	11
zuò	做	to do, manage	8, 13, 19, 24
zuò shì	做事	to do something, handle matters	18
zuǒbian/ zuǒmian	左边/左面	(to the) left (of)	11
zuòjiā	作家	writer	1, 20
zuótiān	昨天	yesterday	4, 5, 6, 7, 8, 10, 11, 14, 16, 22, 25
zuòwén	作文	composition	8
zuòyè	作业	homework, coursework	8, 13
zuǒyòu	左右	roughly, about, around	2, 17

FURTHER READING

Chao, Yuen Ren (1968) *A Grammar of Spoken Chinese*, Berkeley: University of California Press.

Fang Yuquing (1996) *Shiyong Hanyu Yufa* ('Practical Chinese Grammar'), Beijing: Beijing Language Institute Press.

Gao Gengsheng et al. (1984) *Xiandai Hanyu* ('Modern Chinese'), Shandong Education Press.

Henne, H. et al. (1977) *A Handbook of Chinese Language Structure*, Oslo: Universitetsforlaget.

Hu Yushu (ed.) (1986) *Xiandai Hanyu* ('Modern Chinese'), Shanghai: Shanghai Education Press.

Huang Borong and Liao Xudong (1983) *Xiandai Hanyu* ('Modern Chinese'), Lanzhou: Gansu People's Press.

Kratochvil, P. (1968) *The Chinese Language Today*, London: Hutchinson.

Li, C. N. and Thompson, S. A. (1981) *Mandarin Chinese: A Functional Reference Grammar*, Berkeley: University of California Press.

Li Dejin and Cheng Meizhen (1988) *A Practical Chinese Grammar for Foreigners*, Beijing: Sinolingua.

Lin Xiangmei (ed.) (1991) *Xiandai Hanyu* ('Modern Chinese'), Beijing: Language Press.

Liu Yuehua, Pan Wenyu and Gu Wei (1983) *Shiyong Xiandai Hanyu Yufa* ('Chinese Grammar'), Beijing: Foreign Languages Teaching and Research Press.

Norman, J. (1988) *Chinese*, Cambridge: Cambridge University Press.

INDEX